Essential

JavaFX™

GAIL ANDERSON • PAUL ANDERSON

PRENTICE
HALL

Upper Saddle River, NJ • Boston • Indianapolis • San Francisco
New York • Toronto • Montreal • London • Munich • Paris • Madrid
Capetown • Sydney • Tokyo • Singapore • Mexico City

Contents

Preface

As we complete the final edits and our printing deadline looms, we're excited and grateful to be involved with JavaFX. In February 2009, JavaFX reached the 100,000,000th download of the JavaFX runtime.[1] The ranks of JavaFX developers will undoubtedly grow as more developers see the flexibility and power of JavaFX. This synergy, we believe, will fuel continued development of the language and enhancements to the runtime environment.

This book is designed to get you up to speed quickly with JavaFX. JavaFX is a scripting language. It's not Java, but it's built on top of the Java runtime. You don't need experience with Java to succeed with JavaFX. Indeed, JavaFX's declarative syntax makes life easier if you *don't* think like a developer. Instead, JavaFX encourages you to think like a designer.

What does it mean to "think like a designer"? Basically, it means to visualize the structure of your application or widget and compose your scene out of simple shapes and other building blocks. In JavaFX, you compose a scene by declaring objects.

Let's take an example. Say you visualize a sky with the sun, the sea, and an island (think South Pacific). The sky is the background, reflecting the blues of a bright cloudless day (think of a linear gradient, going from "blue sky" to "azure"). The sun is a Circle, with a radial gradient consisting of yellows and oranges. The island is a quadratic curve (think of a cone-shaped volcano-type island paradise filled with a gradient of rich browns and tropical greens). And there you have your scene, as shown in Figure 1 (in a black and white approximation).[2]

Not only can you declare visual objects with JavaFX, but you can also declare animations. Animations give your objects life. Returning to our island paradise, visualize the beginning of the day. The colors are muted as the morning light slowly gives shape to an ethereal world. The sun rises and the island takes form. The sun continues

---

1. Jonathan Schwartz's Blog: *JavaFX Hits 100,000,000 Milestone!* February 13, 2009. URL: http://blogs.sun.com/jonathan/entry/javafx_hits_100_000_000
2. You'll find widget Island Paradise with the other JavaFX examples on the authors' web site at http://www.asgteach.com/javafx.

Figure 1. Visualizing an island paradise

higher in the sky and the whole world brightens. When the sun reaches its zenith, the colors of the sea and sky are saturated with "sea green," "azure," and "sky blue." But, it's a temporary brightness. The sun follows its path and eventually falls back into the sea in a glow of warm reds. The sky darkens. The sea fades. Eventually the island disappears. Everything is black. You build these behaviors with animation and a powerful JavaFX language construct called *binding*. (Binding lets you declare dependencies among objects—when a variable changes, JavaFX automatically updates all objects bound to that variable.)

JavaFX animation lets you move objects along a path (the sun rises and sets in an arc) and fade objects in and out with timelines. Our "island paradise" controls day and night with black and red rectangle "filters." These filters color the scene as night, dawn, daytime, evening, dusk, and back to night, all cycling through an accelerated Circadian clock. Animation and binding make it all work.

If you're a Java programmer, you will feel at home in JavaFX with packages and import statements, classes, things called public, and static type checking. (Don't worry about these things if you're not a Java programmer.) If you're a JavaScript programmer, you will appreciate the value of static type checking coupled with a sophisticated type inference engine in JavaFX. (Type inference eases the burden of having to specify types everywhere.) But most importantly, we hope you'll appreciate the simplicity of the JavaFX declarative style. For example, take this one-line JavaFX object "literal."

```
Circle { centerX: 200 centerY: 40 radius: 25 fill: Color.YELLOW }
```

If you think the above describes a yellow circle, then you're on your way! And, if you think perhaps it describes a yellow sun, that's even better.

About the Audience

This book is aimed at developers with some previous programming experience (in any language). We don't assume you know Java and we assume you've never written a JavaFX script before. (The term *script* in this book refers to both the programs you write and the individual files that contain these programs.)

We hope to show you how to use JavaFX effectively. There is a diversity to JavaFX: you can use it to build games, create effective web-service-based widgets, or build snazzy front-ends to your desktop applications. You can use Swing-based components, "native" JavaFX components, or roll your own. You can collaborate with designers and import images and other assets to incorporate into your scene graph. Our aim is to expose some of this diversity so that you can forge ahead with your own successful JavaFX projects.

How to Use This Book

Chapter 1 gets you started with JavaFX. We show you how to download JavaFX and begin building projects with the NetBeans IDE. (We use NetBeans to build our examples, but you can also use Eclipse.)

Chapter 2 gives you a broad overview of JavaFX. It takes you through an example (a Guitar Tuner), pointing out how things are done with JavaFX. If you want to get a "feel" for the language, this chapter introduces you to many trademark JavaFX features.

Chapter 3 through Chapter 5 are "reference-oriented" chapters. Chapter 3 describes the JavaFX language, Chapter 4 describes graphical objects, and Chapter 5 discusses user interface components. These chapters are organized with small examples to help you find information quickly (how do I bind an object or generate a sequence with a for loop?). The language chapter covers everything from JavaFX built-in types to mixin inheritance. Graphical objects are the basic JavaFX shapes you use to build scene graphs and layout objects (islands in the sun, for example). The components chapter shows you the JavaFX Swing components and the JavaFX "native" UI components. We also show you how to build custom UI components in a more advanced section.

Chapter 6 shows you how to design and structure a JavaFX application. It introduces a building-block approach with a nod towards object oriented design principles.

Chapter 7 is all about JavaFX animation and timelines. JavaFX animation is both powerful and flexible. Transitions are "pre-packaged high-level" animations that help build straightforward motions quickly, such as fade-ins and fade-outs, scaling, and moving.

Chapter 8 discusses viewing and manipulating images. One example shows you how to design an animated photo carousel.

Chapter 9 covers web services. JavaFX provides two important utility classes that make it easier to work with web services. An HttpRequest class handles asynchronous web requests and a PullParser class simplifies processing the response data. We take you through several Flickr-based web service API calls.

Chapter 10 discusses the JavaFX mobile environment and explores the differences between desktop JavaFX and the JavaFX mobile runtime. We discuss guidelines for targeting mobile devices and how to make an application mobile-friendly.

About the Examples

You can download the source code for all book examples from the authors' web site at

```
http://www.asgteach.com/javafx
```

In addition, example applications are deployed so you can try them out.

Notational Conventions

We've applied a rather light hand with font conventions in an attempt to keep the page uncluttered. Here are the conventions we follow.

Element	Font Example
JavaFX class	Shape, Circle, Color
JavaFX property	`layoutBounds, opacity, height`

JavaFX code	`def sunPath = Path {`
	`    elements: sunElements`
	`    stroke: Color.GRAY`
	`}`

URL	`http://javafx.com/`
file name	**Main.fx, Carousel.fx**
key combinations	**Ctrl+Space**
NetBeans menu selections	**Properties** menu item
code within text	The animation varies property `opacity` from . . .

code highlighting (to show modified or relevant portions)	`def sunPath = Path {`
	`    `**`elements: sunElements`**
	`    stroke: Color.GRAY`
	`}`

Acknowledgments

We'd first like to thank Greg Doench, our editor at Prentice Hall, for making the impossible a reality. While we were pushing the limits of how quickly one can respond to changes and making our manuscript reflect reality, he lassoed the right people and made it happen. We're extremely grateful to have worked with Greg on this book and on so many other projects in the past.

We'd also like to thank Octavian Tanase of Sun Microsystems for giving us the opportunity to write a book on JavaFX. Learning JavaFX has enriched our technical toolbox and for that we thank Octavian.

Brian Goetz, Richard Bair, Robert Field, and Marvin Ma from the JavaFX team provided us with technical guidance. In particular, Brian read over portions of our manuscript and helped us think in the "JavaFX way." He gave us insights into the language and, more importantly, into the philosophy that makes JavaFX unique. Richard Bair and Marvin Ma gave us up-to-the-minute details on new JavaFX developments, including access to early versions of the JavaFX 1.2 SDK.

We had invaluable assistance from our son, Kellen Anderson, who created two significant examples for us. GuitarTuner (discussed in Chapter 2) and Banker, a game-based widget that puts JavaFX through its paces, accurately reflecting the physics of a rolling, banking ball. You can try out Banker on the authors' web site.

Matthew Duggan proved invaluable as a reviewer, providing insightful comments, catching errors and inconsistencies, and improving the manuscript in many places. A special thanks to you, Matt!

William Krainski, Kellen Anderson, Mike Shelton, and Peter Dibble provided valuable feedback that improved the manuscript. Jasper Liu and Scott Ng worked under a very tight time schedule to get the Chinese translation done. Chuti Prasertsith came up with an awesome cover design. And finally, the Pearson production staff, headed by John Fuller, brought this book to press under the most dire scheduling constraints.

Gail and Paul Anderson
Anderson Software Group, Inc., www.asgteach.com
May 2009

1 Getting Started with JavaFX

Welcome to JavaFX. This chapter tells you what JavaFX is, what it does, how to get it, and how to get started. After you finish this chapter, you should be able to start working with JavaFX right away.

What You Will Learn

- What is JavaFX and why should I care?
- What is in the JavaFX Bundle
- Where to get JavaFX
- Using JavaFX with the NetBeans IDE

1.1 What Is JavaFX?

JavaFX is a software technology that lets you create and deliver Rich Internet Applications (RIAs) with media and content across a wide variety of platforms and devices. The language was originally called F3 (Form Follows Function) and was developed primarily by Chris Oliver, now at Sun Microsystems. The name was changed to JavaFX in 2007.

On Java platforms, JavaFX is a compiled, statically typed, declarative scripting language. The language offers automatic data binding, triggers, animation, and an expression syntax where code blocks yield values. Sequences, function types, and inferred types make JavaFX a concise scripting language. Developers can use object-oriented JavaFX features to simplify complexity and handle errors with Java-like exceptions. JavaFX also lets you easily access the complete Java API, which includes an enormous number of third-party Java libraries.

Figure 1.1 is the big picture for JavaFX. This block diagram shows the various pieces you can leverage when creating JavaFX applications. As the diagram shows, there are extensions for three environments: Desktop, Mobile and TV. All three environments support the common API (labeled Common Elements in Figure 1.1). As of this writing, the runtime for the JavaFX TV environment does not yet exist. There is a runtime for the JavaFX mobile environment, which supports the common API only. (We discuss the JavaFX mobile environment in Chapter 10.)

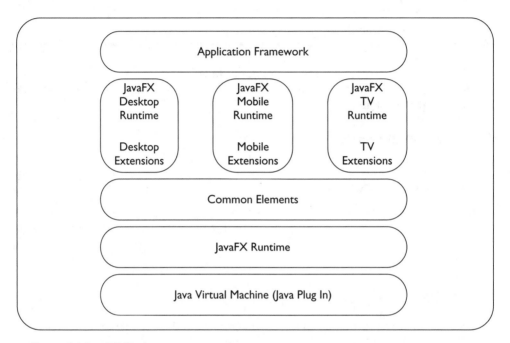

Figure 1.1 JavaFX Platform

On the desktop, JavaFX runs on Windows XP, Vista, and Mac OS. Linux support is forthcoming (as of this writing). JavaFX is also capable of running on Android, Windows Mobile, and other mobile operating systems.

1.2 The JavaFX Bundle

The JavaFX platform release currently includes three major components.

JavaFX SDK

The JavaFX SDK (Software Development Kit) includes the JavaFX compiler, runtime tools, graphics, media, and web services. It also includes libraries that let you create RIAs (Rich Internet Applications) for desktop, browser, and mobile platforms.

NetBeans IDE

NetBeans is a sophisticated IDE (Integrated Development Environment) that lets you build, preview, and debug JavaFX applications. The code editor supports JavaFX syntax checking, code completion, hyperlinked documentation, and other developer-friendly features. To decrease development time, the editor offers drag-and-drop from palettes of GUI controls, event handlers, transformations, effects, and animation. For Mobile applications, NetBeans also supports a Mobile emulator to simulate applications running on mobile devices.

Currently, JavaFX is a plug-in component for NetBeans. A community-supported plug-in for Eclipse IDE users is also available.

JavaFX Production Suite

The JavaFX Production Suite is a set of tools and plug-ins to help designers export JavaFX graphics from third-party applications (Adobe Illustrator and Photoshop). Using the JavaFX Graphics Viewer, you can preview how graphics will render when you deploy to desktop and mobile environments. An SVG (Scalable Vector Graphics) conversion tool lets you convert SVG files to JavaFX format.

1.3 Where to Get JavaFX

To access the JavaFX downloads, go to `http://java.sun.com/javafx/downloads`. You will see downloads for the following components.

- JavaFX SDK

- NetBeans for JavaFX

- JavaFX Production Suite

Follow the instructions on the web site to download and install the component you want. You can download and install NetBeans with JavaFX together or you can install the JavaFX plug-in separately if you already have NetBeans installed.

Here are some other valuable links for JavaFX.

- `http://java.sun.com/javafx`—Main site for JavaFX

- `http://javafx.com`—Samples and demos for JavaFX

- `http://java.sun.com/javafx/`*`num`*`/docs/api`—JavaFX documentation (version *num*)

- `http://www.netbeans.org`—NetBeans site

- `https://openjfx-compiler.dev.java.net`—OpenJFX Compiler Project

Once you have NetBeans and JavaFX installed, you are ready to try out JavaFX.

Create a NetBeans Project

In this section, we show you how to build a NetBeans project for a JavaFX application, compile a short program, and run it.

Launch NetBeans and choose **File>New Project** as shown in Figure 1.2.

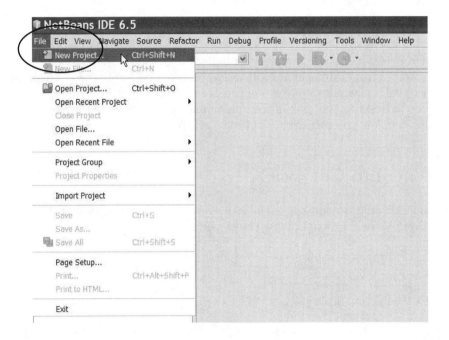

Figure 1.2 NetBeans Create New Project

You will see the New Project dialog, as shown in Figure 1.3.

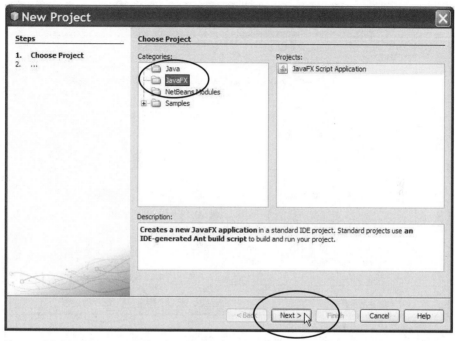

Figure 1.3 NetBeans New Project Dialog

Under Categories, select **JavaFX** and click **Next** as shown. Another dialog will appear that lets you chose a Project name, location, and project configuration, as shown in Figure 1.4.

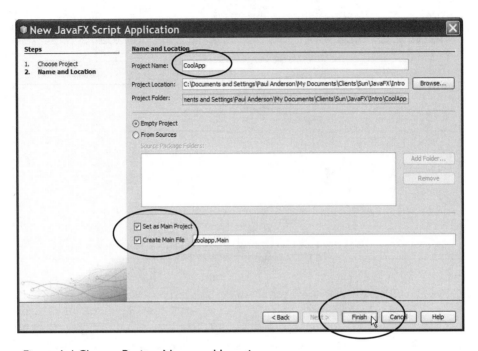

Figure 1.4 Choose Project Name and Location

To finish specifying your JavaFX project, perform these steps:

1. Specify **CoolApp** for the Project Name.

2. Accept the default for **Project Location** or click the **Browse** button to change the location of this project.

3. Make sure the checkboxes for **Set as Main Project** and **Create Main File** are checked.

4. Click **Finish**.

Netbeans creates the CoolApp application and brings you up into the source editor as shown in Figure 1.5.

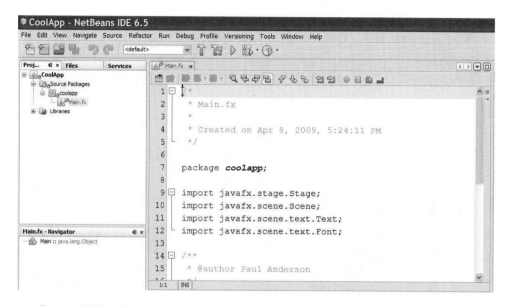

Figure 1.5 CoolApp Application

Edit JavaFX Source Code

You are now ready to edit the source code. Move the scrollbar in the editor window to the bottom, as shown in Figure 1.6.

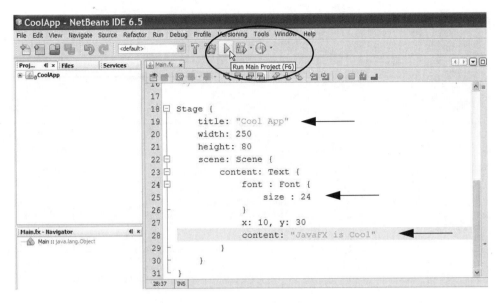

Figure 1.6 Edit Source Code

Perform these steps to edit the source code. (The line numbers in your edit window may not exactly match. We reference the line numbers in Figure 1.6.)

1. Show line numbers. (Place the mouse in the left column of the editor window, right click, and select **Show Line Numbers** from the context menu.)

2. Change "`Application title`" to **"`Cool App`"** (line number 19 in Figure 1.6).

3. In line number 25, change 16 to **24**. The line should now read `size : 24`.

4. Change "`Application content`" to **"`JavaFX is Cool`"** (line number 28).

Compile and Run

Click the green chevron on the tool bar to Run the Main Project, as shown in Figure 1.6. This will compile and run your application. You should see the application in a window on your screen, as shown in Figure 1.7.

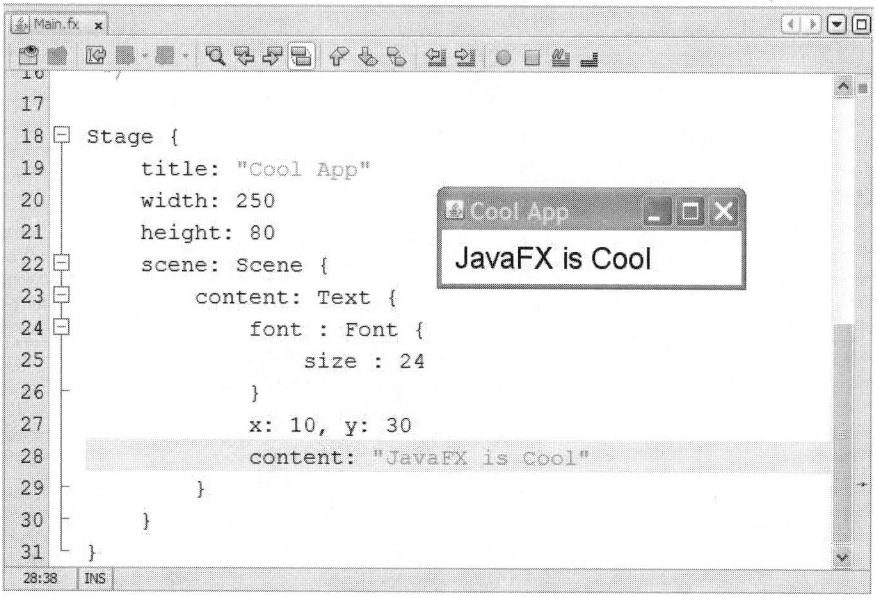

```
Main.fx  x
16
17
18 ⊟  Stage {
19          title: "Cool App"
20          width: 250
21          height: 80
22 ⊟       scene: Scene {
23 ⊟           content: Text {
24 ⊟               font : Font {
25                      size : 24
26                  }
27                  x: 10, y: 30
28                  content: "JavaFX is Cool"
29              }
30          }
31   }
28:38    INS
```

Figure 1.7 Run CoolApp Application

Execution Models

Netbeans lets you run your JavaFX programs in several different environments. Your choices are as follows.

- Standard Execution (default)
- Java Web Start
- Run in Browser
- Run in Mobile Emulator

Standard Execution (the default) is for desktop applications. The Mobile Emulator simulates the Mobile environment. You can also run your application in a browser or use Java Web Start, a tool for deploying desktop applications with the Java Network Launching Protocol (JNLP).

To choose a deployment option, right-click the CoolApp project in the Project view, and choose **Properties** from the drop-down list, as shown in Figure 1.8.

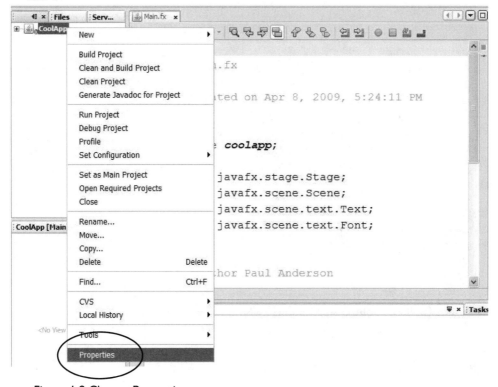

Figure 1.8 Choose Properties

NetBeans displays the Project Properties dialog. Select **Run** under Categories as shown in Figure 1.9.

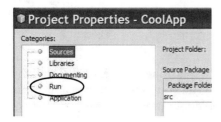

Figure 1.9 Choose Run under Categories (Project Properties)

NetBeans now displays a new Project Properties dialog, as shown in Figure 1.10.

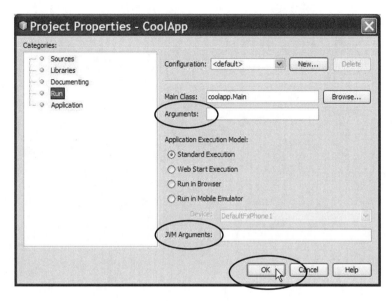

Figure 1.10 Run CoolApp Application

The Standard Execution is pre-selected for you, but you can change to any of the other execution models. After you make your selection, click **OK**. When you run your application with the green chevron on the tool bar as before (see Figure 1.6 on page 8), your application will run in the environment you selected.

NetBeans Tip

The Project Properties dialog lets you specify arguments to your program when you run it. You can also specify JVM (Java Virtual Machine) arguments.

2 A Taste of JavaFX

As the preface hints, JavaFX has a combination of features that makes it unique. This chapter gives you a taste of the language and some of these features. Our goal is to choose a representative example so you get a feel for the kinds of programs possible with JavaFX. The example (a guitar tuner) illustrates language constructs while keeping the discussion concrete. We'll veer away from the example at times to illustrate additional JavaFX features that are relevant. While this overview is in no way complete (remember, it's just a taste), we hope to entice you to explore JavaFX further.

The source code for GuitarTuner appears at the end of the chapter (see "Source Code for Project GuitarTuner" on page 36). To keep the text flowing, we'll show snippets from this application throughout the overview.

What You Will Learn

- What makes JavaFX unique as a scripting language

- All about object literals and declarative constructs

- Introducing the JavaFX scene graph

- Declaring variables, properties, and objects

- Initializing objects and object properties

- Basics in container coordinate space and layout

- Creating a custom node

- Manipulating objects with color, effects, and gradients

- Getting things done with binding, event handlers, and animation

2.1 Introducing JavaFX

What is JavaFX? JavaFX is a scripting language with static typing. You can call a Java API as needed from JavaFX and create new object types with classes, but JavaFX also provides an easy declarative syntax. (Declarative means you say what you want and the system figures out how to do it for you.) JavaFX provides properties for manipulating objects within a 2D coordinate system, specifying fill and pen stroke colors, and creating special effects. You can create shapes and lines, manipulate images, play videos and sounds, and define animations.

Let's begin exploring JavaFX by introducing the basics. Our introduction begins with project GuitarTuner where you'll see the main structure of a JavaFX program. Then, you'll explore a few JavaFX language constructs and see how to improve the appearance of your applications. Finally, you'll see how to make applications do things.

JavaFX in a Nutshell

JavaFX is statically typed, meaning program data types are known at compile time. JavaFX also uses type inference. This means you don't have to declare the type of every variable because JavaFX can generally figure it out for you. This gives JavaFX the efficiency of a statically typed language combined with the ease of a declarative language.

2.2 Project GuitarTuner

Project GuitarTuner helps you tune your guitar. It displays a visual guitar fret board with six strings. The letter (note) corresponding to the guitar string appears next to the fret board. When you click a string with the mouse, you'll hear a synthesized guitar note for the selected string as it vibrates visually. Project GuitarTuner uses the Java `javax.sound.midi` API to generate the sounds. Figure 2.1 shows this application running when the A string is vibrating. The corresponding JavaFX graphical objects are labeled.

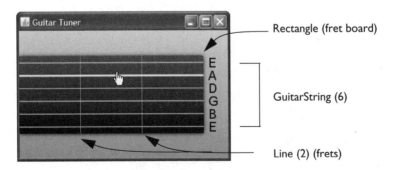

Figure 2.1 JavaFX application GuitarTuner

The Scene Graph Metaphor

JavaFX programs with a graphical user interface define a *stage* and a *scene* within that stage. The stage represents the top level container for all JavaFX objects; that is, the content area for an applet or the frame for a widget. The central metaphor in JavaFX for specifying graphics and user interaction is a *scene graph*. A scene defines a hierarchical node structure that contains all the scene's components. *Nodes* are represented by graphical objects, such as geometric shapes (Circle, Rectangle), text, UI controls, image viewers, video viewers, and user-created objects (such as GuitarString in our example). Nodes can also be containers that in turn hold more nodes, letting you group nodes together in hierarchical structures. (For example, Group is a general-purpose container node, HBox provides horizontal layout alignment, and VBox provides vertical layout alignment.) The scene graph is this hierarchical node structure.

Figure 2.2 shows the scene graph for project GuitarTuner. Compare the visual graphical elements in Figure 2.1 with the scene graph depicted in Figure 2.2.

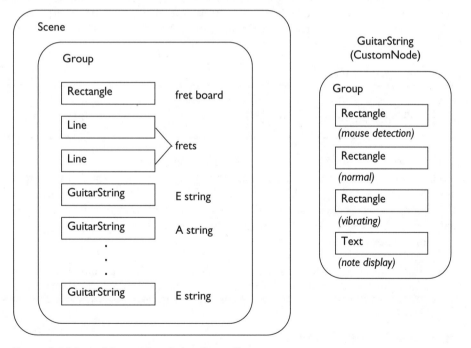

Figure 2.2 Nested Scene Graph for GuitarTuner

In general, to construct a JavaFX application, you build the scene graph, specifying the look and behavior of all its nodes. Then, your application just "runs." Some applications need input to go—user actions that activate animations or affect component properties. Other applications just run on their own. (Building the scene graph is analogous to winding up a toy. When you're done, the application just runs.)

JavaFX Scene Graph

The power of the scene graph is that, not only do you capture the entire structure of your application in a data structure, but you can change the display simply by modifying properties of the objects in the scene graph. (For example, if you change a node's visible *property to* false, *that node, and any nodes it contains, disappears. If you change a node's location, it moves.)*

Within the scene graph for project GuitarTuner, you see the Scene at the top level, which contains a Group. Within the Group there is a Rectangle for the fret board (the guitar neck), two Line nodes representing frets, and six GuitarStrings. Each GuitarString is in turn its own Group consisting of three Rectangles and a Text node. Nodes that contain other nodes (such as Scene and Group) include a content property that holds subnodes. The hierarchical nature of the scene graph means that all nodes at the same level share the same coordinate space. You therefore build node structures (such as GuitarString) that use a relative coordinate system. You'll see shortly why this is useful.

Think Like A Designer

JavaFX encourages you to think like a designer. As a first step, visualize the structure of your application or widget and compose your scene out of simple shapes and other building blocks.

The order of nodes within a parent container affects their rendering. That is, the first node in the container is "drawn" first. The final node is "drawn" last and is on top of the view. Nodes (depending on their placement within the coordinate system) may visually block or "clip" previously drawn nodes. In GuitarTuner, the nodes must be in a specific order. You draw the fret board first, then the frets, and finally the guitar strings, which appear on top.

Changing the relative order of nodes in a container is easy. The toFront() function brings a node to the front (top) and the toBack() function sends a node to the back (bottom).

Hierarchical Scene Graph

Figure 2.3 also shows a scene graph of project GuitarTuner. Figure 2.2 and Figure 2.3 depict the same structure, but Figure 2.3 shows the hierarchical relationship among the nodes in the scene using a graphical tree view. Nodes at the same level share the same coordinate space. For example, the three Rectangles and Text nodes in the GuitarString share the same coordinate system.

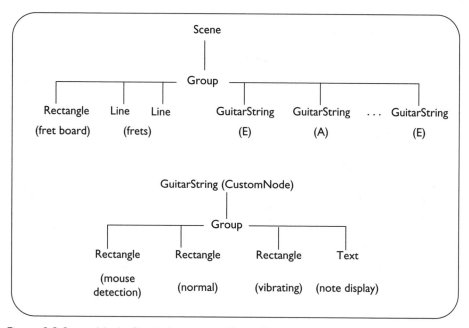

Figure 2.3 Scene Node Graph for project GuitarTuner

2.3 JavaFX Program Structure

JavaFX program structure is simple. For programmers who are used to traditionally compiled programs, programming in JavaFX will feel different. With static typing, JavaFX gives you feedback at compile time when you use types incorrectly. This greatly enhances your ability to write correct code. Furthermore, with the NetBeans IDE, you can access JavaDocs for all JavaFX types (classes) and dynamically query these class properties and functions, essentially getting feedback at edit time.

Let's see how the Stage and Scene form the JavaFX program structure.

Stage and Scene

The Stage is the top-level container and contains the Scene. The Scene, in turn, holds nodes that make up the scene graph. Every JavaFX program that has graphical objects declares a Stage object.

Here is a top-level implementation of the scene graph for GuitarTuner from Figure 2.2 (or Figure 2.3). (We'll look at GuitarString's node graph shortly.)

```
// Stage and Scene Graph
Stage {
   title: "Guitar Tuner"
   Scene {
      // content is sequence of SceneGraph nodes
      content: [
         Group {
            content: [
               Rectangle { ... }
               Line { ... }
               Line { ... }
               GuitarString { ... }
               GuitarString { ... }
               GuitarString { ... }
               GuitarString { ... }
               GuitarString { ... }
               GuitarString { ... }
            ]
         } // Group
      ]
   } // Scene
} // Stage
```

Object Literals

The Stage and Scene objects are instantiated with object literal expressions, or *object literals*. Object literals provide a declarative style of programming. Intuitively, declarative means "tell me what you want, not how to do it." As you will see, the real declarative part of JavaFX is *binding*. We show why this is so powerful later in the chapter.

Object literals require an object (or class) type (such as Stage or Scene) followed by curly braces { }. Any properties you need to initialize appear inside the braces. (Stage has a title property and Scene and Group both have content properties.) Each property has a name, followed by a colon : and an initial value for the property. You separate properties with commas, line breaks, or white space. Here, for example is an object literal that initializes a Rectangle (properties x and y designate the upper-left corner origin).

```
Rectangle { x: 10, y: 20, height: 15, width: 150 }
```

The above Stage, Scene, and Group objects are defined with object literals. Note that the Scene object nests inside the Stage object. Likewise, a Group nests inside the Scene. Square brackets [ ] define a sequence of items for the content property in a Scene or Group. Here, the Scene object's content property is a sequence of all of the top-level nodes of the Scene. In the GuitarTuner application, this is a Group node (see Figure 2.2 or Figure 2.3). The Group node likewise includes a content property with all of its subnodes (Rectangles, Lines, and a custom GuitarString). How you nest these nodes determines the structure of the scene graph.

Here's the top-level implementation for GuitarString from its scene graph in Figure 2.2 (and Figure 2.3).

```
// GuitarString - defined as custom class
Group {
    content: [
        Rectangle { ... }
        Rectangle { ... }
        Rectangle { ... }
        Text { ... }
    ]
} // Group
```

The GuitarString consists of a Group node whose content property defines a sequence containing three rectangles and a Text object. You'll see how this fits into the Guitar-Tuner application later on.

2.4 Key JavaFX Features

GuitarTuner is a fairly typical JavaFX example application. It has a graphical representation and responds to user input by changing some of its visual properties (as well as producing guitar sounds). Let's look at some of the key JavaFX features it uses to give you a broad look at the language.

Signature JavaFX Features

Included in any list of key JavaFX features are binding, node event handlers, and animation. We discuss each of these important constructs in their own section (see "Doing Things" on page 31).

Type Inference

JavaFX provides def for read-only variables and var for modifiable variables.

```
def numberFrets = 2;      // read-only Integer
var x = 27.5;             // variable Number
var y: Number;            // default value is 0.0
var s: String;            // default value is ""
```

The compiler *infers types* from the values you assign to variables. Read-only numberFrets has inferred type Integer; variable x has inferred type Number (Float). This means you don't have to specify types everywhere (and the compiler tells you when a type is required.)

Strings

JavaFX supports dynamic string building. Curly braces { } within a String expression evaluate to the contents of the enclosed variable. You can build Strings by concatenating these String expressions and String literals. For example, the following snippet prints "Greetings, John Doe!".

```
def s1 = "John Doe";
println("Greetings, {s1}!");      // Greetings, John Doe!
```

Shapes

JavaFX has numerous shapes that help you create scene graph nodes. There are shapes for creating lines (Line, CubicCurve, QuadCurve, PolyLine, Path) and shapes for creating geometric figures (Arc, Circle, Ellipse, Rectangle, Polygon). The Guitar-Tuner application uses only Rectangle and Line, but you'll see other shape examples throughout this book.

Let's look at shapes Rectangle and Circle. They are both standard JavaFX shapes that extend class Shape (in package javafx.scene.shape). You define a Circle by specifying values for its radius, centerX, and centerY properties. With Rectangle, you specify values for properties height, width, x, and y.

Shapes share several properties in common, including properties fill (type Paint to fill the interior of the shape), stroke (type Paint to provide the outline of the shape), and strokeWidth (an Integer for the width of the outline).

Here, for example, is a Circle with its center at point (50,50), radius 30, and color Color.RED.

```
Circle {
    radius: 30
    centerX: 50
    centerY: 50
    fill: Color.RED
}
```

Here is a Rectangle with its top left corner at point (30, 100), height 30, width 80, and color Color.BLUE.

```
Rectangle {
    x: 30, y: 100
    height: 30, width: 80
    fill: Color.BLUE
}
```

All shapes are also Nodes (javafx.scene.Node). Node is an all-important class that provides local geometry for node elements, properties to specify transformations (such as translation, rotation, scaling, or shearing), and properties to specify functions for mouse and key events. Nodes also have properties that let you assign CSS styles to specify rendering.[1] We discuss graphical objects in detail in Chapter 4.

Sequences

Sequences let you define a collection of objects that you can access sequentially. You must declare the type of object a sequence will hold or provide values so that its type can be inferred. For example, the following statements define sequence variables of GuitarString and Rectangle objects.

```
var guitarStrings: GuitarString[];
var rectangleSequence: Rectangle[];
```

These statements create read-only sequences with def. Here, sequence noteValues has an inferred type of Integer[]; sequence guitarNotes has an inferred type of String[].

```
def noteValues = [ 40,45,50,55,59,64 ];
def guitarNotes = [ "E","A","D","G","B","E" ];
```

Sequences have specialized operators and syntax. You will use sequences in JavaFX whenever you need to keep track of multiple items of the same object type. The GuitarTuner application uses a sequence with a for loop to build multiple Line objects (the frets) and GuitarString objects.

```
// Build Frets
for (i in [0..<numberFrets])
    Line { . . . }

// Build Strings
for (i in [0..<numberStrings])
    GuitarString { . . . }
```

The notation [0..<n] is a sequence literal and defines a range of numbers from 0 to n-1, inclusive.

You can declare and populate sequences easily. The following *declarative approach* inserts Rectangles into a sequence called rectangleSequence, stacking six Rectangles vertically.

```
def rectangleSequence = for (i in [0..5])
    Rectangle {
```

---

1. Cascading Style Sheets (CSS) help style web pages and let designers give a uniform look and feel throughout an application, widget, or entire web site. You can use CSS to similarly style JavaFX nodes. (See "Cascading Style Sheets (CSS)" on page 148 for details on applying styles to JavaFX nodes.)

```
        x: 20
        y: i * 30
        height: 20
        width: 40
    }
```

You can also insert number values or objects into an existing sequence using the insert operator. The following *imperative approach* inserts the six Rectangles into a sequence called varRectangleSequence.

```
    var varRectangleSequence: Rectangle[];
    for (i in [0..5])
       insert Rectangle {
           x: 20
           y: i * 30
           height: 20
           width: 40
       } into varRectangleSequence;
```

JavaFX Tip

The declarative approach with rectangleSequence *is always preferred (if possible). By using* def *rather than* var *and declaring sequences rather than inserting objects into them, type inference will more likely help you and the compiler can optimize the code more effectively.*

You'll see more uses of sequence types throughout this book.

Calling Java APIs

You can call any Java API method in JavaFX programs without having to do anything special. The GuitarString node "plays a note" by calling function noteOn found in Java class SingleNote. Here is GuitarString function playNote which invokes SingleNote member function noteOn.

```
    function playNote(): Void {
       synthNote.noteOn(note);     // nothing special to call Java methods
       vibrateOn();
    }
```

Class SingleNote uses the Java javax.sound.midi package to generate a synthesized note with a certain value (60 is "middle C"). Java class SingleNote is part of project GuitarTuner.

Extending CustomNode

JavaFX offers developers such object-oriented features as user-defined classes, over-riding virtual functions, and abstract base classes (there is also "mixin" inheritance).

GuitarTuner uses a class hierarchy with subclass GuitarString inheriting from a JavaFX class called CustomNode, as shown in Figure 2.4.

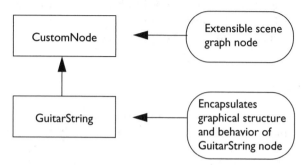

Figure 2.4 GuitarString Class Hierarchy

This approach lets you build your own graphical objects. In order for a custom object to fit seamlessly into a JavaFX scene graph, you base its behavior on a special class provided by JavaFX, *CustomNode*. Class CustomNode is a scene graph node (a type of Node, discussed earlier) that lets you specify new classes that *extend* from it. Just like Java, "extends" is the JavaFX language construct that creates an inheritance relationship. Here, GuitarString extends (*inherits from*) CustomNode. You then supply the additional structure and behavior you need for GuitarString objects and override any functions required by CustomNode. JavaFX class constructs are discussed in more detail in Chapter 3 (see "Classes and Objects" on page 67).

Here is some of the code from GuitarTuner's GuitarString class. The `create` function returns a Node defining the Group scene graph for GuitarString. (This scene graph matches the node structure in Figure 2.2 on page 15 and Figure 2.3 on page 17. Listing 2.2 on page 38 shows the `create` function in more detail.)

```
public class GuitarString extends CustomNode {
   // properties, variables, functions
   . . .
   protected override function create(): Node {
      return Group {
         content: [
            Rectangle { ... }
            Rectangle { ... }
            Rectangle { ... }
            Text { ... }
         ]
      } // Group
   }
} // GuitarString
```

Geometry System

In JavaFX, nodes are positioned on a two-dimensional coordinate system with the origin at the upper-left corner. Values for x increase horizontally from left to right and y values increase vertically from top to bottom. The coordinate system is always relative to the parent container.

Layout/Groups

Layout components specify how you want objects drawn relative to other objects. For example, layout component HBox (horizontal box) evenly spaces its subnodes in a single row. Layout component VBox (vertical box) evenly spaces its subnodes in a single column. Other layout choices are Flow, Tile, and Stack (see "Layout Components" on page 119). You can nest layout components as needed.

Grouping nodes into a single entity makes it straightforward to control event handling, animation, group-level properties, and layout for the group as a whole. Each group (or layout node) defines a coordinate system that is used by all of its children. In GuitarTuner, the top level node in the scene graph is a Group which is centered vertically within the scene. The subnodes are all drawn relative to the origin (0,0) within the top-level Group. Centering the Group, therefore, centers its contents as a whole.

Benefits of Relative Coordinate Space

Nodes with the same parent share the same relative coordinate space. This keeps any coordinate space calculations for subnodes separate from layout issues of the parent container. Then, when you move the parent, everything under it moves, keeping relative positions intact.

JavaFX Script Artifacts

Defining the Stage and Scene are central to most JavaFX applications. However, JavaFX scripts can also contain package declarations, import statements, class declarations, functions, variable declarations, statements, and object literal expressions. You've already seen how object literal expressions can initialize nodes in a scene graph. Let's discuss briefly how you can use these other artifacts.

Since JavaFX is statically typed, you must use either import statements or declare all types that are not built-in. You'll typically define a package and then specify import statements. (We discuss working with packages in Chapter 3. See "Script Files and Packages" on page 86.) Here is the package declaration and import statements for GuitarTuner.

```
package guitartuner;

import javafx.scene.effect.DropShadow;
```

```
import javafx.scene.paint.Color;
import javafx.scene.paint.LinearGradient;

    . . . more import statements . . .

import javafx.stage.Stage;
import noteplayer.SingleNote;
```

If you're using NetBeans, the IDE can generate import statements for you (type **Ctrl+Shift+I** in the editor window).

You'll need script-level variables to store data and read-only variables (def) for values that don't change. In GuitarTuner, we define several read-only variables that help build the guitar strings and a variable (singleNote) that communicates with the Java midi API. Note that noteValues and guitarNotes are def sequence types.

```
def noteValues = [ 40,45,50,55,59,64 ];
def guitarNotes = [ "E","A","D","G","B","E" ];
def numberFrets = 2;
def numberStrings = 6;
var singleNote =  SingleNote { };
```

When you declare a Stage, you define the nested nodes in the scene graph. Instead of declaring nodes only as object literal expressions, it's also possible to assign these object literals to variables. This lets you refer to them later in your code. (For example, the Scene object literal and the Group object literal are assigned to variables in order to compute the offset for centering the group vertically in the scene.)

```
var scene: Scene;
var group: Group;

scene: scene = Scene { ... }
group = Group { ... }
```

You may also need to execute JavaFX script statements or define utility functions. Here's how GuitarTuner makes the SingleNote object emit a "guitar" sound.

```
singleNote.setInstrument(27);           // "Clean Guitar"
```

Once you set up the Stage and scene graph for an application, it's ready to ready to run.[2] In GuitarTuner, the application waits for the user to pluck (click) a guitar string.

---

2. Java developers may wonder where function main() is. As it turns out, the JavaFX compiler generates a main() for you, but from a developer's view, you have just a script file.

2.5 Making Things Look Good

Using JavaFX features that enhance the appearance of graphical objects will help your application look professionally designed. Here are some simple additions you can apply.

Gradients

Gradients lend a depth to surfaces and backgrounds by gradually varying the color of the object's fill property. In general, use linear gradients with rectangular shapes and radial gradients with circles and ovals. In GuitarTuner, the background is a linear gradient that transitions from Color.LIGHTGRAY (at the top) to the darker Color.GRAY (at the bottom) as shown in Figure 2.5. The guitar fret board also uses a linear gradient.

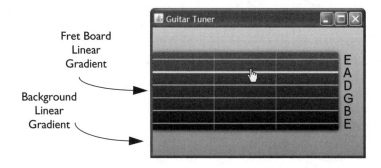

Figure 2.5 Gradients in the GuitarTuner Application

Here is the LinearGradient for the background scene in GuitarTuner, defined for property fill. Note that specifying gradients is declarative; you identify the look you want and the system figures out how to achieve it, independent of screen resolution, color depth, etc.

```
fill: LinearGradient {
    startX: 0.0
    startY: 0.0
    endX: 0.0
    endY: 1.0
    proportional: true
    stops: [
        Stop {
            offset: 0.0
            color: Color.LIGHTGRAY
        },
        Stop {
            offset: 1.0
```

```
            color: Color.GRAY
        }
    ]
}
```

The background gradient changes color along the y axis and the color is constant along the x axis (properties `startX` and `endX` are the same). Property `stops` is a sequence of Stop objects containing an `offset` and a `color`. The offset is a value between 0 and 1 inclusive; each succeeding offset must have a higher value than the preceding one.

Property `proportional` indicates whether start and end values are proportional (defined between [0..1] if `true`) or absolute (absolute coordinates if `false`).

Radial gradients work well for circular shapes, as shown in Figure 2.6. Here you see three Circle shapes, all with radial gradients. The first circle defines a gradient with its center in the lower left quadrant (`centerX` is `0.25` and `centerY` is `0.75`). The second circle's gradient is centered (`centerX` and `centerY` are both `0.5`), and the third circle's gradient appears in the upper right quadrant (`centerX` is `0.75` and `centerY` is `0.25`).

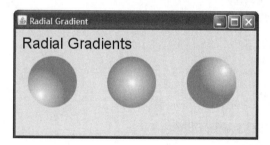

Figure 2.6 Radial Gradients work well with circular shapes

Here is the radial gradient for the middle circle.

```
fill: RadialGradient {
    centerX: 0.5        // x center of gradient
    centerY: 0.5        // y center of gradient
    radius: 0.5         // radius of gradient
    stops: [
        Stop {
            offset: 0
            color: Color.WHITE
        },
        Stop {
            offset: 1
```

```
        color: Color.DODGERBLUE
    }
  ]
}
```

Note that the gradient is half the size of the circle (radius is 0.5). Making the gradient less than the full size lets the last stop color appear more prominent (the dark color predominates).

Color

You specify a shape's color with property fill. JavaFX has many predefined colors ranging alphabetically from Color.ALICEBLUE to Color.YELLOWGREEN. (In the NetBeans IDE, press **Ctrl+Space** when the cursor is after the dot in Color to see a complete list, as shown in Figure 2.7.)

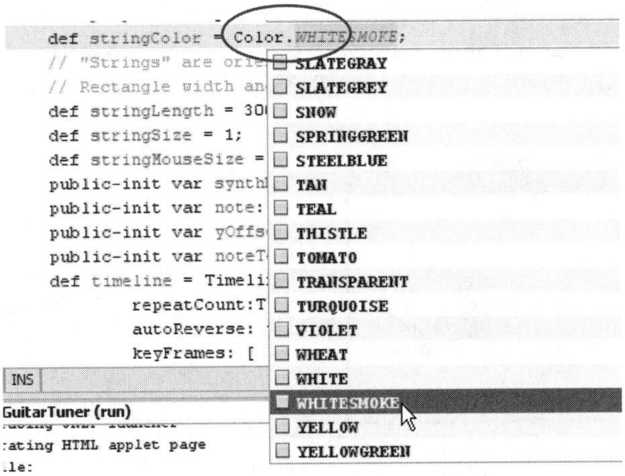

Figure 2.7 Explore color choices with the NetBeans IDE

You can also specify arbitrary colors with Color.rgb (each RGB value ranges from 0 to 255), Color.color (each RGB value ranges from 0 to 1), and Color.web (a String corresponding to the traditional hexadecimal-based triad). An optional final argument sets the opacity, where 1 is fully opaque and 0 is fully translucent. You can also make a shape transparent by setting its fill property to Color.TRANSPARENT.

Here are several examples of color settings. Each example sets the opacity to .5, which allows some of the background color to show through.

```
def c1 = Color.rgb(10, 255, 15, .5);       // bright lime green
def c2 = Color.color(0.5, 0.1, 0.1, .5);   // dark red
def c3 = Color.web("#546270", .5);         // dark blue-gray
```

Numeric-based color values (rather than hexadecimal strings or predefined colors) let you write functions and animations that numerically manipulate gradients, colors, or opacity. For example, the following `fill` property gets its `Color.rgb` values from a `for` loop's changing value i. The loop produces three different shades of green, depending on the value of i.

```
def rectangleSequence = for (i in [0..2])
    Rectangle {
        x: 60 * i
        y: 50
        height: 50
        width: 40
        fill: Color.rgb(10 + (i*50), 100 + (i*40), i*50)
    }
```

Figure 2.8 shows the resulting set of rectangles with different `fill` values.

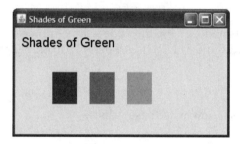

Figure 2.8 Manipulating numeric-based Color values

Rectangles with Arcs

You can soften the corners of Rectangles by specifying properties `arcWidth` and `arcHeight`, as shown in Figure 2.9. The first Rectangle has regular, square corners. The second Rectangle sets `arcHeight` and `arcWidth` to 15, and the third one uses value 30 for both. Here's the object literal for the third Rectangle.

```
Rectangle {
    x: 180
    y: 0
    height: 70
    width: 60
    arcHeight: 30
    arcWidth: 30
    fill: LinearGradient { . . . }
}
```

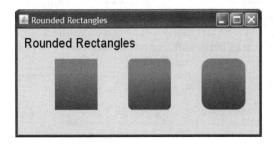

Figure 2.9 Soften Rectangles with rounded corners

DropShadows

One of the many effects you can specify is DropShadow (effects are declarative).
Effect DropShadow applies a shadow to its node, giving the node a three-dimensional
look. In project GuitarTuner, the fret board (guitar neck) uses a default drop shadow,
as follows.

```
effect: DropShadow { }
```

The default object literal provides a drop shadow with these values.

```
effect: DropShadow {
    offsetX: 0.0
    offsetY: 0.0
    radius: 10.0
    color: Color.BLACK
    spread: 0.0
}
```

You can manipulate the location of the shadow by changing offsetX and offsetY.
Negative values for offsetY set the shadow above the object and negative values for
offsetX set the shadow to the left. Positive values for offsetX and offsetY place the
shadow to the right and below, respectively. You can also change a shadow's size
(radius), color, and spread (how "sharp" the shadow appears). A spread value of 1
means the shadow is sharply delineated. A value of 0 provides a "fuzzy" appearance.
Figure 2.10 shows three rectangles with drop shadows that fall below and to the right
of the rectangles, using these offsets.

```
effect: DropShadow {
    // shadow appears below and to the right of object
    offsetX: 5.0
    offsetY: 5.0
}
```

Figure 2.10 Drop shadows provide a three-dimensional effect

2.6 Doing Things

JavaFX has three main constructs for doing things: binding, node properties that define event handlers, and animation. Together, these constructs provide powerful yet elegant solutions for modifying scene graphs based on user input or other events. Let's see how GuitarTuner uses these constructs to get its tasks done.

Binding

Binding in JavaFX is a powerful technique and a concise alternative to specifying traditional callback event handlers. Basically, binding lets you make a property or variable depend on the value of an expression. When you update any of the "bound to" objects in the expression, the dependent object automatically changes. Suppose, for example, we bind area to height and width, as follows.

```
var height = 3.0;
var width = 4.0;
def area = bind height * width;        // area = 12.0

width = 2.5;                           // area = 7.5
height = 4;                            // area = 10.0
```

When either height or width changes, so does area. Once you bind a property (or variable), you can't update it directly. For example, you get a compile-time error if you try to directly update area.

```
area = 5;                 // compile time error
```

If you make area a var and provide a binding expression, you'll get a runtime error if you try to update it directly.

In GuitarTuner, the vibrating string changes both its location (property translateY) and its thickness (property height) at run time to give the appearance of vibration. These properties are bound to other values that control how a guitar string node changes.

```
var vibrateH: Number;
var vibrateY: Number;

Rectangle {
    x: 0.0
    y: yOffset
    width: stringLength
    height: bind vibrateH       // change height when vibrateH changes
    fill: stringColor
    visible: false
    translateY: bind vibrateY  // change translateY when vibrateY changes
}
```

GuitarTuner also uses bind to keep the fret board centered vertically by binding property layoutY in the top level group.

```
group = Group {
    layoutY: bind (scene.height - group.layoutBounds.height) /
                 2 - group.layoutBounds.minY
    . . .
}
```

Node property layoutBounds provides bounds information for its contents. If a user resizes the window, the top level group is automatically centered vertically on the screen. Binding helps reduce event processing code because (here, for example) you don't have to write an event handler to detect a change in the window size.

Binding is Good

Binding is good for many things. For example, you can change the appearance of a node based on changes to the program's state. You can make a component visible or hidden. You can also use binding to declaratively specify layout constraints. Not only does binding produce less code, but the code is less error-prone, easier to maintain, and often easier for the compiler to optimize.

Mouse Events

JavaFX nodes have properties for handling mouse and key events. These properties are set to callback functions that the system invokes when an event triggers. In Guitar-Tuner, the "mouse detection" rectangle has the following event handler to detect a mouse click event.

```
onMouseClicked: function(evt: MouseEvent): Void {
    if (evt.button == MouseButton.PRIMARY) {
        // play and vibrate selected "string"
    }
}
```

The if statement checks for a click of the primary mouse button (generally the left mouse button is primary) before processing the event. The event handler function (shown in the next section) plays the note and vibrates the string.

Animations

JavaFX specializes in animations. (In fact, we dedicate an entire chapter to animation. See Chapter 7 beginning on page 205.) You define animations with timelines and then invoke Timeline functions play or playFromStart (there are also functions pause and stop). Timelines consist of a sequence of key frame objects that define a frame at a specific time offset within the timeline. (Key frames are declarative. You say "this is the state of the scene at this key time" and let the system figure out how to render the affected objects.) Within each key frame, you specify values, an action, or both. Traditionally, people think of animations as a way to move objects. While this is true, you'll see that JavaFX lets you animate any writable object property. You could, for instance, use animation to fade, rotate, resize, or even brighten an image.

Figure 2.11 shows a snapshot of a program with simple animation. It moves a circle back and forth across its container.

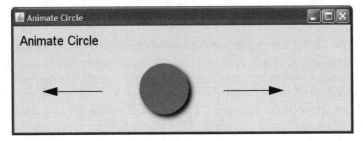

Figure 2.11 Timelines let you specify animations

Here is the timeline that implements this animation using a specialized shorthand notation for KeyFrames. The timeline starts out by setting variable x to 0. In gradual, linear increments, it changes x so that at four seconds, its value is 350. Now, it performs the action in reverse, gradually changing x so that in four more seconds it is back to 0 (autoReverse is true). This action is repeated indefinitely (or until the timeline is stopped or paused). Constants 0s and 4s are Duration literals.

```
var x: Number;
Timeline {
    repeatCount: Timeline.INDEFINITE
    autoReverse: true
    keyFrames: [
        at (0s) { x => 0.0 }
        at (4s) { x => 350 tween Interpolator.LINEAR }
    ]
}.play();                   // start Timeline
    . . .
Circle {
    . . .
    translateX: bind x
}
```

The JavaFX keyword tween is a key frame operator that lets you specify how a variable changes. Here, we use Interpolator.LINEAR for a linear change. That is, x doesn't jump from 0 to 350, but gradually takes on values in a linear fashion. Linear interpolation moves the Circle smoothly from 0 to 350, taking four seconds to complete one iteration of the timeline.

JavaFX has other interpolators. Interpolator DISCRETE jumps from the value of one key frame to the second. Interpolator EASEIN is similar to LINEAR, except the rate of change is slower at the onset. Similarly, EASEOUT is slower at the finish and EASEBOTH provides easing on both ends of the timeline.

To make this animation apply to the Circle node, you bind the Circle's translateX property to the variable manipulated by the timeline (x). Property translateX represents a node's change in the x direction.

Now let's examine how GuitarTuner uses animation to vibrate the guitar string and play its note. Each GuitarString object uses two rectangles to implement its visible behavior. One rectangle is a stationary, thin "string" and represents the string in a static state. This motionless rectangle is always visible in the scene. The second rectangle is only visible when the string is "played." This rectangle expands and contracts its height quickly using animation (a Timeline). This moving rectangle gives users the illusion of a vibrating string.

To get a uniform vibrating effect, the rectangle must expand and contract evenly on the top and bottom. The animation makes the string appear to vibrate by varying the height of the rectangle from 1 to 3 while keeping it vertically centered by varying its translateY property between 5 and 4. When the string is clicked, the string's note plays and the rectangle vibrates for the allotted time. When the timeline stops, only the stationary rectangle is visible.

Let's first look at the timeline that plays the note. This timeline appears in the event handler for the GuitarString node (see the code for GuitarString in Listing 2.2 on page 38).

```
onMouseClicked: function(evt: MouseEvent): Void {
    if (evt.button == MouseButton.PRIMARY) {
        Timeline {
            keyFrames: [
                KeyFrame {
                    time: 0s
                    action: playNote  // play note and start vibration
                }
                KeyFrame {
                    time: 2.8s
                    action: stopNote  // stop playing note and stop vibration
                }
            ]
        }.play();                     // start Timeline
    }
}
```

Here, the timeline is an object literal defined inside the event handler, invoked with function play. This timeline defines a sequence of KeyFrame objects, where function playNote is invoked at time offset 0 seconds and function stopNote is invoked at time offset 2.8 seconds (2.8s). Here are functions playNote and stopNote.

```
// play note and start vibration
function playNote(): Void {
    synthNote.noteOn(note);
    vibrateOn();
}

// stop playing note and stop vibration
function stopNote(): Void {
    synthNote.noteOff(note);
    vibrateOff();
}
```

Function synthNote.noteOn calls a Java class API to play the guitar string. Function vibrateOn causes the string vibration.

```
function vibrateOn(): Void {
    play.visible = true;    // make the vibrating rectangle visible
    timeline.play();        // start the vibration timeline
}
```

Here is the vibration timeline.

```
def timeline = Timeline {
    repeatCount: Timeline.INDEFINITE
    autoReverse: true
    keyFrames: [
```

```
        at (0s) { vibrateH => 1.0 }
        at (.01s) { vibrateH => 3.0 tween Interpolator.LINEAR }
        at (0s) { vibrateY => 5.0 }
        at (.01s) { vibrateY => 4.0 tween Interpolator.LINEAR }
    ]
};
```

This timeline uses the shorthand notation discussed earlier for key frames and animates two variables: vibrateH and vibrateY. Variable vibrateH changes the height of
the rectangle that represents the vibrating string. Variable vibrateY changes the vertical position of the rectangle to keep it centered as the oscillating height changes.

2.7 Source Code for Project GuitarTuner

Listing 2.1 and Listing 2.2 show the code for class GuitarString in two parts.
Listing 2.1 includes the class declarations, functions, class-level variables, and properties for class GuitarString. Note that several variables are declared public-init. This
JavaFX keyword means that users of the class can provide initial values with object literals, but otherwise these properties are read-only. The default accessibility for all
variables is *script-private*, making the remaining declarations private.

Use def for read-only variables and var for modifiable variables. The GuitarString
class also provides utility functions that play a note (playNote) or stop playing a note
(stopNote). Along with the sound, guitar strings vibrate on and off with vibrateOn and
vibrateOff. These functions implement the behavior of the GuitarString class.

Listing 2.1 Class GuitarString—Properties, Variables, and Functions

```
package guitartuner;

import javafx.animation.Interpolator;
import javafx.animation.KeyFrame;
import javafx.animation.Timeline;
import javafx.scene.Cursor;
import javafx.scene.CustomNode;
import javafx.scene.Group;
import javafx.scene.input.MouseButton;
import javafx.scene.input.MouseEvent;
import javafx.scene.Node;
import javafx.scene.paint.Color;
import javafx.scene.shape.Rectangle;
import javafx.scene.text.Font;
import javafx.scene.text.Text;
import noteplayer.SingleNote;

public class GuitarString extends CustomNode {
```

```
// read-only variables
def stringColor = Color.WHITESMOKE;
// "Strings" are oriented sideways, so stringLength is the
// Rectangle width and stringSize is the Rectangle height
def stringLength = 300;
def stringSize = 1;
def stringMouseSize = 15;
def timeline = Timeline {
    repeatCount: Timeline.INDEFINITE
    autoReverse: true
    keyFrames: [
        at (0s) { vibrateH => 1.0 }
        at (.01s) { vibrateH => 3.0 tween Interpolator.LINEAR }
        at (0s) { vibrateY => 5.0 }
        at (.01s) { vibrateY => 4.0 tween Interpolator.LINEAR }
    ]
};

// properties to be initialized
public-init var synthNote: SingleNote;
public-init var note: Integer;
public-init var yOffset: Number;
public-init var noteText: String;

// class variables
var vibrateH: Number;
var vibrateY: Number;
var play: Rectangle;

function vibrateOn(): Void {
    play.visible = true;
    timeline.play();
}
function vibrateOff(): Void {
    play.visible = false;
    timeline.stop();
}
function playNote(): Void {
    synthNote.noteOn(note);
    vibrateOn();
}
function stopNote(): Void {
    synthNote.noteOff(note);
    vibrateOff();
}
```

Listing 2.2 shows the second part of the code for the GuitarString class.

Every class that extends CustomNode must define a function create that returns a Node object.[3] Often the node you return will be a Group, since Group is the most general Node type and can include subnodes. But, you can return other Node types, such as Rectangle (Shape) or HBox (horizontal box) layout node.

The scene graph for GuitarString is interesting because it actually consists of three Rectangle nodes and a Text node. The first Rectangle, used to detect mouse clicks, is completely translucent (its opacity is 0). This Rectangle is wider than the guitar string so the user can more easily select it with the mouse. Several properties implement its behavior: property cursor lets a user know the string is selected and property onMouseClicked provides the event handling code (play the note and vibrate the string).

The second Rectangle node defines the visible string. The third Rectangle node (assigned to variable play) "vibrates" by both moving and changing its height. This rectangle is only visible when a note is playing and provides the vibration effect of "plucking" a string. The movement and change in height are achieved with animation and binding. The Text node simply displays the letter (E, A, D, etc.) associated with the guitar string's note.

Listing 2.2 Scene Graph for GuitarString

```
protected override function create(): Node {
    return Group {
        content: [
            // Rectangle to detect mouse events for string plucking
            Rectangle {
                x: 0
                y: yOffset
                width: stringLength
                height: stringMouseSize
                // Rectangle has to be "visible" or scene graph will
                // ignore mouse events. Therefore, we make it fully
                // translucent (opacity=0) so it is effectively invisible
                fill: Color.web("#FFFFF", 0)    // translucent
                cursor: Cursor.HAND
                onMouseClicked: function(evt: MouseEvent): Void {
                    if (evt.button == MouseButton.PRIMARY){
                        Timeline {
                            keyFrames: [
                                KeyFrame {
```

---

3. Well, almost. If you don't define function create, then you must declare the class abstract. The Piano example (see "Project Piano" on page 167) uses an abstract class.

```
                                   time: 0s
                                   action: playNote
                               }
                               KeyFrame {
                                   time: 2.8s
                                   action: stopNote
                               }
                           ]   // keyFrames

                       }.play();  // start Timeline
                   } // if
               }
           }   // Rectangle
           // Rectangle to render the guitar string
           Rectangle {
               x: 0.0
               y: 5 + yOffset
               width: stringLength
               height: stringSize
               fill: stringColor
           }
           // Special "string" that vibrates by changing its height
           // and location
           play = Rectangle {
               x: 0.0
               y: yOffset
               width: stringLength
               height: bind vibrateH
               fill: stringColor
               visible: false
               translateY: bind vibrateY
           }
           Text {       // Display guitar string note name
               x: stringLength + 8
               y: 13 + yOffset
               font: Font {
                   size: 20
               }
               content: noteText
           }
       ]
   }   // Group
   }
} // GuitarString
```

Listing 2.3 shows the code for **Main.fx**, the main program for GuitarTuner.

Listing 2.3 Main.fx

```
package guitartuner;
import guitartuner.GuitarString;
import javafx.scene.effect.DropShadow;
import javafx.scene.Group;
import javafx.scene.paint.Color;
import javafx.scene.paint.LinearGradient;
import javafx.scene.paint.Stop;
import javafx.scene.Scene;
import javafx.scene.shape.Line;
import javafx.scene.shape.Rectangle;
import javafx.stage.Stage;
import noteplayer.SingleNote;

def noteValues = [ 40,45,50,55,59,64 ];   // numeric value required by midi
def guitarNotes = [ "E","A","D","G","B","E" ];
// guitar note name
def numberFrets = 2;
def numberStrings = 6;
var singleNote =  SingleNote{};
singleNote.setInstrument(27);            // "Clean Guitar"

var scene: Scene;
var group: Group;
Stage {
    title: "Guitar Tuner"
    visible: true
    scene: scene = Scene {
      fill: LinearGradient {
         startX: 0.0
         startY: 0.0
         endX: 0.0
         endY: 1.0
         proportional: true
         stops: [
            Stop {
               offset: 0.0
               color: Color.LIGHTGRAY
            },
            Stop {
               offset: 1.0
               color: Color.GRAY
            }
         ]
      }
      width: 340
      height: 200
      content: [
          group = Group {
              // Center the whole group vertically within the scene
              layoutY: bind (scene.height - group.layoutBounds.height) /
```

```
                2 - group.layoutBounds.minY
        content: [
            Rectangle {              // guitar neck (fret board)
                effect: DropShadow { }
                x: 0
                y: 0
                width: 300
                height: 121
                fill: LinearGradient {
                startX: 0.0
                startY: 0.0
                endX: 0.0
                endY: 1.0
                proportional: true
                stops: [
                    Stop {
                        offset: 0.0
                        color: Color.SADDLEBROWN
                    },
                    Stop {
                        offset: 1.0
                        color: Color.BLACK
                    }
                ]
            }
        } // Rectangle
            for (i in [0..<numberFrets])   // two frets
                Line {
                    startX: 100 * (i + 1)
                    startY: 0
                    endX: 100 * (i + 1)
                    endY: 120
                    stroke: Color.GRAY
                }
            for (i in [0..<numberStrings])   // six guitar strings
                GuitarString {
                    yOffset: i * 20 + 5
                    note: noteValues[i]
                    noteText: guitarNotes[i]
                    synthNote: singleNote
                }
        ]
    }
    ]
    }
}
```

3 JavaFX Language

Now that you've seen JavaFX code in the overview application example, let's discuss the JavaFX scripting language in more detail. This chapter covers the essential aspects of the JavaFX language.

What You Will Learn

- Declaring variables and defining their types
- Using operators and expressions
- Using sequences
- Writing functions with arguments and return values
- Using function types
- Defining classes, instance variables, and instance functions
- Creating objects from classes with object literals
- Using inheritance and overriding functions
- Writing init and postinit blocks
- Using abstract classes and mixin inheritance
- Using binding and triggers
- Packaging classes and writing script files
- Exception handling

3.1 Variables and Types

In JavaFX, you define modifiable variables with the keyword var. Use the keyword def for read-only variables. Attempts to directly modify def variables result in compile-time errors.

```
def maxLength = 100;        // read-only
```

```
var count = 0;           // readable and writable
count++;                 // count is writable
maxLength = 500;         // compiler error
```

You can also use def with variables that change through binding (see "Binding Expressions" on page 52). Using def allows the compiler to generate more efficient code and check the correctness of your program.

Programming Tip

If something can be def, *it probably should be.*

You may have noticed that the above var and def statements did not specify any *types* for the declarations. This is because JavaFX has a sophisticated inference engine that determines types by their use. Type inference makes your code more concise. Of course, you can always specify types explicitly if you need to.

```
def maxLength: Integer = 100;    // read-only
var count: Integer = 0;          // readable and writable
```

JavaFX Types

JavaFX is a statically-typed language with the following built-in types: Boolean, Integer, Number, String, Duration, and Void. Use Boolean for boolean variables, Integer for integral variables, Number for floating variables, and String for strings. Use Void with functions that do not return values. (Note that the Void keyword begins with a capital V in JavaFX.) Duration types support time literals.

Let's look at the built-in JavaFX types in more detail.

Boolean

The Boolean type is handy for variables representing flags and any application-specific internal state. Use the keywords true and false for boolean values. The default value for Boolean is false.

```
var isElement: Boolean;    // Boolean type, default is false
var flag = true;           // Boolean type inferred
isElement = 1;             // compiler error
flag++;                    // compiler error
```

Integer

The `Integer` type is signed integral values representing 32 bits. You can use octal (prefix with `0`) or hexadecimal notation (prefix with `0x` or `0X`) to initialize or assign values. The default value for `Integer` is `0`.

```
var counter: Integer;        // Integer type (32 bits), default is 0
def length = 80;             // Integer type inferred
var byte = 0x3f;             // hexadecimal value
var word = 037;              // octal value
```

Number

Use `Number` when you need 32-bit floating-point precision. The default value for `Number` is `0.0`.

```
var radius: Number;          // Number type, default is 0.0
var value = 1.1;             // Number type inferred
var big = 1.56e10;           // big number
var small = 6.32e-25;        // small number
```

String

The String type represents character strings of any length. You can use double quotation marks (") or single quotation marks (') to enclose character string literals. Single quotation marks are legal within double-quoted strings without being escaped (and vice versa). The compiler also merges adjacent string literals for you at compile-time, making it convenient to define strings on multiple lines. Use curly braces "{}" to embed expressions in strings. The default value for `String` is `""`.

```
var s: String;               // String type, default is ""
var a = "datapoint";         // String type inferred
var b = "I can't figure it out, that's too hard";
def c = "Hello "             // adjacent strings
"and Goodbye";               // "Hello and Goodbye"
var s1 = 'duck';             // single quotes ok
var s2 = 'soup';             // single quotes ok
var s3 = "{s1} {s2}";        // "duck soup"
var s4 = s1 s2;              // compiler error
var s5 = "alpha" "bet";      // "alphabet"
```

Duration

The `Duration` type represents floating values for units of time. Durations are denoted with time literals (`ms` for milliseconds, `s` for seconds, `m` for minutes, and `h` for hours). You typically use `Duration` types with animation in JavaFX. The default value for `Duration` is `0ms`.

```
var timeSlice: Duration;    // Duration type, default is 0ms
var period = 100ms;         // Duration type inferred, 100 milliseconds
var halfMinute = 30s;       // 30 seconds
var halfHour = 30m;         // 30 minutes
var halfDay = 12h;          // 12 hours
var halfPast = .5h;         // half hour
```

Void

Use the Void type to define a function that does not return a value.

```
function startSimulation(): Void {
    simulate(100ms);
    // no return value
}
```

(See "Functions" on page 61 for more details about JavaFX functions.)

But Wait, There's More . . .

You can also use Java wrapper types in JavaFX, but you probably won't need them very often. These types are primarily used for interoperability with Java classes that use primitives in their interfaces. Use Character for 16-bit Unicodes, Byte for 8 bits, Short for 16 bits, Integer for 32 bits, and Long for 64 bits (all signed integral values). For floating values, use Float (32 bits) or Double (64 bits). In JavaFX, the Number type is Float (32 bits). Here are some examples.

```
var ch: Character = 120;    // Unicode character (16 bits) - 'x'
var ts: Byte = 127;         // 8 bits
var data: Byte = 500;       // compiler error - too large for 8 bits
var ts: Short = 10;         // Short (16 bits)
var sdata: Short = 50000;   // compiler error - too large for 16 bits
var tl: Long = 100000;      // Long (64 bits)
var tg: Double = 3.45;      // Double (64 bits)
var tf: Float = 1.23;       // Float type (32 bits) - same as Number
```

Printing Variables

Printing the values of JavaFX variables on the console screen is easy. The function print(var) prints the value of *var* and println(var) prints the value of *var* followed by a newline. Here are some examples.

```
var b = true;               // Boolean type
println(b);                 // true
var i = 12;                 // Integer type
println(i);                 // 12
var f = 3.45;               // Number type
println(f);                 // 3.45
var s = "javafx";           // String type
```

```
println(s);              // javafx
var d = 100ms;           // Duration type
println(d);              // 100.0ms
var a: Character = 97;   // Character type
println(a);              // 'a'
print("last");           // last (no newline)
println("");             // empty string with newline
```

You can also use curly braces "{}" to embed variable values in string expressions.

```
var i = 12; var s = "javafx";
println("i = {i}, s = {s}");          // i = 12, s = javafx
```

For more sophisticated formatting, "printf-like" formats are available within "{}".

```
var i = 12; var s = "javafx";
println("i = {%3d i}, s = {%.4s s}");  // i =  12, s = java
var v = 56.789;
println("v = {%8.2f v}");             // v =    56.79
```

The first `println()` prints integer i right-justified in a field of 3 characters followed by the first four characters of the string s. The second `println()` prints floating value v in a field of 8 characters with 2 digits to the right of the decimal point. Refer to the Javadoc for `java.lang.System.printf()` to learn more about these formatting options.

Pseudo Variables

JavaFX supports several pre-defined variables that you can use in your programs. These variables are script-level read-only `def` variables.

Table 3.1 shows the JavaFX pseudo-variables.

TABLE 3.1 Built-In JavaFX pseudo variables

Name	Description
__PROFILE__	Environment ("mobile", "desktop", "browser")
__FILE__	Script file name (full path name)
__DIR__	Script file directory (full path name)

3.2 Operators

JavaFX has arithmetic, assignment, unary, relational, and logical operators. The `instanceof` operator determines variable types. Let's look at each of these operators separately.

Arithmetic Operators

The arithmetic operators are add (+), subtract (-), multiply (*), divide (/) and divide with integer remainder (mod). Here are several examples with Integer variables.

```
var val = 25; var nt = 4;
var a = val + nt;           // a is 29
var b = val - nt;           // b is 21
var c = val * nt;           // c is 100
var d = val / nt;           // d is 6
var e = val mod nt;         // e is 1
```

Mixed type arithmetic will do what is reasonable, as these examples show.

```
var fv = 6.5;               // fv is Number type
var ic = 6;                 // ic is Integer type
var td = 100ms;             // td is Duration type
var tg = 10ms;              // tg is Duration type

var gv = fv * ic;           // gv is Number type
var tf = td / fv;           // tf is Duration type
var hm = td / tg;           // hm is Number type
var mm = td * tg;           // compiler error
```

Assignment Operators

Besides conventional assignments with =, you can also form compound assignments with arithmetic operators. Here are some examples with Integer variables.

```
var val = 25; var nt = 4;
val += nt;                  // val = val + nt; (val is 29)
val -= nt;                  // val = val - nt; (val is 25)
val *= nt;                  // val = val * nt; (val is 100)
val /= nt;                  // val = val / nt; (val is 25)
```

The mod operator is not allowed in a compound assignment. Instead, you must do

```
val = val mod nt;           // val is 1
```

You can also assign a sequence of values with [].

```
var summerMonths = ["June", "July", "August"];
var powersOfTen = [10, 100, 1000, 10000];
```

For more on assignments with sequences, see "Sequence Literals" on page 54.

Unary Operators

Although most operators in JavaFX are binary (two operands), there are several unary (one operand) operators. These are ++ (preincrement, postincrement), -- (predecrement, postdecrement), - (negation), and not (logical complement). Here are some examples.

```
var data = 10;
var negate = -data;              // negate is -10
var m; var n;
var s = 5; var t = 5;
m = s++;                         // m is 5, s is 6
n = ++s;                         // n is 7, s is 7
m = t--;                         // m is 5, t is 4
n = --t;                         // n is 3, t is 3
var enabled = false;
var start = not enabled;         // start is true
```

Relational Operators

The relational operators compare values (>, >=, <, <=) and test for equality (==, !=). Here are several examples.

```
var f = 10.5; var g = 20.5; var h;
h = (f == g);                    // h is false
h = (f != g);                    // h is true
h = (f > g);                     // h is false
h = (f < g);                     // h is true
h = (f >= g);                    // h is false
h = (f <= g);                    // h is true
h = (f > 10);                    // h is true
```

Note that the inferred type is Boolean for variable h in these examples. The last example compares different types (Number and Integer). In this case, the Integer is first converted to Number before the comparison.

With Strings, the equality operators (==, !=) in JavaFX perform *value* comparisons (this is different than Java).

```
def input: String = getInput();     // get input String
var exit = (input == "quit");       // true if input string is "quit"
```

Logical Operators

The and operator and the or operator let you combine boolean expressions.

```
var i = 2; var j = 3; var k = 4;
var p = (j > i and j < k);       // p is true
var q = (j > k or i < k);        // q is true
```

Both operators have "short-circuit" behaviors; that is, if the first expression of operator and is false, the second expression is not evaluated. Likewise, the second expression of operator or is not evaluated if the first expression is true.

Instanceof Operator

The `instanceof` operator tells you if an object is a specific type, returning `true` for a correct type match. Here are several examples.

```
def u = "string of chars";        // String
var v = u instanceof String;      // v is true
def w = 6.5;                      // Number (Float)
v = w instanceof java.lang.Float;  // v is true
```

You typically use `instanceof` with the as operator to determine if an object is an instance of a specific class at runtime. (See "As Operator" on page 80.)

3.3 Expressions

JavaFX is an expression language with *value expressions*. Many forms of blocks, loops, and conditionals in JavaFX are actually expressions in themselves with a value and a type. In certain cases, for instance, you can use the return value of an `if` statement in an assignment statement or the return value from a `for` loop to create a new sequence. You can also bind expressions.

Let's look at JavaFX expressions in more detail.

Block Expressions

A block in JavaFX is a list of expressions enclosed by curly braces. The value of the block expression is the value of the last expression. Blocks can be empty (their type is `Void`) and `var` and `def` statements are expressions, too (their value is the value of the new variable).

Typically, blocks are used for function bodies and with `if` statements, `for` loops, and `while` loops. Blocks can have local `var` variables and `def` constants whose scope is defined only within the block where they are declared. However, blocks can also return values in JavaFX.

```
var a = 10; var b = 20; var c = 30;
var sum = {                  // start of block
   def d = 40; def e = 50;
   a + b + c + d + e         // value of last expression
}                            // end of block
println(sum);                // sum is 150
```

A block's type and value is the type and value of the last expression in the block, which does not require a terminating semicolon.

If Expressions

An if expression alters program flow based on the value of a boolean expression as a conditional.

```
var num;
var i: Integer = getNumber();
if (i >= 0 and i <= 9)
    num = "single digit";
```

The else keyword can also be used with if expressions.

```
var num;
var i: Integer = getNumber();
if (i >= 0 and i <= 9) {
    num = "single digit";
} else if (i >= 10 and i <= 99) {
    num = "two digits";
} else
    num = "three digits or more";
```

Since if expressions are value expressions in JavaFX, we can collapse all this code into the following terse form (no braces needed).

```
var i: Integer = getNumber();
var num = if (i >= 0 and i <= 9) "single digit"
          else if (i >= 10 and i <= 99) "two digits"
          else "three digits or more";
```

Note that if controls the execution of one expression. If that expression includes one statement, a block with braces is optional. If that expression includes more than one statement, you must use a block.

For Expressions

A for loop is an easy way to do something a certain number of times.

```
for (i in [1..5]) {
    doSomething();           // call function five times
}
```

The notation [1..5] generates a sequence literal (see "Sequence Literals" on page 54).

A for loop is also convenient for going through a sequence of items.

```
var strings = ["straight", "forward", "thinking"];
for (s in strings) {
    writeText(s);           // call function three times with s
}
```

This for loop fetches three strings from a sequence, one at a time, assigns each one to variable s, and passes it as an argument to function writeText.

Programming Tip

Note that you do not declare loop variables with var *or* def *before the keyword* in. *You cannot modify a loop variable and its scope is the loop where it is defined.*

A for loop is actually an expression that returns a sequence. We show you how to use this powerful technique in "Creating Sequences with for" on page 56.

While Expressions

A while expression loops until a given condition is false. While expressions do not return a value. While loops are typically used when you can easily express the loop continuation condition as a boolean. Here is an example.

```
var u = 1234;              // count number of digits in number
var numDigits = 0;
while (u != 0) {
    numDigits++;
    u /= 10;
}
println(numDigits);        // numDigits is 4
```

Break and Continue

The keywords break and continue may only appear inside for and while expressions. Use continue to skip to the next iteration and break to exit a loop immediately.

```
var str: String = getString();
for (weekDay in ["Mon", "Tues", "Wed", "Thu", "Fri"]) {
    if (weekDay == "Wed") continue;    // skip Wed
    . . .
    if (str == weekDay) break;         // exit loop
}
```

Binding Expressions

One of the most powerful features of JavaFX is *binding*. The idea is to bind a variable in your program to something that changes when your program runs. This creates a *dependency* between your variable and what is changing. When dependencies change, your variable automatically updates. JavaFX lets you bind def or var variables to expressions (blocks, conditionals, functions, for loops, and object literals).

The format for binding expressions is

```
def v = bind expression;
```

When *expression* changes, *v* is updated.

Let's look at several examples. Suppose you are calculating a product between two numbers. When either number changes, you want the product value to stay current. Binding the product expression does the job.

```
var a = 10; var b = 2;
def product = bind a * b;    // bind to expression
println(product);            // 20
a = 100;
println(product);            // 200
b = 5;
println(product);            // 500
product = 10;                // compiler error
```

The compiler lets you declare bound variables with var, but you cannot modify them (see "Overriding bind" on page 75). If you try, you get a runtime error rather than a compiler error.

```
var prod = bind a * b;       // bind to expression
prod = 10;                   // AssignToBoundException at runtime
```

Here's an example that calls a getNumber function to update variable top. Binding the if expression insures that top gets a value no greater than 100.

```
def top = bind if (num <= 100) num else 100; // bind to conditional
var num = getNumber();       // suppose num is 50
println(top);                // top is 50
num = getNumber();           // suppose num is 500
println(top);                // top is 100
```

Here's another example that binds the addition of variables in a block expression to a sum variable.

```
a = 10; b = 20; var c = 30;
def sum = bind {             // bind to block expression
   def d = 40; def e = 50;
   a + b + c + d + e         // binds to this statement
}
println(sum);                // sum is 150
b = 50; c = 50;
println(sum);                // sum is 200
```

Recall that the value of a block expression is the value of its last expression. With bind, all other expressions in the block must be defined with def or var.

Bidirectional Binding

Bidirectional binding is often used with user interactions to make sure that stored values and displayed values are in sync. The format for bidirectional binding is

```
var v = bind w with inverse;
```

This format allows updates to occur in both directions. Variable v updates if w changes, and vice versa. Note that var must be used with bidirectional binding, since v is modifiable.

Here's an example that keeps two variables (field and name) in sync.

```
var field = "one";
var name = bind field with inverse;  // name is "one"
field = "two";                       // name is "two"
name = "three";                      // field is "three"
```

3.4 Sequences

A sequence is an ordered list of items in JavaFX, similar to arrays in other languages. Sequences are very powerful in JavaFX, because you can use them to store any data type, including objects. In this section, we show you how to create sequences and access sequence items, as well as insert items into sequences and delete items from sequences. We also discuss comparing sequences, sequence slices, predicates, and binding sequences.

Sequence Literals

Sequence literals are created with a comma-separated list of items within [].

```
def primeNumbers = [2, 3, 5, 7, 11, 13];          // Integer values
var brothers = ["groucho", "chico", "harpo"];     // String values
```

When you declare a sequence, use var if you intend to modify the sequence; otherwise use def. The JavaFX compiler can usually determine sequence types by inference, but you can include an explicit type (using []) if it's necessary (the compiler will let you know when you need to do this).

```
def primeNumbers: Integer[] = [2, 3, 5, 7, 11, 13];
var brothers: String[] = ["groucho", "chico", "harpo"];
```

There is a convenient notation in JavaFX for generating sequences of values.

```
def nineties = [1990..1999];    // [1990, 1991, 1992, ..., 1999]
```

The notation [v..w] generates a sequence literal with an increasing range of values, where v and w are Integer or Number types. Each new value in the range is one more than the previous one. Here are some more examples.

```
var g = [1..5];        // same as [1, 2, 3, 4, 5]
var h = [1.1..5.1];    // same as [1.1, 2.1, 3.1, 4.1, 5.1]
var j = [1..<5];       // same as [1, 2, 3, 4];
```

```
var k = [1..5.0];              // same as [1.0, 2.0, 3.0, 4.0, 5.0]
var m = [4.5..7];              // same as [4.5, 5.5, 6.5]
var n = [5..1];                // no incrementing values, same as []
```

The default increment for each new range number is 1, but you can use the notation [*v*..*w* step *n*] to step by different values (*n* is a positive or negative Integer or Number type). This makes it easier to generate more arbitrary sequences.

```
var p = [0..9 step 2];         // same as [0, 2, 4, 6, 8]
var q = [5..1 step -1];        // same as [5, 4, 3, 2, 1]
var r = [1..3 step .5];        // same as [1.0, 1.5, 2.0, 2.5, 3.0]
```

The sizeof operator gives you the length of a sequence.

```
def primeNumbers = [2, 3, 5, 7, 11, 13];
var length = sizeof(primeNumbers);      // length is 6
var length = sizeof primeNumbers;       // same thing
```

The reverse operator reverses items in a sequence.

```
var brothers = ["groucho", "chico", "harpo"];
var revBros = reverse brothers;        // ["harpo", "chico", "groucho"]
```

And, if you nest sequences, you get a "flattened" sequence.

```
def boys = ["billy", "joey"];
def girls = ["mary", "susie"];
var kids = [boys, girls];              // ["billy", "joey", "mary", "susie"];
```

Printing Sequences

You can use print() or println() directly to print all values of a sequence.

```
def primeNumbers = [2, 3, 5, 7, 11, 13];
println(primeNumbers);         // [ 2, 3, 5, 7, 11, 13 ]
println("{primeNumbers}");     // 23571113
```

Programming Tip

A sequence name (primeNumbers) with println() makes the sequence values easy to read for debugging. In contrast, the string expression "{primeNumbers}" with println() displays a string of characters.

If you need to print sequence elements individually, use a for loop.

```
def primeNumbers = [2, 3, 5, 7, 11, 13];
for (n in primeNumbers) {
    print("{n} ");
}
println("");               // 2 3 5 7 11 13
```

The indexof operator gives you a sequence item's integer index number (zero-based). This operator can only be applied to a loop induction variable. Here is an example using the indexof operator in a for loop.

```
var colors = ["red", "blue", "green"];
for (c in colors) {
    println("{c} is color #{indexof c}");
}
```

Each iteration of this for loop displays a color name and the index number (zero-based) in the sequence.

```
red is color #0
blue is color #1
green is color #2
```

Creating Sequences with for

A for expression returns a sequence, so you can use for loops to create new sequences. Here are some examples.

```
var oddNumbers = for (n in [1..9 step 2]) n; // [1, 3, 5, 7, 9]
var cubes = for (n in [1..5]) n * n * n;      // [1, 8, 27, 64, 125]
```

The following example generates a sequence of integers in a for loop (a pair at a time), where the second integer is twice the value of the first integer. (Bracket notation [] is required in the body of the for loop here.)

```
def seq = for (n in [2..6]) [n, 2*n];  // [2, 4, 3, 6, 4, 8, 5, 10, 6, 12]
```

A for expression can have more than one in clause. Here's an example that calculates a sequence of cross products.

```
var row = [10, 100];
var col = [5, 15];
var crossProduct = for (r in row, c in col) r * c;
println(crossProduct);          // [ 50, 150, 500, 1500 ]
```

Note that the for expression acts like two for loops with loop variable r in the outer loop and loop variable c in the inner loop.

A for expression can also have a where clause, which must be a boolean expression. This *constrains* selections, as the following example shows.

```
var numbers = for (r in row, c in col where r * c < 500) r * c;
println(numbers);               // [ 50, 150 ]
```

Here's a variant of the same example.

```
for (r in row, c in col where r * c < 500) {
    print("r = {r} c = {c}, ");    // r = 10 c = 5, r = 10 c = 15,
}
```

Accessing Sequence Items

Use the expression *seq*[*index*] to access items in sequence *seq*, where *index* is zero-based. If *index* is outside the bounds of the sequence (positive or negative), the expression evaluates to the default value for that item's type.[1]

Here are several examples.

```
var brothers = ["groucho", "chico", "harpo"];
var firstBro = brothers[0];        // firstBro is "groucho"
var lastBro = brothers[2];         // lastBro is "harpo"
var noBro = brothers[3];           // noBro is ""
var nonBro = brothers[-1];         // nonBro is ""
```

You can also use for loops with sizeof to access or modify sequence elements.

```
var list = [1, 2, 3, 4];
for (i in [0..<sizeof(list)]) {
    print(list[i]);
}
println("");               // 1234

for (i in [0..<sizeof(list)]) {
    list[i] = -1;          // set each element to -1
}
```

Here are some alternative ways to set sequence elements to specific values with for.

```
for (n in list) list[indexof n] = -1;  // set each element to -1
list = for (n in list) {-1};           // set each element to -1
```

Inserting Items into Sequences

The insert keyword lets you insert new items into sequences. You may insert items at the end of a sequence (insert into), before an indexed element (insert before), or after an indexed element (insert after). Here are some examples.

```
var colors = ["red", "blue"];
insert "green" into colors;       // ["red", "blue", "green"]
insert "pink" after colors[1];    // ["red", "blue", "pink", "green"]
insert "cyan" before colors[0];   // ["cyan", "red", "blue", "pink", "green"]
```

Inserting before or after a negative indexed element inserts at the beginning of the sequence. Inserting before or after an indexed element beyond the end of a sequence inserts at the end.[2]

---

1. This is an example of "The show must go on" philosophy of JavaFX.
2. Again, "The show must go on."

Programming Tip

Assigning sequences copies values. Look at the following example.

```
var s = [1..5];
var t = s;              // makes a copy
insert 6 into s;
println(t);             // [ 1, 2, 3, 4, 5 ]
println(s);             // [ 1, 2, 3, 4, 5, 6 ]
```

This shows that values are copied when you assign a sequence to another sequence. The same is true when you pass a sequence as an argument to a function.

Here's a for loop that inserts Circles into a sequence.

```
var theCircles: Circle[];
for (i in [1..3])
   insert Circle {
       radius: 5
       fill: Color.RED
   } into theCircles;
```

Here's a more efficient way to build a sequence of Circles using the expression-nature of for loops.

```
def theCircles = for (i in [1..3])
    Circle {
       radius: 5
       fill: Color.RED
    }
```

Deleting Items from Sequences

The delete keyword lets you delete items from sequences. Table 3.2 shows you the different delete formats.

TABLE 3.2 Sequence Delete Formats

delete *sequence*[*index*]	Delete item at *index* of *sequence*. If no element at that index, ignore the delete
delete *sequence*[*low..high*]	Delete the items from *low* to *high* inclusive (slice)
delete *value* from *sequence*	Delete all occurrences of *value* from *sequence*. If no *value* found, ignore the delete
delete *sequence*	Delete all elements from *sequence* but not the sequence itself (sequence is empty)

Here are some examples of delete.

```
var bros = ["groucho", "chico", "harpo", "zeppo", "gummo"];
```

```
delete bros[4];              // delete "gummo"
delete bros[2..3];           // delete "harpo" and "zeppo"
delete "chico" from bros;    // delete "chico"
delete bros;                 // delete "groucho" (empty sequence)
```

Comparing Sequences

Use the == and != relational operators to compare sequences. Two sequences are equal if they have the same values for all items and they have the same length. Both comparison expressions return boolean values (true or false). Here are some examples.

```
var sample = [1, 3, 5, 7, 9];
var a = (sample == [1..10 step 2]);    // a is true
var b = (sample == [1..5 step 2]);     // b is false
var c = (sample != [1..10 step 3]);    // c is true
```

The other relational operators (<, <=, >, >=) cannot be used with sequences.

Sequence Slices

The expression *sequence[low..high]* is called a sequence *slice*. The values for *low* and *high* (Integer or Number types) are the beginning and ending of a sequence range (inclusive on both ends). Here are several examples.

```
var bros = ["groucho", "chico", "harpo", "zeppo", "gummo"];
var funnyBros = bros[0..2];    // ["groucho", "chico", "harpo"]
var otherBros = bros[3..];     // ["zeppo", "gummo"]
var movieBros = bros[0..<4];   // ["groucho", "chico", "harpo", "zeppo"]
bros[3..4] = ["Z", "G"];       // ["groucho", "chico", "harpo", "Z", "G"]
```

Predicates

A predicate is a boolean expression that helps generate new sequences as *subsets* of existing sequences. A predicate is used with sequences in JavaFX as follows.

```
seq[name | BooleanExpression]
```

Here, seq is the source sequence, *name* is the selection variable, | is the predicate separator, and *BooleanExpression* is the constraint. Elements are selected from the source sequence if and only if the constraint is true.

The following example generates a sequence of numbers whose square is less than 50.

```
def seq = [1..100];
def newSeq = seq[n | (n*n) < 50];    // [1, 2, 3, 4, 5, 6, 7]
```

Here, n is the selection variable from the source seq. An item is only selected for the new sequence (newSeq) if its square (n*n) is less than 50.

Note that you can use a for loop with a where clause to generate the same sequence without a predicate.

```
def newSeq = for (n in [1..100] where (n*n) < 50) {n};
```

Binding Sequences

The format for binding sequences is

```
def newSeq = bind seq;
```

If seq changes, newseq is updated. Here's an example.

```
var seq = [1, 2, 3];
def myseq = bind seq;        // bind to sequence
insert 4 into seq;
println(myseq);              // [ 1, 2, 3, 4 ]
delete 2 from seq;
println(myseq);              // [ 1, 3, 4 ]
```

In a graphical context, binding property content keeps a scene graph current. Here, a Group object literal binds its content property to sequence nodeSequence. Changes to nodeSequence updates the Group's content.

```
Group {
    content: bind nodeSequence
      . . .
}
```

You can also bind for expressions, since they return sequences. The format is

```
def newSeq = bind for (elem in seq) expression;
```

If sequence seq changes, a new sequence newSeq is created. Existing sequence elements are not recalculated unless you insert or delete elements.

Here's an example that updates a scaled sequence of numbers.

```
var scale = 10;
def t = bind for (item in [1..5]) item * scale; // bind to for expression
println(t);              // [ 10, 20, 30, 40, 50 ]
scale = 100;
println(t);              // [ 100, 200, 300, 400, 500 ]
```

The for loop multiplies five numbers in a sequence by a scale variable and is bound to variable t. If variable scale changes, sequence t is updated.

3.5 Functions

Functions help you centralize code from different places in your scripts. Functions can take arguments and can return values. You can also bind functions, pass program arguments to scripts, and use functions as special types.

Defining Functions

The keyword `function` defines a function and its block of code. If the function doesn't return anything, use the keyword `Void` for its return type. Here is a function that prints a message when it has been called.

```
function myPrint(): Void {
    println("myPrint called");
}
```

Passing Arguments to Functions

To pass arguments to functions, include the names and types in the function's signature. Here function `printStrings` prints its two string arguments. The function doesn't return anything (`Void` return type).

```
function printStrings(a: String, b: String): Void {
    println("{a}{b}");
}

printStrings("alpha", "bet");       // prints "alphabet"
```

Of course, JavaFX's inference engine can deduce argument types and return types for you, so here is a more compact and general version of `printStrings`.

```
function printStrings(a, b) {
    println("{a}{b}");
}

printStrings("alpha", "bet");       // prints "alphabet"
```

One important point about JavaFX function parameters: they are passed by *value* inside functions. This makes it impossible to write certain functions in JavaFX, like the following swap function which attempts to swap the values of its arguments.

```
function swap(a, b) {
    var tmp = a;
    a = b;              // won't compile
    b = tmp;            // won't compile
}
```

Programming Tip

If you pass a sequence to a function as an argument, you cannot change its elements in the function (this is different from Java arrays).Object references are also passed by value (see "Classes and Objects" on page 67).

Returning Values from Functions

If a function returns a value, you can include its return type when you define the function. Here's a concat function that concatenates its parameters into a new string and returns it.

```
function concat(a: String, b: String): String {
    return "{a}{b}";
}
var s = concat("set", "up");        // s is "setup"
```

Of course we can rely on inference to write a more compact version of concat.

```
function concat(a, b) {
    return "{a}{b}";
}
var s = concat("alpha", "bet");     // s is "alphabet"
```

These have all been simple examples, so let's show you a more interesting one. The following gcd function calculates the greatest common denominator from two integers passed to the function.

```
function gcd(x: Integer, y: Integer) {
    var a = x; var b = y;
    while (b != 0) {
        var t = a;
        a = b;
        b = t mod a;
    }
    return a;
}
```

Here's a for loop to try out gcd.

```
for (n in [1..10]) {
    println("gcd of 12 and {n} is {gcd(12, n)}");
}
```

The output looks like this.

```
gcd of 12 and 1 is 1
gcd of 12 and 2 is 2
gcd of 12 and 3 is 3
gcd of 12 and 4 is 4
gcd of 12 and 5 is 1
```

```
gcd of 12 and 6 is 6
gcd of 12 and 7 is 1
gcd of 12 and 8 is 4
gcd of 12 and 9 is 3
gcd of 12 and 10 is 2
```

Binding Function Calls

In addition to binding expressions, you can also bind function calls. The format for binding function calls is

```
def v = bind function(arg1, arg2, ...);
```

The binding concept is similar to binding expressions. When any of the arguments (arg1, arg2, ...) change in the function call, v is updated with the value returned by the function.

Let's show you an example. Suppose you have a hypot function that calculates the hypotenuse for right triangles. Here's an example that binds the hypot function to variable hypotenuse to keep its value current when the base or height change.

```
import java.lang.Math;

function hypot(a, b) {
    return Math.sqrt(a * a + b * b);
}
var base = 3; var height = 4;
def hypotenuse = bind hypot(base, height);   // bind to function call
println(hypotenuese);                 // 5.0
base = 30; height = 40;
println(hypotenuse);                  // 50.0
```

Bound Functions

It may not be sufficient to bind to a function and update only when the function arguments change. You may want to update when variables in the function body change, too. To do this, you need a *bound* function. The format for a bound function is

```
bound function functionName(arg1, arg2, ...) { . . . }
```

All expressions in the function body must be defined with def or var. If you call bound functions in a non-bind context, they are ordinary functions.

To see how useful bound functions are, here is an example that uses a bound function getTotal to update the contents of a Text object when selections are made with GUI components.

```
bound function getTotal(): String {
    def item1 = if (itemOne.selected) .75 else 0;
    def item2 = if (itemTwo.selected) .50 else 0;
```

```
    def item3 = if (itemThree.selected) .25 else 0;
    def total = item1 + item2 + item3;
    return "$ {total}";
}

def finalOrder = Text {
    content: bind getTotal()          // must use bind here
    font: Font {
        size: 18
    }
}
```

The Text content property is automatically updated to a new total when any of the selections (itemOne.selected, itemTwo.selected, itemThree.selected) inside the getTotal function body change.

Think of bound functions as "black boxes." The dependencies of an ordinary function call in bind context are the dependencies of its arguments. Bound functions calculate the dependencies dynamically, based on what actually goes into the calculation.

Bound functions are not automatically treated as if their result is bound. You need to use bind (as shown in the above example).

Program Arguments

In certain situations (applets, command line scripts) you may want to pass arguments to your JavaFX programs at runtime. These program arguments are available to your JavaFX programs as strings. To access program arguments, you can specify a run function.[3]

To demonstrate, here's a program that echoes its program arguments to the console screen in reverse order.

```
// Echo.fx - Echo program arguments in reverse
function run(args: String[]) {
    for (arg in reverse args)
        print("{arg} ");
    println("");
}

$ javafxc Echo.fx
$ javafx Echo one two three
three two one
```

The program arguments are passed to run as a sequence of Strings. The for loop calls reverse to create a new sequence with the strings in reverse order. Inside the for loop,

---

3. Like main in Java, run is a magic name.

the `print` function prints each argument from this sequence to the screen followed by a space. Outside the for loop, the `println` supplies the newline.

Programming Tip

You can also call `FX.getArguments` *to access program arguments. This approach does not require a* run *function.*

```
var args = FX.getArguments();
for (arg in reverse args)
    print("{arg} ");
println("");
```

Function Types

A more advanced topic with JavaFX functions is *function types*. In addition to returning built-in types and class types, JavaFX functions can *return* a function, or more specifically, a function literal type. Why would you want to do this? Using a technique called *closures*, function literals make libraries more reusable. Let's investigate this technique and show you how to use it.

Suppose you are interested in scaling data in your application; that is, multiplying variables in your program by scaling factors at run time. Let's look at a technique that sets up this concept in three steps. The first step is to define a function, as follows.

```
function scale(n) {
    function(x) { x * n }          // function literal
}
```

The interesting thing about this `scale` function is that it doesn't return a value. Instead, `scale` accepts a scaling factor (n) and returns a *function literal* that multiplies its parameter (x) by n. Note that this function literal (an anonymous function) is *not* called when `scale` is invoked.

The second step is to call the `scale` function with a scaling factor (100) and assign the returned function literal to a variable.

```
var scaleHundred = scale(100);      // returns function literal
```

Now you can use `scaleHundred` to call the anonymous function in the function literal. Think of it as a pointer or reference to a function that accepts a single argument.

The third step is to use the `scaleHundred` variable to call the anonymous function in the function literal with a variable in your program.

```
var m = 5;
println(scaleHundred(m));            // prints 500
```

Note that in order to make this work, the scale function must "remember" the scaling factor (100) that was passed to it in the second step. This construct is called a *closure*.[4] When the function in the function literal is invoked with an argument in step three, the value of this argument is multiplied by the scaling factor. Of course we can always change the scaling factor at run time, which is the point of all this.

```
scaleHundred = scale(200);          // change scaling factor to 200
println(scaleHundred(m));            // prints 1000
```

To see what's going on under the hood, here is the scale function again, fully defined.

```
function scale(n: Number): function(x: Number): Number {
    return function(x: Number): Number { x * n }
}
```

The scale function accepts a Number argument and returns a function literal. This function literal takes a Number argument and returns a Number type, which is the new scaled value. Fortunately, type inference in JavaFX makes explicit type declarations like this unnecessary in most cases.

All this seems like a lot of work just to multiply two values. The real power of function types and closures is with sequences. Here is an example that multiplies all the values of a sequence by a scaling factor of 10.

```
function mult(n: Integer) {
    function(seq: Integer[]) {
        var thisSeq = seq;
        for (i in thisSeq) { thisSeq[indexof i] *= n; }
    }
}

var seq = [1, 2, 3, 4, 5];          // original sequence
var multTen = mult(10);              // scaling factor is 10
var newSeq = multTen(seq);           // generate new sequence
println(newSeq);                     // [ 10, 20, 30, 40, 50 ]
```

The mult function accepts a scaling factor as an argument and returns a function literal (an explicit return is not necessary here). This function literal takes a sequence of Integers as an argument and returns a new sequence of Integers. Inside the function, a for loop multiplies each sequence element by the scaling factor. The variable thisSeq is necessary because JavaFX does not allow you to modify function parameters (seq).

We could also use the mult function to scale our original sequence.

```
var seq = [1, 2, 3, 4, 5];          // [ 1, 2, 3, 4, 5 ]
var multTen = mult(10);              // scaling factor is 10
```

---

4. Specifically, a function literal implements a closure because it retains references to variables that are outside the function's scope (*i.e.*, variables that appear free in the closure).

```
seq = multTen(seq);           // generate new sequence, replace old one
println(seq);                 // [ 10, 20, 30, 40, 50 ]
```

Remember, the mult function generates new sequences. Instead of changing the original sequence, you are reassigning a new sequence to the original sequence variable.

A common use of function types is with event handlers for graphical objects. JavaFX nodes, for instance, let you specify function types for properties that describe event handlers. The following example shows a Rectangle component with an event handler that acknowledges when a user clicks inside the Rectangle with the mouse.

```
Rectangle {
    x: 40
    y: 40
    width: 40
    height: 40
    fill: Color.RED
    onMouseClicked: function(e: MouseEvent): Void {
        println("You clicked me");
    }
}
```

Here, property onMouseClicked has function type function(e: MouseEvent): Void.

3.6 Classes and Objects

Besides built-in types, JavaFX lets you create your own data types in applications. This powerful feature is the concept behind object-oriented design techniques that work well in complex "real world" applications. In this section, we show you how to define your own classes and create objects in JavaFX. You'll also learn how to use inheritance to create new classes from existing ones.

Classes

Let's begin with a simple Point class.[5]

```
public class Point {
    public var x: Number;
    public var y: Number;
    public function clear(): Void {
        x = 0;
        y = 0;
```

5. The Point class is in **Point.fx** and the code that creates and uses Point objects is in **Main.fx**. See "Access Modifiers" on page 88 for a more detailed discussion of how to use public and other access modifiers with classes.

```
        }
    }
```

The Point class manages x and y coordinates (both Number types). Every Point object has its own x and y (these are called *instance variables*). Since the instance variables are both Number types, they have default values of 0.0. The clear function sets the x and y instance variables to zero. Note that clear is defined *inside* the Point class. This is called an *instance function*. As you will see shortly, instance functions are always called with object *references*. This implies that the instance variables of the object are always in the scope of the instance function body. The class, instance variables, and instance function are all declared public so that code in separate files may access them.

Object Literals

Most object-oriented languages use special class functions called constructors to create objects from classes. In JavaFX, you build an object from a class with an *object literal expression*. Here are several examples with the Point class.

```
// object literal initializes instance variables
var p = Point { x: 10, y: 20 };
println("p = ({p.x}, {p.y})");      // p = (10.0, 20.0)

// empty object literal uses defaults for instance variables
var q = Point {};
println("q = ({q.x}, {q.y})");      // q = (0.0, 0.0)
```

Object literals begin with a class name followed by curly braces "{}" containing initializers with : separating instance variables from their values. If you assign an object literal to a variable (object reference) in your program, you can call instance functions later with the object reference. An empty object literal uses defaults for the instance variables. JavaFX lets you use commas, semicolons, or newlines to separate initializers. Here we use an object literal on one line, but you can use separate lines for each initializer if you want.

Programming Tip

In addition to instance variable initializers, you can also declare local variables and define functions in object literals. Here's an example that sets the x and y instance variables in a Point object literal using the return value of a function.

```
var r = Point {
    var n = getNumber()
    x: n
    y: n + 10
}
```

There are lots of advantages to creating objects with object literal expressions. First of all, you see the values that each instance variable is initialized to at the point where you construct the object. Second, object literals nest well, so you can use an object literal inside other object literals. Third, sequences of object literals may appear inside object literals. Fourth, you can construct object graphs without creating unnecessary temporary variables. All this makes object literals useful in the design of complicated things (graphical user interfaces, for instance), as you will see later on.

Recall that the Point class has a `clear` instance function. When you call this function with a Point object reference, it resets that object's x and y coordinates to zero.

```
p.clear();
println("p = ({p.x}, {p.y})");      // p = (0.0, 0.0)
```

Using public-init

Once you define a Point object, moving to a new spot is straightforward.

```
var p = Point { x: 10, y: 20 };
p.x = 30; p.y = 40;                 // move to (30, 40)
```

But there is a potential problem. Suppose our Point objects can only have positive values for their x and y coordinates. With our current class definition, an application could do the following.

```
var p = Point { x: 10, y: 20 };
p.x = -1;                           // change x coordinate to -1
p.y = -1;                           // change y coordinate to -1
```

This compiles and runs, but it's not the behavior we want. We need a Point class with a more controlled interface. Let's restrict the accessibility of instance variables x and y and control how users move Point objects.

```
public class Point {
    public-init var x: Number;
    public-init var y: Number;
    init {
        if (x < 0) x = 0;
        if (y < 0) y = 0;
    }
    public function move(newX: Number, newY: Number): Void {
        if (newX >= 0 and newY >= 0) {
            x = newX;
            y = newY;
        }
    }
    public function clear(): Void {
        x = 0;
        y = 0;
    }
}
```

To change the location of point objects, the Point class has a new instance function called move. Note that this function won't move to a different spot unless the new x and y values are legal (not negative). But what's to prevent users from changing x and y directly like before? The answer is a `public-init` *access modifier* with the declarations of instance variables x and y.

With instance variables, the `public-init` access modifier allows an application to initialize its value in an object literal, but the instance variable is read-only after that.

Init Blocks

The other new feature introduced in this Point class is an *init block*.

```
init {
    if (x < 0) x = 0;
    if (y < 0) y = 0;
}
```

Init blocks are optional in classes, but if you write one and create an object with an object literal, the init block is executed immediately after the instance variables receive their values.

We don't want users to set x and y to negative values in object literals, so we use an init block to set them to zero if they are negative. Init blocks help you implement tasks during initialization and mimic things you typically do with constructors. JavaFX also has postinit blocks (see page 78).

These enhancements implement the behaviors we want.

```
var p = Point { x: 10, y: 20 };      // (10.0, 20.0)
p.move(30, 40);                      // move to (30.0, 40.0)
p.move(-10, -10);                    // does not move
p.x = -1;                            // compiler error
p.y = -1;                            // compiler error
var q = Point { x: -10, y: -20 };    // (0.0, 0.0)
```

Using public-read

Next, let's suppose Point objects must maintain their distance from the origin (0,0). Here's a version of Point that implements this new feature.

```
import java.lang.Math;

public class Point {
    public-init var x: Number;
    public-init var y: Number;
    public-read def distance = bind Math.sqrt(x * x  + y * y);
    init {
        if (x < 0) x = 0;
```

```
      if (y < 0) y = 0;
    }
    public function move(newX: Number, newY: Number): Void {
      if (newX >= 0 and newY >= 0) {
        x = newX;
        y = newY;
      }
    }
    public function clear(): Void {
      x = 0;
      y = 0;
    }
}
```

The Point class now has a def instance variable called `distance`. The keyword `public-read` makes `distance` *read-only* when accessed by applications.

```
var p = Point { x: 10, y: 20 };              // (10.0, 20.0)
println("length of p = {p.distance}");       // length of p = 22.36068
p.move(30, 40);                              // move to (30.0, 40.0)
println("length of p = {p.distance}");       // length of p = 50.0
```

However, `distance` cannot be changed or used in an object literal.

```
p.distance = 50;                             // compiler error
var q = Point { x: 3, y: 4, distance: 5 };   // compiler error
```

The `distance` variable also receives its value from the Java `Math.sqrt` function. Note that we use `bind` with `distance` and `Math.sqrt`. This makes `distance` update *automatically* when x changes or y changes. Without `bind`, `Math.sqrt` would be called only once. Binding is critical here, since it keeps `distance` up to date as you create, move, or clear Point objects.

Properties

Instance variables that are `public`, `public-init`, or `public-read` are exposed to code outside the class. These specialized instance variables are called properties.

Using this

The `move` instance function for class Point can also be written this way.

```
public function move(x: Number, y: Number): Void {
  if (x >= 0 and y >= 0) {
    this.x = x;
    this.y = y;
  }
}
```

Here, the function's parameters have the same names (x, y) as the instance variables in our Point class. Consequently, we need the keyword this to distinguish between them. The expression this.x refers to the instance variable in the class and x refers to the local function parameter.

Using null

Recall that all JavaFX built-in types have default values. What about defaults for object references? If you don't initialize or assign a reference to an object you create, its default is null. You can also assign null to object references.

```
var p: Point;                        // p is null (default)
p = Point { x: 10, y: 20 };          // p refers to Point(10.0, 20.0)
p = null;                            // p is null
```

A common use for null is to check the validity of a function's argument when it is a class type.

```
function calculate(p: Point) {
    if (p == null) {
        /* object not initialized */
    }
}
```

JavaFX Tip

JavaFX does not throw exceptions for null references. If you call an instance function with a null reference, the call is ignored. If you access an instance variable with a null reference, default values are used.

Using Java Objects

If you need to create Java objects in your JavaFX programs, use operator new and pass arguments directly to the Java class constructor, if necessary. To illustrate, here's an example that uses the Java Date and DateFormat objects to give you the current time.

```
var today = new java.util.Date();
var timeNow = java.text.DateFormat.getTimeInstance().format(today);
println(timeNow);        // 4:41:30 PM
```

A new Java Date object is passed to getTimeInstance().format and called with java.text.DateFormat to return the current time as a string.

Here's an example that uses Java character strings. Suppose you have an input string containing leading spaces and fields of substrings delimited by colons. You want to strip leading spaces and replace the colon characters in the input string with spaces.

JavaFX strings are immutable, so you can't modify the input string directly. But you can call Java functions `trim` and `replace` with JavaFX strings, as follows.

```
var str = "  Ted Smith:123 Elm St.:10105";
str = str.trim();                       // trim leading spaces
def space: Character = 32;              // "space" character
def colon: Character = 58;              // ":" character
str = str.<<replace>>(colon, space);
println(str);                           // Ted Smith 123 Elm St. 10105
```

Since `replace` is a JavaFX keyword, use `<<replace>>` to call the Java string function `replace`. Note that both functions return new strings, which we use to update the originals.

Alternatively, you can use a Java StringBuffer object inside a JavaFX `replaceSpaces` function. Here's the code.

```
function replaceSpaces(input: String): String {
    def space: Character = 32;
    def colon: Character = 58;
    var str = new java.lang.StringBuffer(input); // StringBuffer
    var index = 0;
    // strip any initial spaces first
    while ((index <= str.length()-1) and (str.charAt(index) == space))
        str.deleteCharAt(index);
    for (i in [0..str.length()-1])
        if (str.charAt(i) == colon)
            str.setCharAt(i, space);     // replace colon with space
    return str.toString();               // return as String
}

var newString = replaceSpaces("  Ted Smith:123 Elm St.:10105");
println(newString);          // Ted Smith 123 Elm St. 10105
```

Inside function `replaceSpaces`, variable `str` is a StringBuffer object created from the Java StringBuffer class using string `input` as the argument to its constructor. The while loop calls StringBuffer methods `charAt` and `deleteCharAt` to find and delete leading spaces. The for loop uses StringBuffer method `setCharAt` to replace colon characters with space characters.

Binding with Object Literals

In JavaFX, you can bind directly to an object literal or bind any subset of its initializers. Binding directly to an object literal creates a new instance.

```
def v = bind ClassName {
    w: expression;
}
```

If *expression* changes, a new instance of `ClassName` is created and assigned to v with w having *expression*'s value.

Binding to an initializer in an object literal does not create a new instance.

```
def v = ClassName {
   w: bind expression;
}
```

If *expression* changes, w is updated from *expression*'s value in the same object.

Binding initializers in object literals is most useful with component properties. Here's an example that loads images in a web service call (only skeletal code is shown here).

```
var loadComplete = false;
var description: String;

function makeServiceCall() {
   description = "Loading Photos...";
   . . .
   loadComplete = true;
}

function alert(msg: String): Void {
   loadComplete = false;
   description = "Loading Error: {msg}";
}

scene: Scene {
   content: [
      VBox {
         visible: bind not loadComplete      // bind to visible property
         content: [
            Text {
               content: bind description      // bind to Text content
            }
         ]
      }
   ]
}
```

Two component properties are bound here. The `visible` property of a VBox is bound to the `loadComplete` boolean and the `content` property of a Text component is bound to a `description` string. Both bind expressions update the scene graph dynamically.

A call to `makeServiceCall` starts loading images. The `loadComplete` boolean is initially false, so the VBox is visible and its Text component displays `"Loading Photos"`. When image loading has completed, `makeServiceCall` sets `loadComplete` to true and the VBox becomes invisible. If an error occurs, the `alert` function sets `loadComplete` to false and changes the description string to an error message. This makes the visible Text component now display the error message.

Programming Tip

Binding component properties is a powerful JavaFX idiom that lets you update your scene graph dynamically.

Overriding bind

You can bind class instance variables with the keyword var. This lets you override the bind with an object literal initialization. Here's an example.

```
var size = 100;

public class Thing {
    var num = bind size;          // num binds to size
}

var t1 = Thing { };               // t1.num is 100
size = 500;                       // t1.num is 500
var t2 = Thing { num: 50 };       // t2.num is 50
size = 300;                       // t1.num is 300, t2.num is 50
```

Since num is directly initialized in the object literal for t2, the binding of size does not apply to that object.

3.7 Inheritance

Code reuse is a major goal of object-oriented programming. When designing a new class, you can derive it from an existing one. This is called *inheritance* and represents an "is-a" relationship between classes. Inheritance makes it easy to hook into existing frameworks and use existing APIs. With inheritance, you can retain the state and behavior of an existing class and specialize certain aspects of it to suit your needs.

In JavaFX, inheritance is implemented by *extending* classes (just like Java). When you use the extends keyword to inherit one class from another, the public functions of the "parent" class become part of the public functions of the "child" class. The parent class is often called a *superclass* and the child class a *subclass*.

JavaFX Tip

JavaFX classes can extend at most one Java or JavaFX class, and any number of Java interfaces or JavaFX mixins (see "Mixin Inheritance" on page 81).

Overriding Functions

Even if you don't use the extends keyword explicitly when you create a new class, the JavaFX compiler implicitly extends your new class from superclass Object. Let's return to our Point class to see what this means.

```
public class Point extends Object {
    public-init var x: Number;
    public-init var y: Number;
    . . .
    public override function toString(): String {
        return "({x}, {y})";
    }
}
```

The Object superclass includes an instance function called toString that returns a String type for every object in JavaFX. Using the override keyword, you can provide a different implementation for your extended class. In our Point class, for instance, the toString function now returns the x and y coordinates as an ordered pair (x, y). This means you can use a Point object in any expression that expects a String type and you'll get a nicely formatted ordered pair.

```
var p = Point { x: 10, y: 20 };    // (10.0, 20.0)
println("p = {p}");                // p = (10.0, 20.0)
var spot = "{p}";                  // spot is a String
println("spot = {spot}");          // spot = (10.0, 20.0)
```

You'll see more examples of overriding functions in the next section.

Programming Tip

The default conversion for class types to Strings is the address of the object. To display an object's state in a more meaningful way, override the toString() *function.*

Using super

Suppose a Pixel class needs to manage color with x and y coordinates. You could design this class from scratch, but it would be a lot of work. Why not reuse the Point class and extend Pixel from Point? A Pixel, after all, is a Point object with color.

Here is the Pixel class.[6] As you see, there is not a lot of code to write when you use inheritance.

```
import javafx.scene.paint.Color;
```

---

6. The Pixel class is in **Pixel.fx** and the Point class is in **Point.fx**.

```
public class Pixel extends Point {
    public var color: Color;
    public override function toString(): String {
        return "({color}, {x}, {y})";
    }
    public override function clear(): Void {
        super.clear();              // call clear() in Point class
        color = null;
    }
}
```

A Pixel class manages a public color instance variable. Its type (Color) is accessible via the import statement shown. When a class defines an instance variable with public, applications have read *and* write access to that variable. (Contrast this with public-init in the Point class for x and y, which grants only read access of these instance variables to applications after object literal initialization).

The Pixel class also overrides toString to convert Pixel objects to the string "(color, x, y)". Clearing a Pixel object is also desirable. The behavior is to reset the x, y coordinates to zero and make the Pixel object have no color (null). To accomplish this, you need a way to call the clear instance function in the Point class. That's what super.clear() does. Without this super keyword, clear would call itself recursively and the Pixel's x and y coordinates would never change.

Let's create several Pixel objects now and try them out.

```
var p = Pixel { color: Color.RED, x: 30, y: 40 };
println("p = {p}"); // p = ([red=255,green=0,blue=0,...], 30.0, 40.0)
println("length of p = {p.distance}");     // length of p = 50.0

var q = Pixel {};                          // default values (color = null)
q.color = Color.BLUE;                      // change color
q.move(10, 10);                            // move to (10, 10)
println("q = {q}"); // q = ([red=0,green=0,blue=255,..], 10.0, 10.0)
println("length of q = {q.distance}");     // length of q = 14.142136

p.clear();                                 // clear Pixel
println("p = {p}");                        // p = (null, 0.0, 0.0)
println("length of p = {p.distance}"); // length of p = 0.0
```

The first Pixel object (p) has a red color at position (30.0, 40.0). The second Pixel object (q) is at the origin (0, 0) with no color initially, but we change its color to blue and move it to (10.0, 10.0). When we clear Pixel object p, its color is set to null and its x, y values are set to zero. Note that distance (defined in class Point) is inherited and accessible with Pixel objects.

From these examples, you see that a Pixel is a Point with public-init properties for x, y, and read-only for distance. What makes a Pixel different from a Point is its color property, which you can modify. Like Points, Pixels may be moved or cleared.

PostInit Blocks

JavaFX supports init blocks and postinit blocks inside classes. An init block runs immediately after the instance variables have been initialized. A postinit block executes right after an object has been completely initialized. Here is an example with inheritance that shows you both.

```
class Superclass {
    var m: Integer;
    init { println("Superclass.init"); }
    postinit { println("Superclass.postinit"); }
}
class Subclass extends Superclass {
    var n: Integer;
    init { println("Subclass.init"); }
    postinit { println("Subclass.postinit"); }
}
var s = Subclass { m: 2, n: 3 };
```

The output shows init blocks in both the superclass and subclass always execute before any postinit blocks, even postinit blocks in the superclass.

```
Superclass.init
Subclass.init
Superclass.postinit
Subclass.postinit
```

JavaFX Tip

Postinit blocks are rarely used. Their primary purpose is to register listeners or otherwise publish a completely initialized object.

Abstract Base Classes

Another concept in object-oriented programming is a class that you can't instantiate. These classes define abstract functions that you cannot invoke directly and exist only to specify contracts for state and behavior. Abstract functions must be overridden in subclasses.

If a class defines abstract functions (and possibly members), it's called an *abstract class*. An *interface* contains only abstract functions. JavaFX does not support interfaces with the keyword interface like Java does,[7] but it does have abstract base classes.

---

7. Java treats abstract classes as separate from interfaces, even if the abstract class has only abstract methods.

In JavaFX, the keyword abstract defines abstract classes. The abstract keyword also defines a function with no code. Here's an abstract class called Shape2d that defines a two-dimensional shape with an area function.

```
public abstract class Shape2d {             // abstract class
    public abstract function area(): Number;  // abstract function
}
```

The Shape2d class does not have state, so no instance variables are necessary. Since the specific type of Shape2d is unknown at this point, area must be abstract with no code. This class exists only to be inherited from, so let's define two simple shapes, a Circle and a Square.

```
import java.lang.Math;

public class Circle extends Shape2d {
    public var radius: Number;
    public override function area(): Number {    // redefine area
        Math.PI * radius * radius;
    }
    public override function toString(): String {// redefine toString
        return "Circle";
    }
}

public class Square extends Shape2d {
    public var side: Number;
    public override function area(): Number {    // redefine area
        side * side;
    }
    public override function toString(): String {// redefine toString
        return "Square";
    }
}
```

You *must* override function area in both Circle and Square (and any other class that extends Shape2d) because it's defined as abstract in Shape2d. If you do not, compilation errors occur. However, overriding toString in both classes is *not* required (this function has default code in class Object and is not abstract). Here, toString is overridden to return the name of the class as a string.

Let's create two shape objects and try them out.

```
var shapes: Shape2d[] = [
    Circle { radius: 10 },
    Square { side: 20 }
];

for (s in shapes) {
    println("{s} has area {s.area()}");
}
```

Variable shapes is a sequence containing Circle and Square objects of type Shape2d. The for loop fetches each object from the sequence and prints their Shape names and areas. Here's the output.

```
Circle has area 314.15927
Square has area 400.0
```

JavaFX Tip

When you create a custom graphical node in JavaFX, you extend CustomNode. You must override function create *because CustomNode defines abstract function create.*

As Operator

Earlier in the chapter, we introduced the Boolean instanceof operator (see "Instanceof Operator" on page 50), which returns true if its argument is a specific type. JavaFX also includes an as operator that returns a subclass type if its argument is an object of that type at runtime. With Object types, the instanceof and as operators let you specialize tasks for specific subclass types.

To illustrate, suppose you need to access the width of a Rectangle component in an event handler.

```
onMouseClicked: function(e: MouseEvent): Void {
    println(e.node.width);    // does not compile
}
```

The println statement does not compile because e.node is not a Rectangle type. To make this work correctly, you need the instanceof and as operators.

```
onMouseClicked: function(e: MouseEvent): Void {
    if (e.node instanceof Rectangle) {
        var w = (e.node as Rectangle).width;
        println("Rectangle is {w} wide");
    }
}
```

The instanceof operator verifies that expression e.node is a Rectangle before the as operator converts it to a Rectangle type. Now you can access the width of the Rectangle and print it with println.

Programming Tip

It's a good idea to use the instanceof *and* as *operators together to check for specific types at runtime. Without* instanceof, *the* as *operator fails and throws a* ClassCastException *if you give it the wrong type.*

Mixin Inheritance

Occasionally you'll want to combine behaviors and state from more than one class. This is called *mixin inheritance*. Using the mixin keyword, you can create a *mixin class*. Recall that a JavaFX class can extend at most one Java or JavaFX class and any number of Java interfaces. A JavaFX class can also extend any number of JavaFX mixin classes.

The format for a mixin class is

```
mixin class MixinClass { . . . }
```

Mixin classes cannot be instantiated, just like abstract classes. A class that extends a mixin class with the keyword extends is called a *mixee*.

```
class Mixee extends MixinClass { . . . }
```

A mixin class is a type, so you can use its name with the instanceof and as operators.

Mixin classes can have public abstract functions that mixees must override, which is similar to abstract base classes and Java interfaces. If a mixin class has a non-abstract function, the mixee has the option of overriding the function in a subclass or using the default implementation from the mixin class.

Here's an example that overrides functions with mixins.

```
public mixin class Mixin {
    public function write(obj: Object): Void {
        println("Mixin write");
    }
    public abstract function log(entry: String): Void; // no implementation
}

public class Base { . . . }

public class Derived extends Base, Mixin {
    public override function write(obj: Object): Void {
        println("Derived write");
    }
    public override function log(entry: String): Void {   // must override
        println("Derived log");
    }
}

var d = Derived { };
d.write("something");          // Derived write
d.log("Derived");              // Derived log
```

The Mixin class defines a write function with a default implementation and an abstract log function. A mixee must implement a version of log but is not required to provide an implementation for write. Here, the mixee (Derived) uses override to implement its own version of write. A call to d.write("something") invokes Derived's write function but if Derived did not override write, the one in the Mixin class would be called.

Programming Tip

You must use the keyword mixin *here. When you extend from more than one JavaFX class, only one non-mixin based class is allowed.*

With mixin classes, you can resolve ambiguities in overridden functions with class names. To illustrate, look at the following classes.

```
public mixin class Log {
    public function write(str: String): Void {
        println("Log write");
    }
}

public class Document {
    public function write(str: String): Void {
        println("Document write");
    }
}

public class LogFile extends Document, Log {
    public override function write(str: String): Void {
        Log.write(str);
    }
}
LogFile{}.write("something");                 // Log write
```

Class LogFile extends from Document and a Log mixin class. The Log and Document classes both define write functions with the same signature. LogFile overrides the write function to call Log.write(str) in the Log class. A call to Document.write(str) would invoke the write function in Document. Note that compilation errors occur with LogFile{}.write("something") if LogFile does not override the write function.

Mixin classes can also declare variables. A variable declaration has a name, type, optional default value, and possibly an on replace trigger. A mixin with variable x means mixees must also have an x (an x is provided if the mixee does not already have one; there is only one x in any case). Just like abstract functions, mixees have the option of using defaults for the mixin variable or extending the definition with the override keyword. This allows the mixee to override the default value and/or add a different on replace trigger. Triggers work with mixin classes just as they do with ordinary classes. (See "On Replace with Variables" on page 83.)

Here's an example that overrides variables with mixins.

```
public mixin class Mixin {
   public var value: Number = 1.1;
   public function getValue(): Number {
      return value;
   }
}

public class Base { . . .}

public class Derived extends Base, Mixin {
   public override var value = 2.2;
}

var d = Derived { };
println(d.getValue());              // 2.2
```

The Mixin class defines a Number variable that the Derived mixee class overrides with a new value. In Derived, a type is not required for value, since Number is inferred. A call to d.getValue() returns the overridden value (2.2). If Derived does not override value, d.getValue() returns the Mixin value (1.1).

JavaFX Tip

Mixin inheritance is not the same as multiple inheritance. Unlike multiple inheritance, which can inherit variables with the same name and type from multiple superclasses, mixin inheritance guarantees that only one variable of that name and type will be "mixed" in. This resolves ambiguities and makes mixin classes easier to work with.

3.8 Triggers

JavaFX has another feature that lets you execute code when variables in your program change their values. This is called a *trigger* and is implemented with the on replace keywords. Triggers are similar to binding block expressions except that you are not limited to def and var statements inside your blocks (see binding block expressions on page 53). In JavaFX, you can use triggers with variables, properties, sequences, and with bind. Let's look at several examples and show you how triggers work.

On Replace with Variables

The simplest use of on replace is to react to a change in the value of a variable in your program. The format is

```
var v = value on replace oldvalue {
   . . .
}
```

When variable *v* changes, the statements in the block execute. The `oldvalue` name is optional and is set to the previous value of v. The block also executes when you initialize variable *v* the first time.

Here's an example of `on replace` that only inserts positive values in a sequence.

```
var seq: Integer[];
var value = 0 on replace {
   if (value > 0) insert value into seq;
}

value = 12; value = -5;    // no negatives in seq
println(seq);              // [ 12 ]
value = 20;
println(seq);              // [ 12, 20 ]
```

When `value` changes, the `on replace` block executes. The `if` statement makes sure that `value` is positive before inserting it into the sequence.

If you need the previous value when an `on replace` block executes, include a name after the keyword `replace` (any non-keyword name will do). Here's an example that shows you how this works.

```
var number = 4 on replace old {
   println("old = {old} new = {number}");    // old = 0 new = 4
}

number = 8;      // // old = 4 new = 8
```

Note that `println` executes twice here, once when `number` receives its initial value (4) and again when `number` changes to 8. The `old` variable is 0 the first time because that's the default value for `number`.

On Replace with Sequences

You can use `on replace` with sequences, too. The format is

```
var seq = [sequence] on replace oldValue[low..high] = newSeq {
   . . .
}
```

When sequence *seq* changes, *oldValue* is the previous sequence, *low* and *high* are the indices of the sequence that changed, and *newSeq* is the new sequence. (You can use any non-keyword for these names.) Note that *oldValue[low..high]* is a sequence slice.

Here's an example to see how all this works.

```
var chars = ['a','b','c'] on replace old[lb..ub] = newchars {
   println("old = {old} low = {lb} high = {ub} newchars = {newchars}");
}                        // old =  low = 0 high = -1 newchars = abc
```

```
insert 'd' into chars;      // old = abc low = 3 high = 2 newchars = d
delete 'a' from chars;      // old = abcd low = 0 high = 0 newchars =
chars[1..2] = ['i', 't'];   // old = bcd low = 1 high = 2 newchars = it
println(chars);             // [ b, i, t ]
```

When the chars sequence is initialized, old is empty and newchars is the new sequence. Because this is an insertion, low is 0 and high is -1 (one less than low). The other sequence expressions generate the values shown (left as an exercise to the reader). Note that newchars is empty when you delete from the sequence.

On Replace with isInitialized

The isInitialized function returns true if its argument has been previously set. This can be important in on replace blocks, since they always execute at least once. If a variable in your program receives a default value, you may not want to execute the statements in an on replace block. The isInitialized function can prevent this.

To illustrate, here's a Distance object that converts miles to kilometers and vice versa.

```
class Distance {
    def factor = 1.609344;
    var miles: Number on replace {
        if (isInitialized(miles))
            kilometers = miles * factor;
    }
    var kilometers: Number on replace {
        if (isInitialized(kilometers))
            miles = kilometers * 1.0 / factor;
    }
    function print() {
        println("Miles = {%6.3f miles}, Kilometers = {%6.3f kilometers}")
    }
}

Distance{miles: 60}.print();         // Miles = 60.000, Kilometers = 96.561
Distance{kilometers: 500}.print();   // Miles = 310.686, Kilometers = 500.000
```

Programming Tip

Inside both on replace *blocks,* isInitialized *verifies that variables* miles *and* kilometers *are set before they are used. This avoids executing the conversions for this situation.*

```
Distance{}.print();        // Miles = 0.000, Kilometers = 0.000
```

On Replace with Bind

Another nice technique with on replace is to use it with bind. The format is

```
def v = bind w on replace oldValue {
    . . .
}
```

Here, if w changes, v is updated to w's value and then the code in the on replace block executes. As before, oldValue is optional.

Programming Tip

Using def *gives you compiler errors if you modify v. If you use* var, *you'll get an* AssignTo-BoundException *at runtime. In general, use* def *in declarations with* bind. *(The exception occurs with class instance variables when users can override binding with an object literal. See "Using this" on page 71.)*

To see an example of on replace with bind, let's return to our image loading example from earlier (see page 74). Recall that a loadComplete boolean was set to true by function makeServiceCall when image loading was completed. Here is a code snippet that binds a loadCarousel variable to the loadComplete boolean and starts up the carousel when all the images are loaded.

```
def loadCarousel: Boolean = bind loadComplete on replace {
    if (loadComplete) {
        println("starting carousel");
        carousel.play();
    }
}
```

Programming Tip

Remember, the on replace *block executes when you first initialize the* loadComplete *boolean to false. Here we check the flag and make sure it's true before starting up the carousel.*

3.9 Script Files and Packages

This section discusses program structure, how to access variables and functions from different script files, and how to organize your code into packages.

JavaFX lets you structure code as a collection of script level statements (statements that are not inside a function or class) or as reusable packages. Let's look at these two approaches in more detail and show you how JavaFX keywords help control the accessibility of your variables, objects, and functions.

Variable Scope

There are three types of variables in JavaFX: script variables, class instance variables, and local variables. Script variable declarations appear at the top-level of a JavaFX script *outside* of function definitions. Their values are visible everywhere in the script file (and, if public, everywhere in the program). The lifetime of a script variable starts when the script is loaded and ends when the program terminates. Local variable declarations only appear *inside* blocks (curly braces); their lifetime ends when you exit the block. Class instance variables appear inside JavaFX class definitions. Their scope is tied to the lifetime of the object they belong to.

Here is an example of variable declarations and their scope.

```
var interval = 100ms;                    // script variable

class Thing {
    var val: Integer;                    // instance variable
}

function doSomething(t: Thing): Void {
    var timeSlice = t.val * interval;   // local variable
    simulate(timeSlice);
}
```

Function Scope

JavaFX lets you write script functions and class instance functions. A script function is callable from anywhere in the script file where it's defined. Instance functions, on the other hand, are defined inside class declarations and must be called with object references.

Here are examples of script functions and instance functions.

```
function totalSum(seq: Integer[]) {         // script function
    var sum;
    for (i in seq) sum += i;
    return sum;
}

class Square {
    var side: Number;
    function area(): Number { side * side; } // instance function
}
```

As you will see shortly, you can control the accessibility of your JavaFX variables and functions with access modifiers.

Script Files

If you want to write JavaFX code quickly and check out its behavior, JavaFX lets you organize a program into script files. With this approach, it's not necessary to include a run function or use packages. This can be very useful when you are learning or just want to check out a portion of JavaFX code.

To illustrate, here's a script file that defines a Complex class and an add function to add Complex objects.

```
class Complex {
    var real: Number;
    var imag: Number;
    override function toString(): String {
        return "({real}, {imag})";
    }
}

function add(a: Complex, b: Complex): Complex {
    return Complex { real: a.real + b.real, imag: a.imag + b.imag; }
}

// script-level statements
var c1 = Complex{ real: 1.2, imag: 3.4 };
var c2 = Complex{ real: 3.1, imag: 2.5 };
var c3 = add(c1, c2);
println(c3);            // (4.3, 5.9)
```

Programming Tip

If you designate any function or variable public *in a script file, script-level statements will not compile. You have to put script-level statements in a* run *function. A script file is a compilation unit in JavaFX.*

Access Modifiers

To make JavaFX programs more modular and reusable, you can use access modifiers in your script files. Table 3.3 lists the primary access modifiers that apply to creating and using classes, calling functions, and reading and writing script variables or instance variables. These access modifiers also apply when overriding and setting or binding object literals of instance variables.

TABLE 3.3 Primary Access Modifiers

(no access modifier)	Script-private. Accessible only within script where it is defined (default). Readable and writable.
`package`	Only accessible from within package where it is defined. Readable and writable.
`protected`	For class instance variables and functions, accessible to subclasses of the class where it is defined. For script variables and script functions, accessible from the same package. Readable and writable.
`public`	Accessible anywhere. Readable and writable.

JavaFX Tip

JavaFX does not have a private access modifier like other languages (Java, C++). The default (no access modifier) is script-private.

Table 3.4 lists the variable access modifiers. You can use `protected` and `package` with `public-read` and `public-init` to grant additional write permissions as indicated in Table 3.4.

TABLE 3.4 Variable Access Modifiers

`public-read`	Writable only within the current script. Read-only outside the script.
`public-init`	Writable only within the current script. Can be initialized in an object literal and read anywhere outside the script. Read-only after initialization outside the script.
`protected public-read`	Writable with sub-classes; otherwise read-only outside the script.
`protected public-init`	Writable with sub-classes outside the script; otherwise init-only.
`package public-read`	Writable in the same package; otherwise read-only.
`package public-init`	Writable in the same package; otherwise init-only.

Packages

Let's restructure the previous Complex script file and show you how to use it with packages. Here's the approach.

```
// Complex.fx - Complex class
```

```
package complex;

public class Complex {
    public var real: Number;
    public var imag: Number;
    public override function toString(): String {
        return "({real}, {imag})";
    }
}

public function add(a: Complex, b: Complex): Complex {
    return Complex { real: a.real + b.real, imag: a.imag + b.imag; }
}
```

The file **Complex.fx** contains the code for class Complex and the add script function. All members and functions have public access specifiers and belong to package complex.

Here's a **Main.fx** program that instantiates Complex objects and adds them.

```
// Main.fx - Complex objects
package complex;

var c1 = Complex { real: 1.2, imag: 3.4 };
var c2 = Complex { real: 3.1, imag: 2.5 };
var c3 = Complex.add(c1, c2);
println(c3);            // (4.3, 5.9)
```

The package statement lets you access public members (Complex, add). Note that Complex.add is required to call the add function. Access to public members is also possible with import statements.

Programming Tip

With functions, type inference can generally determine the types of your arguments and return values. However, you must explicitly provide types for functions that you intend to call from other script files.

JavaFX does not support static member variables and static member functions like other languages (Java, C++). You can, however, use script variables with appropriate access modifiers to simulate static behaviors. Here's an example.

```
// Thing.fx - Thing class
package thing;

public def size1 = 100;
public-read var size2 = 200;

public class Thing {
    public var num: Integer;
```

```
        public function func() {
            return size1 + size2;
        }
    }

    public function myFunction() {
        size1 = 300;                        // compiler error
        size2 = 400;                        // ok
    }


    // Main.fx - Main program
    package thing;

    var th = Thing { num: 10 };
    println(th.func());                     // 300
    println(thing.Thing.size2);             // 200
    thing.Thing.size2 = 500;                // compiler error
```

In **Thing.fx**, size2 is modifiable but in other files (**Main.fx**) it is not. The notation
thing.Thing (package name and file name) is necessary to access script variables in
Thing.fx. Note that public-read is legal with script variables.

3.10 Exception Handling

In most cases, the JavaFX compiler does a good job of reporting errors at compile time
when you do something wrong. Occasionally, however, unexpected runtime errors
occur. In some situations, you might want to deal with runtime errors in some specific
way. This is called *exception handling*. In this section, we show you how to handle
exceptions in your JavaFX programs.

Try, Catch, Finally

Use the keywords try, catch, and finally for thrown exceptions. The formats are

```
try {
    // critical code
} catch (e: myException) {
    // exception handler code
}
finally {
    // always executes
}

try {
    // do something here
    return;
}
```

```
finally {
   // always executes
}
```

A try block encloses code where an exception could be thrown. A catch handler has a signature with an exception type (*myException*) and catches the thrown exception if the type matches. You can have more than one catch handler (each with a different signature) and a handler can rethrow the same exception or a different one. A finally block is optional and always executes, regardless of whether an exception was thrown or not. If you omit a catch handler after a try block, you must include a finally block. The finally block typically includes cleanup code.

Exceptions can easily be thrown in a JavaFX program, especially if you are using Java API methods. Here's an example with a run function that converts program arguments.

```
// Numbers.fx - Program argument conversions
import java.lang.*;

function run(args: String[]) {
   try {
      def intVal = Integer.parseInt(args[0]);
      def doubleVal = Double.parseDouble(args[1]);
      println(intVal);
      println(doubleVal);
   } catch (e: NumberFormatException) {
      println(e);
   }
}
```

Without try and catch, the program throws an exception at runtime and terminates if the program arguments have illegal characters for integers or doubles. To detect these runtime errors under program control, enclose the code in a try block with a catch handler that prints the error message.

```
$ javafx Numbers 123 45.67
123
45.67

$ javafx Numbers badchars
java.lang.NumberFormatException: For input string: "badchars"
```

Throwing Exceptions

The keyword throw lets you throw exceptions in JavaFX. The format is

```
throw new myException(args);
```

Note that you must use operator new to create an exception object from the *myException* class. The constructor arguments typically contain information pertinent to the error. You can throw built-in Java exception objects or user-defined exception objects.

Here's a checkArgument function that throws an IllegalArgumentException if its integer argument is negative.

```
import java.lang.*;

function checkArgument(num: Integer): Void {
    if (num < 0)
        throw new IllegalArgumentException("neg value");
}
```

JavaFX Tip

Unlike Java, JavaFX does not have throws clauses on script functions or instance functions that throw exceptions.

3.11 JavaFX Keywords

Table 3.5 lists the keywords and reserved words in JavaFX.

TABLE 3.5 JavaFX Keywords and Reserved Words

abstract	after	and	as	assert	at
attribute	before	bind	bound	break	catch
class	continue	def	delete	else	exclusive
extends	false	finally	first	for	from
function	if	import	indexof	in	init
insert	instanceof	into	inverse	last	lazy
mixin	mod	new	not	null	on
or	override	package	postinit	private	protected
public-init	public	public-read	replace	return	reverse
sizeof	static	step	super	then	this
throw	trigger	true	try	tween	typeof
var	where	while	with		

Use <<*keyword*>> to escape a keyword.

```
    str = str.<<replace>>(colon, space);     // call Java function replace
```

4 Graphical Objects

Graphical objects and their manipulation are where JavaFX excels. This chapter shows you how to define and control graphical objects in JavaFX.

We begin at the top-level Stage and its Scene, followed by the all-important Node class. Nodes share a wealth of properties that let you manipulate graphical objects in a consistent way.

Nodes specialize into different types: there are nodes that are Shapes, nodes for grouping and layout, or developer's can define their own nodes. Shapes come in all forms: Circle, Polygon, Line, and even Path—a shape that lets you describe your own Shape.

JavaFX graphical objects also include user interface components. We cover these in the next chapter.

What You Will Learn

- Top-level JavaFX objects Stage and Scene
- Node class and its properties
- Mouse and key event handler properties
- Cursor types
- Group and CustomNode
- Shapes, Paths, and Path Elements
- Layout components and bounding rectangles

4.1 Setting the Stage

JavaFX programs that render graphical material include a top-level Stage. The Stage includes a Scene object, which in turn includes a sequence of Nodes. By default the Stage style is set to StageStyle.DECORATED, which is rendered differently depending on the environment (Windows Vista, Mac OS, Windows XP). StageStyle.UNDECORATED removes the decoration from the window. Both styles are shown in Figure 4.1.

```
Stage {
    title: "Stage Title"
    width: 180
    height: 150
    style: StageStyle.UNDECORATED
    scene: Scene {
        fill: Color.BISQUE
        content: // content here
    }
}
```

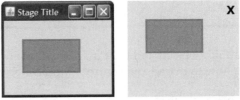

Default Stage style   StageStyle.UNDECORATED

Figure 4.1 Top-level Stage

JavaFX Tip

If you set the Stage's style to StageStyle.UNDECORATED, *you can provide your own "window close" button. See the code in Figure 4.19 on page 116 for an example.*

Scene

The JavaFX Scene class is the root for all content in a scene graph. The background of the scene is specified by the fill property (default is Color.WHITE). The sequence of Nodes in the content sequence is rendered on the scene.

Node

Class Node is the base class for all objects in the scene graph. You can add Node objects (subtypes of Node) to a scene graph, specify their properties, and apply transformations. Node has many properties that let you customize its look and behavior, such as event handlers, clip, effect, opacity, rotate, properties for scaling and translating, visible, focusable, disable, bounding rectangles, and other properties listed in Table 4.1 and Table 4.2.

Figure 4.2 shows a class hierarchy diagram of some of the JavaFX graphical objects discussed in this chapter.

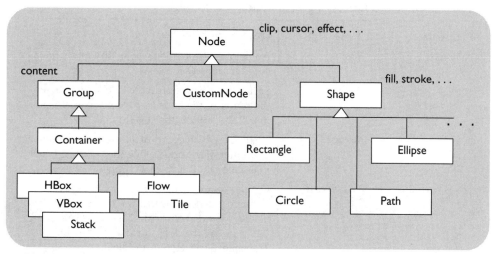

Figure 4.2 Node class hierarchy (partial)

Nodes have different subtypes, and as such, exhibit different specializations. For example, Group is a type of node that contains multiple subnodes in a content sequence. Layout nodes are all types of Container, which is a kind of Group. (See "Layout Components" on page 119 for a description of the layout nodes.) Shape is a type of subnode that is rendered in the coordinate space with properties such as fill and stroke. Path, in turn, is a subtype of Shape that is made up of connected path elements. Circle is also a subtype of Shape. All these Node subtypes share common properties that help customize rendering, shown in Table 4.1. (See "Cascading Style Sheets (CSS)" on page 148 for details on applying styles to JavaFX nodes.)

TABLE 4.1 Node Rendering Properties

Property	Type	Description
clip	Node	Defines the clipping shape for this Node.
cursor	Cursor	Mouse cursor for this node and subnodes. If null, uses the first parent that has a non-null cursor. If still null, uses the cursor of the Scene.
effect	Effect	Specifies the effect to apply to this node. (See Table 8.3 on page 263 for a list of common JavaFX Effects.)
opacity	Number	Specifies how solid (opaque) a node appears (0 is fully translucent and 1 is fully opaque). Note that opacity applies to the entire node, while the opacity argument with fill color affects only the fill (and not the stroke for example).

TABLE 4.1 Node Rendering Properties *(Continued)*

Property	Type	Description
rotate	Number	Angle of rotation about the node's center, measured in degrees.
scaleX	Number	Factor by which coordinates are scaled about the center of the node along the x axis. -1 is normal scale, but the object is flipped.
scaleY	Number	Factor by which coordinates are scaled about the center of the node along the y axis. -1 is normal scale, but the object is flipped.
transforms	Transform[]	Defines sequence of Transform objects that apply to this node. Transformations are applied before translateX, translateY, scaleX, scaleY, and rotate. Transform objects include Translate, Scale, Rotate, or Shear.
translateX	Number	Defines x coordinate of the translation to apply to this node. Used to move a node with animation.
translateY	Number	Defines y coordinate of the translation to apply to this node. Used to move a node with animation.
layoutX	Number	Defines x coordinate layout adjustment to apply to this node. Used to position a node. (New in JavaFX 1.2.)
layoutY	Number	Defines y coordinate layout adjustment to apply to this node. Used to position a node. (New in JavaFX 1.2.)
visible	Boolean	If true, node should be rendered. If false, node is not rendered and will not receive mouse events or keyboard focus.
id	String	Similar to the "id" attribute of an HTML element; useful to assign style elements from external style sheets.
style	String	Provides inline CSS styles. Uses the syntax defined in JavaFX CSS parser.
styleClass	String	Useful to assign style elements from external style sheets to all nodes matching styleClass.

Programming Tip

If you're dealing with movement or animation, use properties translateX *and* translateY*. If you're dealing with node positioning, use properties* layoutX *and* layoutY*.*

Table 4.2 lists Node properties that let you customize how a node handles various input events (mouse and key events) and other properties that affect its event handling.

TABLE 4.2 Node Mouse/Keyboard Event Properties

Property	Type	Description
blocksMouse	Boolean	If true, consumes mouse events in node and does not send them to other nodes further up the scene graph. Commonly used when nodes overlap.
focused	Boolean	If true, node is current input focus owner. Only one node at a time may be the current focus owner.
focusable	Boolean	If true, node can accept focus.
hover	Boolean	If true, node is currently being hovered over (typically with a mouse).
pressed	Boolean	If true, node is pressed (typically, the primary mouse button is down).
disable	Boolean	Sets disabled state of node (and any subnodes).
disabled	Boolean	If true, node is disabled. A disabled node should render itself differently.
onKeyPressed	function(:KeyEvent) :Void	Function called when node has input focus and a key has been pressed.
onKeyReleased	function(:KeyEvent) :Void	Function called when node has input focus and a key has been released.
onKeyTyped	function(:KeyEvent) :Void	Function called when node has input focus and a key has been typed (pressed and released).
onMouseClicked	function(: MouseEvent):Void	Function called when mouse button has been clicked (pressed and released).
onMouseDragged	function(: MouseEvent):Void	Function called when mouse button is pressed and then dragged.
onMouseEntered	function(: MouseEvent):Void	Function called when mouse enters node.

TABLE 4.2 Node Mouse/Keyboard Event Properties *(Continued)*

Property	Type	Description
onMouseExited	function(: MouseEvent):Void	Function called when mouse exits node.
onMouseMoved	function(: MouseEvent):Void	Function called when mouse cursor moves within node but no buttons have been pushed.
onMousePressed	function(: MouseEvent):Void	Function called when mouse button has been pressed.
onMouseReleased	function(: MouseEvent):Void	Function called when mouse button has been released.
onMouseWheel-Moved	function(: MouseEvent):Void	Function called when mouse scroll wheel has moved.

Key Events Tip

Use Node function requestFocus *to request focus for nodes that have key event handlers.*

Event handling for mouse and key events lets the user initiate actions. Let's look at a simple mouse event handler that successively rotates a rectangle by 45 degrees, as shown in Figure 4.3. View A shows the default state of the rectangle. In View B, the user moves the mouse over the rectangle, causing the onMouseEntered event handler to be called, which changes the rectangle's fill color and stroke characteristics. When the user clicks the mouse, the rectangle rotates (View C). When the mouse exits the rectangle, the fill color and stroke are returned to the default settings. A double-click resets the rotation back to zero.

View A   View B   View C

Figure 4.3 Detecting mouse events in a node

Listing 4.1 shows the Rectangle object literal and its three mouse event handlers.

Listing 4.1 Detecting Mouse Events

```
Rectangle {
    x: 30, y: 30
```

```
width: 90, height: 50
stroke: Color.SLATEGRAY
strokeWidth: 3
fill: Color.CORNFLOWERBLUE
onMouseClicked: function(e: MouseEvent): Void {
    if (e.clickCount == 2) { e.node.rotate = 0; }
    else  { e.node.rotate += 45; }
}
onMouseEntered: function(e: MouseEvent): Void {
    (e.node as Shape).fill = Color.BLUE;
    (e.node as Shape).strokeDashArray = [9, 5];
}
onMouseExited: function(e: MouseEvent): Void {
    (e.node as Shape).fill = Color.CORNFLOWERBLUE;
    (e.node as Shape).strokeDashArray = null;
}
}
```

Note that expression (e.node as Shape) is required before accessing Shape-specific properties fill and strokeDashArray. (Expression (e.node as Rectangle) also works for properties fill and strokeDashArray.) The expression is *not* necessary with property rotate, which is a Node property. You also don't need instanceof here, since the event handler object literal appears in a Rectangle, a subtype of Shape.

Cursor

JavaFX provides various cursor types, as shown in Figure 4.4 and listed in Table 4.3. You can set the cursor type of any node with property cursor, as follows.

```
Rectangle {
    cursor: Cursor.HAND
    width: 50
    height: 100
}
```

The cursor type propagates to all subnodes unless a subnode redefines it. If cursor is null, the first parent with a non-null cursor defines the current node's cursor type. If no cursor is defined within the scene graph, the cursor type of the Scene defines the cursor.

Left to right: crosshair, default, hand, move, text, wait, horizontal (east, west) resize, vertical (north, south) resize, northwest or southeast resize, northeast or southwest resize

Figure 4.4 Cursor types

TABLE 4.3 Common Cursor Types

Cursor	Description
CROSSHAIR	cross-shaped cursor
DEFAULT	arrow
HAND	hand
MOVE	4-direction arrow
TEXT	I-bar
WAIT	hour glass

There are also multiple cursor types for specialized resizing operations, as listed in Table 4.4.

TABLE 4.4 Resize Cursor Types

Cursor	Description
H_RESIZE	double ended horizontal arrow
E_RESIZE	
W_RESIZE	
V_RESIZE	double ended vertical arrow
N_RESIZE	
S_RESIZE	
NW_RESIZE	double ended northwest to southeast arrow
SE_RESIZE	
NE_RESIZE	double ended northeast to southwest arrow
SW_RESIZE	

Group

Group is a container class that groups nodes together. Most often, you use Group to construct a portion of a scene graph with related nodes. Once these nodes are inserted into the group's content sequence, you can reposition the group without affecting the relative position of any of its subnodes. You build a Group object literal with subnodes in property content. Alternatively, you can insert nodes under program control, as shown here.

```
var g1 = Group { };        // instantiate Group g1, empty content sequence
insert Rectangle {
    width: 40
    height: 20
```

```
    } into g1.content;        // add a Rectangle to g1 content
```

CustomNode

Class CustomNode is an abstract base class that extends Node. It lets you create custom nodes for scene graphs. When you extend from CustomNode, you provide a create function. Function `create` typically returns a Group node defining other nodes in its content property. Here is the structure of the GuitarString custom node found in Chapter 2 (see Listing 2.1 on page 36 and Listing 2.2 on page 38).[1]

```
public class GuitarString extends CustomNode {
    // properties, variables, functions
    . . .
    protected override function create(): Node {
    // put any initialization code here
       return Group {
          content: [
             Rectangle { ... }
             Rectangle { ... }
             Rectangle { ... }
             Text { ... }
          ]
       } // Group
    }
} // GuitarString
```

See "PianoKey Components" on page 169 for another example that extends CustomNode.

4.2 Shapes

Class Shape is an abstract subclass of JavaFX Node (see Figure 4.2 on page 97). Shape objects inherit all properties in Node and adds new properties such as `fill` and `stroke` (outline drawn around the shape). Property `fill` is type Paint, which can be a color, such as `Color.RED`, or a gradient (LinearGradient or RadialGradient). The default `fill` value for all shapes is `Color.BLACK` except Line, Polyline, and Path, which use default value null. You can make shapes transparent by setting their `opacity` property to 0. You can alternatively provide an opacity argument with a color value or use `Color.TRANSPARENT` for property `fill`. (Property `opacity` affects the entire node, including `stroke`, whereas providing an opacity modifier with a fill color affects the `fill` property only.) See "Gradients" on page 26 and "Color" on page 28 for examples of gradients and color.

---

1. Function `create` is called from the `init` block in class CustomNode. If you need to do any initialization work prior to the custom node's content being created, put that code in `create`.

Property `stroke` is also type Paint. Shapes include several additional properties that let you configure the size, color, and look of a Shape's outline stroke.

Table 4.5 lists a Shape's properties.

TABLE 4.5 Shape Properties

Property	Type	Description
`fill`	`Paint`	Interior of a Shape using the settings of the Paint context. The default value is `Color.BLACK` for all shapes except Line, Polyline, and Path, which use default value null.
`smooth`	`Boolean`	If `true`, antialiasing rendering hints are applied when rendering the Shape.
`stroke`	`Paint`	Parameters of a stroke that is drawn around the outline of a Shape using the settings of the specified Paint. The default value is null for all shapes except Line, Polyline, and Path, which use default value `Color.BLACK`.
`strokeDashArray`	`Number[]`	A sequence representing the lengths of the dash segments. Alternate entries in the sequence represent the lengths of the opaque and transparent segments of the dashes. The pen is opaque when its current cumulative distance maps to an even element of the dash sequence and transparent otherwise.
`strokeDashOffset`	`Number`	Index in the dashing pattern that will correspond to the beginning of the stroke.
`strokeLineCap`	`Stroke-LineCap`	End cap style as one of the following values: `StrokeLineCap.BUTT`, `StrokeLineCap.ROUND`, and `StrokeLineCap.SQUARE`.
`strokeLineJoin`	`Stroke-LineJoin`	Decoration applied where path segments meet as one of the following values: `StrokeLine-Join.BEVEL`, `StrokeLineJoin.MITER`, and `StrokeLineJoin.ROUND`
`strokeMiterLimit`	`Number`	Limit on ratio of miter length to stroke width for `StrokeLineJoin.MITER` line join style.
`strokeWidth`	`Number`	Square pen line width. A value of 0.0 specifies a hairline stroke.

Figure 4.5 shows three different line cap styles with property `strokeLineCap`. The top line uses `StrokeLineCap.SQUARE` (the default), the second one uses `StrokeLine-Cap.ROUND`, and the bottom line uses `StrokeLineCap.BUTT`.

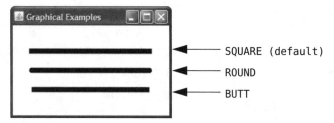

Figure 4.5 Line cap styles

Listing 4.2 shows the object literals for each of the lines shown in Figure 4.5.

Listing 4.2 Property strokeLineCap

```
def line1 = Line {
    startX: 10, startY: 20, endX: 200, endY: 20
    strokeWidth: 8
    stroke: Color.BLACK
    strokeLineCap: StrokeLineCap.SQUARE
}
def line2 = Line {
    startX: 10, startY: 50, endX: 200, endY: 50
    strokeWidth: 8
    stroke: Color.BLACK
    strokeLineCap: StrokeLineCap.ROUND
}
def line3 = Line {
    startX: 10, startY: 80, endX: 200, endY: 80
    strokeWidth: 8
    stroke: Color.BLACK
    strokeLineCap: StrokeLineCap.BUTT
}
```

Figure 4.6 illustrates dashed lines, which are rendered with a sequence of numbers provided in property strokeDashArray. If you specify one number, a dashed line will have equal parts opaque (visible) and equal parts translucent. Otherwise, the numbers in the sequence alternate between the opaque part and the translucent part. The top line uses sequence [8 12], which sets the visible dash size to 8 pixels and the translucent size to 12. The middle line uses [16 4], to make the dash 16 and the translucent part 4. The bottom line uses 10 which provides equal-sized dashes and translucent parts. In general, the wider the stroke (property strokeWidth), the larger you should make your stroke dash sequence numbers.

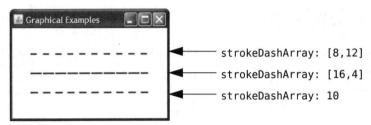

Figure 4.6 Dashed line styles

Listing 4.3 shows the object literals for each of the lines shown in Figure 4.6.

Listing 4.3 Property strokeDashArray

```
def line1 = Line {
    startX: 10, startY: 20, endX: 200, endY: 20
    strokeWidth: 2
    stroke: Color.BLACK
    strokeDashArray: [8,12]
}
def line2 = Line {
    startX: 10, startY: 50, endX: 200, endY: 50
    strokeWidth: 2
    stroke: Color.BLACK
    strokeDashArray: [16,4]
}
def line3 = Line {
    startX: 10, startY: 80, endX: 200, endY: 80
    strokeWidth: 2
    stroke: Color.BLACK
    strokeDashArray: 10
}
```

It's also possible to have more than two numbers in strokeDashArray. Even index numbers map to the opaque part of the dash and odd index numbers map to the translucent part. This lets you build dashed lines with varying-sized dashes. For example, the following strokeDashArray sequence creates a dashed line that cycles through progressively smaller dashes (16, 12, 8, 4) with equal spacing in between (8).

```
    strokeDashArray: [16, 8, 12, 8, 8, 8, 4, 8]
```

When the number of elements in the strokeDashArray is odd, numbers are assigned to opaque and translucent parts in order. In the following example, 20 is assigned to the opaque part in the first cycle and the translucent part in the second cycle.

```
    strokeDashArray: [20, 4, 12]
```

Rectangle

Rectangles have `height` and `width` properties and `x` and `y` properties for the upper left corner origin (default is 0 for the coordinate properties). For rounded rectangles, use properties `arcHeight` and `arcWidth` and specify the vertical and horizontal diameter of the arc at the four corners of the rectangle. Figure 4.7 shows the code for rendering the rounded Rectangle shown.

```
Rectangle {
    x: 30, y: 10
    width: 60, height: 80
    arcWidth: 20
    arcHeight: 20
    fill: Color.CORAL
    stroke: Color.BLUE
}
```

Figure 4.7 Rounded Rectangle example

Book Examples

- "Class WhiteKey—Part 2", Listing 6.3 on page 172, (Chapter 6). Uses a rectangle to render a piano key.

- "Class BlackKey—Part 2", Listing 6.6 on page 177, (Chapter 6). Uses a rectangle to render a piano key.

- "Photo1: Displaying an image", Listing 8.3 on page 254, (Chapter 8). Uses a rectangle to frame an image.

Circle

A Circle has a center point (properties `centerX` and `centerY`) and property `radius`. Figure 4.8 shows an example object literal that renders the Circle shown.

```
Circle {
    centerX: 50, centerY: 50
    radius: 40
    fill: Color.CORAL
    stroke: Color.BLUE
}
```

Figure 4.8 Circle example

Book Examples

- "Class WhiteKey—Part 2", Listing 6.3 on page 172, (Chapter 6). Uses a circle to indicate a mouse event on a piano key.

- "Using Timeline to animate a Circle", Listing 7.1 on page 209, (Chapter 7). Animates a circle.

- "PathBall", Listing 7.21 on page 239, (Chapter 7). Creates a custom node with a circle.

Ellipse

Ellipse is similar to Circle, except that it has separate radius values for the x and y directions. Besides `centerX` and `centerY`, you also specify `radiusX` and `radiusY`. Figure 4.9 shows an example object literal that renders the Ellipse shown.

```
Ellipse {
    centerX: 50, centerY: 50
    radiusX: 50, radiusY: 25
    fill: Color.CORAL
    stroke: Color.BLUE
}
```

Figure 4.9 Ellipse example

Arc

Arcs have a center point (`centerX` and `centerY`) and two radii (`radiusX` and `radiusY`), similar to Ellipse. Arcs also have a starting angle (`startAngle`) and an extent (`length`). Both `startAngle` and `length` are expressed in degrees. Arc objects have three types: `ArcType.ROUND` (close the shape by connecting the ends of the arc to the center point), `ArcType.CHORD` (close the shape by connecting the ends of the arc with a line segment) and `ArcType.OPEN` (leave the shape open).

Angle 0° is at the right axis, 90° is at the top, 180° is at the left axis, and 270° is at the bottom. Positive values for length draw the arc in a counter-clockwise direction and negative values draw the arc in a clockwise direction.

Figure 4.10 show three arc types and the code that creates type ArcType.ROUND. The arc is centered at point (50,50), with a y-axis radius of 25 and an x-axis radius of 50. The sweep of the arc begins at angle 45 and extends to angle 315 (a sweep of 270 degrees).

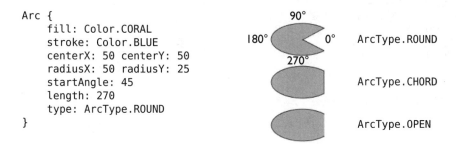

```
Arc {
    fill: Color.CORAL
    stroke: Color.BLUE
    centerX: 50 centerY: 50
    radiusX: 50 radiusY: 25
    startAngle: 45
    length: 270
    type: ArcType.ROUND
}
```

Figure 4.10 Arc examples

Polygon

Polygons have a sequence of x-coordinate and y-coordinate values for property points. A Polygon is a closed shape, so the last point connects to the first point with a line. Figure 4.11 shows an example object literal that renders a "stop sign" octagon.

```
Polygon {
    points: [
        20.0,  0.0, 40.0,  0.0,
        60.0, 20.0, 60.0, 40.0,
        40.0, 60.0, 20.0, 60.0,
         0.0, 40.0,  0.0, 20.0,
    ]
    fill: Color.CORAL
    stroke: Color.BLUE
}
```

Figure 4.11 Polygon example

QuadCurve

The QuadCurve class defines a quadratic Bézier parametric curve segment with a starting and ending point (startX, startY and endX, endY) using a Bézier control point (controlX, controlY). Figure 4.12 shows an example object literal and the resulting

QuadCurve that the code renders. Point A is the starting point (startX, startY), point B is the control point (controlX, controlY), and C is the ending point (endX, endY).

```
QuadCurve {
    startX: 0.0, startY: 100.0
    endX: 50.0, endY: 100.0
    controlX: 25.0, controlY: 0.0
    fill: Color.CORAL
    stroke: Color.BLUE
}
```

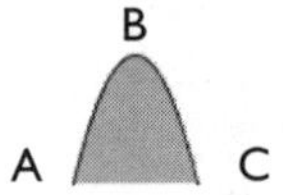

Figure 4.12 QuadCurve example

CubicCurve

The CubicCurve class defines a cubic Bézier parametric curve segment that intersects both a starting and ending point (startX, startY and endX, endY) using the specified Bézier control points (controlX1, controlY1 and controlX2, controlY2). Figure 4.13 shows an example object literal and the resulting CubicCurve that the code renders. Point A is the starting point (startX, startY), points B and C are the control points (controlX1, controlY1 and controlX2, controlY2), and point D is the ending point (endX, endY).

```
CubicCurve {
    startX: 0, startY: 50
    controlX1: 25, controlY1: -50
    controlX2: 75, controlY2: 150
    endX: 100, endY: 50
    fill: Color.CORAL
    stroke: Color.BLUE
}
```

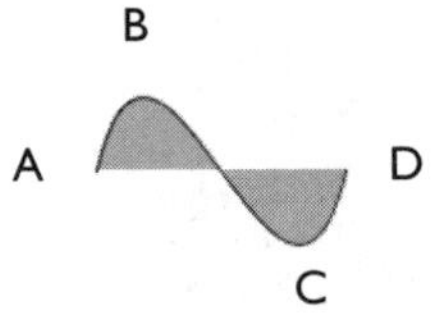

Figure 4.13 CubicCurve example

Line

Lines have starting and ending x and y coordinate points. Property fill defaults to null. Figure 4.14 shows an example object literal and the resulting Line that the code renders. Here, property strokeDashArray renders a dashed line.

```
Line {
    startX: 10, startY: 100
    endX: 200, endY: 20
    stroke: Color.BLUE
    strokeDashArray: [16, 8]
}
```

Figure 4.14 Line example

Polyline

Polylines have a sequence of x-coordinate and y-coordinate values for property points. Polyline is similar to Polygon, except that it does not automatically close. Figure 4.15 shows an example object literal that renders the Polyline shown. Note that the example does not specify a closing side and none is drawn.

```
Polyline {
    points: [
        20.0,  0.0, 40.0,  0.0,
        60.0, 20.0, 60.0, 40.0,
        40.0, 60.0, 20.0, 60.0,
        0.0, 40.0, 0.0, 20.0,
    ]
    fill: Color.CORAL
    stroke: Color.BLUE
    strokeWidth: 6
}
```

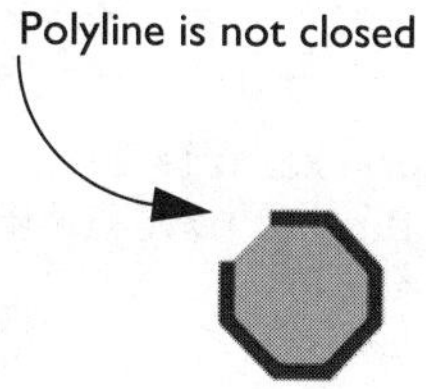

Polyline is not closed

Figure 4.15 Polyline example

SVGPath

SVGPath constructs a shape by parsing SVG (Scalable Vector Graphics) path data from a String.[2] SVGPath parses only SVG path data, which includes commands and point data.

---

2. SVG is a standard for specifying graphics. See http://www.w3.org/TR/SVG/paths.html for a reference on SVG paths.

Table 4.6 lists the available SVGPath commands. Capital letter commands indicate coordinate values with absolute position and lower case letter commands mean coordinate values with relative position.

TABLE 4.6 SVGPath Commands

Command		Description
Absolute	**Relative**	
M	m	move to
L	l	line to
H	h	horizontal line to
V	v	vertical line to
C	c	curve to
S	s	smooth curve to
Q	q	quadratic Bézier curve to
T	t	smooth quadratic Bézier curve to
A	a	elliptical arc
Z	z	close path

Figure 4.16 shows an example object literal that renders the SVGPath shown. This draws a quadratic Bézier curve similar to the QuadCurve object in Figure 4.12 on page 110.

```
SVGPath {
    fill: Color.CORAL
    stroke: Color.BLUE
    strokeWidth: 2
    content : "M0 100"
    "Q25.0 0.0 50 100"
}
```

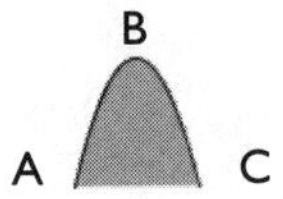

Figure 4.16 SVGPath example

Figure 4.17 shows an SVGPath that produces a spiral graphic. The code that renders this spiral is shown in Listing 4.4.

Figure 4.17 SVGPath that creates a spiral

Listing 4.4 SVGPath that produces a spiral

```
SVGPath {
    fill: Color.CORAL
    stroke: Color.BLUE
    strokeWidth: 2
    content : "M153 334"
      "C153 334 151 334 151 334"
      "C151 339 153 344 156 344"
      "C164 344 171 339 171 334"
      "C171 322 164 314 156 314"
      "C142 314 131 322 131 334"
      "C131 350 142 364 156 364"
      "C175 364 191 350 191 334"
      "C191 311 175 294 156 294"
      "C131 294 111 311 111 334"
      "C111 361 131 384 156 384"
      "C186 384 211 361 211 334"
      "C211 300 186 274 156 274"
}
```

ShapeIntersect/ShapeSubtract

ShapeIntersect and ShapeSubtract are composite shapes. You create them by combining two shapes specified in properties a and b (building block shapes). Building block shapes do not accept Shape properties such as fill or stroke. However, composite shapes do—they are like any other Shape. Figure 4.18 shows several views illustrating ShapeIntersect and ShapeSubtract.

View A shows the two building block shapes: Rectangle for property a and Ellipse for property b.

View B shows ShapeIntersect. The composite shape includes all points in the coordinate space that are in both shapes.

View C shows ShapeSubtract. Here, the composite shape consists of shape a minus shape b.

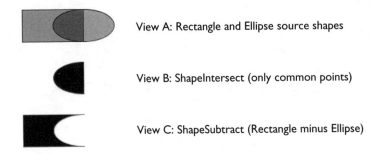

View A: Rectangle and Ellipse source shapes

View B: ShapeIntersect (only common points)

View C: ShapeSubtract (Rectangle minus Ellipse)

Figure 4.18 ShapeIntersect and ShapeSubtract

Listing 4.5 shows the code that renders the views in Figure 4.18.

Listing 4.5 ShapeIntersect and ShapeSubtract

```
// View A
def g1 = Group {
    content: [
        Rectangle {
            width: 100
            height: 50
            stroke: Color.BLUE
            fill: Color.LIGHTSLATEGRAY
        }
        Ellipse {
            centerX: 100
            centerY: 25
            radiusX: 50
            radiusY: 25
            stroke: Color.DARKBLUE
            fill: Color.web("#333333", .5)
        }
    ]
}
// View B
def shapeintersect = ShapeIntersect {
    stroke: Color.DARKCYAN
    a: Rectangle {
        width: 100
        height: 50
    }
    b: Ellipse {
```

```
          centerX: 100
          centerY: 25
          radiusX: 50
          radiusY: 25
      }
}
// View C
def shapeminus = ShapeSubtract {
    stroke: Color.DARKCYAN
    a: Rectangle {
        width: 100
        height: 50
    }
    b: Ellipse {
        centerX: 100
        centerY: 25
        radiusX: 50
        radiusY: 25
    }
}
. . .
VBox {
    content: [ g1, shapeintersect, shapeminus ]
}
. . .
```

Text

Text is a specialized shape for displaying text. Table 4.7 lists the properties for component Text.

TABLE 4.7 Text Properties

Property	Type	Description
content	String	Text to be displayed.
font	Font	Font used to display text.
overline	Boolean	If true, each text line has a line above it.
strikethrough	Boolean	If true, each text line has a line through it.
underline	Boolean	If true, each text line has a line under it.
wrappingWidth	Number	Width constraint. If > 0, text is wrapped at word boundaries to comply.
textAlignment	TextAlignment	Horizontal text alignment; one of TextAlignment.CENTER, TextAlignment.JUSTIFY, TextAlignment.LEFT (default), and TextAlignment.RIGHT

TABLE 4.7 Text Properties *(Continued)*

Property	Type	Description
`textOrigin`	`TextOrigin`	Aligns text with the y coordinate value in local coordinates; one of `TextOrigin.BASELINE` (default), `TextOrigin.BOTTOM`, `TextOrigin.TOP`
x	`Number`	X coordinate of text origin.
y	`Number`	Y coordinate of text origin.

`TextOrigin.BASELINE` aligns the baseline of the text with the y coordinate value, which does not include the space taken by descending characters (such as lower case "g" or "y"). `TextOrigin.BOTTOM` aligns the bottom of the text with the y coordinate value and includes space taken by descending characters. `TextOrigin.TOP` aligns the top of the text with the y coordinate value.

Since Text is a Node, you can easily implement a Text component that responds to an event. For example, Figure 4.19 shows a Text component used as a window close button. This code is useful in a run time environment that does not include a browser.

```
def closeButton = Text {
    content: "X"
    fill: Color.BLACK
    x: 300
    y: 10
    textOrigin: TextOrigin.TOP
    font: Font {
        name: "Bitstream Vera Sans Bold"
        size: 18
    }
    cursor: Cursor.HAND
    visible: bind ("{__PROFILE__}" != "browser")
    onMousePressed: function(e: MouseEvent): Void {
        FX.exit();
    }
}
```

Figure 4.19 Text component as a close button

4.3 Paths

A Path lets you string together a sequence of path elements to define arbitrary shapes. Use Path when you need to customize a shape beyond the standard JavaFX shapes.

You can also use Path to create a PathTransition. This is a specialized animation that lets you move an object along a predefined path.

A Path has path elements. The first path element is always MoveTo. By default, coordinates are expressed in absolute coordinate values. Set property `absolute` to false for relative coordinate values. You'll note that many JavaFX shapes have corresponding path elements (Arc is the shape and ArcTo is the path element).

Table 4.8 lists the standard path elements.

TABLE 4.8 Path Elements

Path Element	Description
MoveTo	Move to specified x and y point. Required first path element.
ArcTo	Forms an arc from the current coordinates to the specified x and y coordinates using `radius`. Boolean property `sweepFlag` specifies clockwise (if `true`) or counter clockwise (if `false`) sweep direction.
HLineTo	Creates a horizontal line from the current point to x.
VLineTo	Creates a vertical line from the current point to y.
LineTo	Creates a line by drawing a line from the current coordinate to the new coordinates.
QuadCurveTo	Creates curved path element, defined by two new points, by drawing a Quadratic Bézier curve that intersects both the current coordinates and the specified coordinates (x, y), using the specified point (`controlX`, `controlY`) as a Bézier control point.
CubicCurveTo	Create curved path element, defined by three new points, by drawing a Cubic Bézier curve that intersects both the current coordinates and the specified coordinates (x, y), using the specified points (`controlX1`, `controlY1`) and (`controlX2`, `controlY2`) as Bézier control points.
ClosePath	Closes current path by drawing a line from the current point to the starting point.

Figure 4.20 shows a Path that forms an elliptical shape and Listing 4.6 is the code that renders it. We first create a sequence of path elements (`pathElements`) and then use them to build a Path. The MoveTo element starts the path at point A, drawing an arc in the counter clockwise direction (`sweepFlag` is `false`) to point B. A second arc starts at point B and finishes back at point A.

B

A

Figure 4.20 Path example using MoveTo and ArcTo

Listing 4.6 Path and PathElements

```
def centerX = 100;
def centerY = 100;
def radiusX = 25;
def radiusY = 50;

// this provides the path elements for the Path
def pathElements = [
    MoveTo {
        x: centerX
        y: centerY + radiusY
    }
    ArcTo {
        x: centerX
        y: centerY - radiusY
        radiusX: radiusX
        radiusY: radiusY
    }
    ArcTo {
        x: centerX
        y: centerY + radiusY
        radiusX: radiusX
        radiusY: radiusY
    }
];

def path = Path {
    stroke: Color.DARKGRAY
    strokeWidth: 2
    elements: pathElements
}
```

JavaFX Tip

With Path you can define a PathTransition, an animation of a node along a sequence of path elements. See "Path Animation" on page 233.

Book Examples

- "Main PathElements", Listing 7.24 on page 242, (Chapter 7). Creates an animation path with CubicCurveTo, LineTo, and MoveTo elements.

- "PathElements that define the PathTransition", Listing 8.17 on page 280, (Chapter 8). Creates a photo carousel path with MoveTo and ArcTo elements.

4.4 Layout Components

Layout components specialize Container and Group (see Figure 4.2 on page 97). They manage their content, which can be a combination of one or more Shapes, Groups, or other layout nodes that make it convenient to arrange nodes in a scene. Table 4.9 describes the layout components available in JavaFX.

TABLE 4.9 Layout Components

Component	Description
HBox	Provides a horizontal layout of its contents in a single row. Control space between subnodes with property spacing. Property hPos is the horizontal position of the row of nodes within this container's width. Property vPos is the vertical position of each node within the space allocated to it in the row.
VBox	Provides a vertical layout of its contents in a single column. Control space between subnodes with property spacing. Property hPos is the horizontal position of each node within the space allocated to it in the column. Property vPos is the vertical position of the column of nodes within this container's height.
Flow	Provides a layout of its contents in either a horizontal or vertical flow (vertical flow if property vertical is true), wrapping at its current width or height boundaries (properties width, height). Use hGap, vGap for spacing. Properties hPos, vPos depend on vertical or horizontal flow. Each cell is sized to fit its content node.
Tile	Provides a layout of its contents in either a horizontal or vertical flow (vertical flow if property vertical is true), wrapping at its current width or height boundaries (properties width, height). Use hGap, vGap for spacing and hPos, vPos to position contents within each cell. All cells are uniform size. Properties tileHeight and tileWidth control cell size.
Stack	Arranges its content nodes in a back-to-front stack. Useful for tab-style nodes or stacks of nodes, such as ImageView components.

HBox and VBox Layout Components

HBox and VBox are layout components that manage a sequence of nodes in property content. HBox provides a horizontal layout of its contents, one after the other, equally spaced and in a single line. (Content that extends beyond the boundaries of the scene is clipped.) Similarly, VBox provides a vertical layout of its contents. You can nest HBox and VBox components as needed, and you can control the amount of space between subnodes with property spacing. Use properties vPos and hPos to control subnode positioning and row/column position.

Figure 4.21 shows a VBox layout component that contains two HBox nodes (each with three rectangles) and a line between them. The rectangles in each HBox have different spacing. The VBox component is positioned with layoutX and layoutY properties.

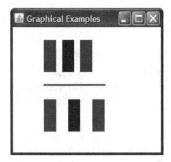

Figure 4.21 Using HBox and VBox layout components

Listing 4.7 shows the code that renders the scene graph from Figure 4.21.

Listing 4.7 HBox, VBox Layout Example

```
def colors = [ Color.RED, Color.BLUE, Color.GREEN ];

def rectangles = for (i in [0..5])
    Rectangle {
        width: 20
        height: 50
        fill: colors[i mod 3]
    }

. . .

VBox {
    layoutX: 50
    layoutY: 20
```

```
    spacing: 20
    content: [
      HBox {
        spacing: 10
        content: [ rectangles[0], rectangles[1], rectangles[2] ]
      }
      Line {
        startX: 0
        startY: 0
        endX: 100
        endY: 0
        stroke: Color.BLACK
        strokeWidth: 2
      }
      HBox {
        spacing: 20
        content: [ rectangles[3], rectangles[4], rectangles[5] ]
      }
    ]
}
    . . .
```

Book Examples

- "Piano—Step 3: Add the keyboard—Part 2", Listing 6.9 on page 183, (Chapter 6). Uses VBox to layout components.

- "Piano—Step 4: Add Swing buttons and note buffer—Part 3", Listing 6.12 on page 187, (Chapter 6). Uses HBox to layout components.

- "Chutes and Ladders Scene Graph", Listing 7.27 on page 246, (Chapter 7). Uses VBox and nested HBox to layout components.

Flow and Tile Layout Components

The Flow layout component provides a layout of its content in either a horizontal (default) or vertical flow (property vertical is true). Flow layout wraps content at its boundaries (specified by properties width and height). Properties hGap and vGap define spacing, depending on whether the flow is horizontal or vertical. For example, property hGap defines the amount of horizontal space between each node in a horizontal flow or the space between columns in a vertical flow. Likewise, properties hPos and vPos depend on vertical or horizontal flow. For horizontal flow, property hPos defines the horizontal position of each flow within the Flow container's width. For vertical flow, property hPos defines the horizontal position of nodes within each cell. Because each node follows the previous node, Flow layout does not necessarily produce a grid layout (see Figure 4.22).

The Tile layout component provides a layout of its content in uniformly sized spaces or "tiles." Tile layout lets you specify the size of tiles with properties tileWidth and tileHeight and the number of columns and rows (properties columns and rows). Properties hGap and vGap define the amount of horizontal space between tiles in a row and vertical space between tiles in a column, respectively. Properties hPos and vPos position a node when the node doesn't fill its space in a tile. (The default value for vPos is VPos.CENTER and for hPos is HPos.CENTER.)

Figure 4.22 shows Flow layout (View A), Tile layout (View B), and Tile layout where vPos is set to VPos.TOP (View C). Listing 4.8 lists the code for each view.

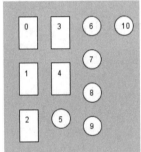

View A: Flow Layout

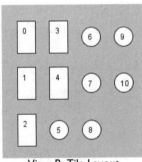

View B: Tile Layout

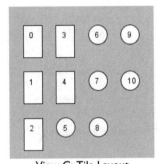

View C: Tile Layout
vPos: VPos.TOP

Figure 4.22 Flow and Tile layout components

Listing 4.8 Flow and Tile Layout Examples

```
// View A: Flow Layout
Flow {
    vertical: true
    width: 200, height: 200
    layoutX: 20, layoutY: 80
    hGap: 20, vGap: 20
    content: [ rectangles, circles ]
}
// View B: Tile Layout
Tile {
    vertical: true
    width: 200, height: 200
    layoutX: 20, layoutY: 80
    hGap: 20, vGap: 20
    content: [ rectangles, circles ]
}
// View C: Tile Layout with vPos
Tile {
```

```
        vPos: VPos.TOP
        vertical: true
        width: 200, height: 200
        layoutX: 20, layoutY: 80
        hGap: 20, vGap: 20
        content: [ rectangles, circles ]
    }
```

Book Example

- "Piano—Step 4: Add Swing buttons and note buffer—Part 3", Listing 6.12 on page 187, (Chapter 6). Uses Flow to layout components.

Stack Layout Component

The Stack layout component arranges its content nodes in a back-to-front stack. That is, each node is "stacked" on top of previously added nodes. Stack layouts are useful for tab-style nodes or stacks of nodes, such as ImageView panels (perhaps a slide show). Figure 4.23 shows an example with a tab-style panel selection mechanism. Selecting the tab brings that panel to the top of the stack.

Figure 4.23 Stack layout component

Listing 4.9 shows the code that renders the layout in Figure 4.23. The tab has an onMouseClicked event handler to move its node to the front with function group.toFront.

Listing 4.9 Stack Layout Example

```
// Build three panels consisting of a tab, tab body, text label, and Text
def panels = for (i in [0..2]) {
    var tab: Rectangle;
    var tabBody: Rectangle;
    var tabLabel: Text;
    var group: Group;
    group = Group {
        effect: DropShadow { }
        content: [
            tab = Rectangle {
                . . .
                cursor: Cursor.HAND
                stroke: Color.BLACK
                onMouseClicked: function(e: MouseEvent): Void {
                    group.toFront();
                }
                arcWidth: 15
                arcHeight: 15
            }
            tabBody = Rectangle { . . . }
            tabLabel = Text { . . . }
            Text { . . . }
        ]
    }
}

// put panels in a Stack layout component
Stack {
    // reverse order so that panels[0] is on top
    content: [ panels[2], panels[1], panels[0]  ]
}
```

4.5 Geometry

A scene is a two-dimensional coordinate space with nodes. JavaFX provides several convenience classes to help you manage this geometry. You also have "bounding" rectangles to manage the relative size and placement of nodes.

Point2D

Class Point2D is a convenience class that encapsulates the x and y coordinates for points. You initialize a point with public-init properties x and y (both Numbers). The Point2D member function distance calculates the distance between two points. Here are some examples.

```
var origin = Point2D { x: 0, y: 0 }
```

```
var newPoint = Point2D { x: 3, y: 4 }
println("distance from origin = {newPoint.distance(origin)}"); // 5.0
println("distance from origin = {newPoint.distance(0,0)}");    // 5.0
```

Bounds/Rectangle2D

Class Bounds (Rectangle2D prior to JavaFX 1.2) is a convenience class that encapsulates geometry properties for bounding rectangles.[3] Bounds lets you query the position or bounds of objects in your scene graph. It's particularly useful when centering or positioning objects based on the dimensions or positions of other objects.

Table 4.10 lists the Bounds properties. Each graphical object has multiple bounding rectangles that define its size and position.

TABLE 4.10 Bounds/Rectangle2D Properties

Property	Type	Description
height	Number	Height of bounding rectangle
width	Number	Width of bounding rectangle
minX	Number	Left x value of bounding rectangle
minY	Number	Top y value of bounding rectangle
maxX	Number	Right x value of bounding rectangle
maxY	Number	Bottom y value of bounding rectangle

Bounding Rectangles

When you add an object (Node) to a scene graph, JavaFX provides four bounding rectangles that describe the node's position and size. Two (boundsInLocal and layoutBounds) are relative to the local coordinate system (the current container). Bounding rectangle boundsInParent is relative to the coordinate system of the parent node. Bounding rectangle boundsInScene is relative to the coordinate system of the scene. Table 4.11 lists the properties for these node bounding rectangles, which are all Bounds objects.

Typically, you'll want to use bounding rectangles for position and size information instead of a node's own dimensions or position properties. Which bounding rectangle you use depends on the bounding rectangle's node and your application. Neither boundsInLocal or layoutBounds responds to the effects of layoutX, layoutY, translateX, translateY, rotate, scaleX and scaleY.

---

3. Beginning with JavaFX 1.2, class Bounds is used to describe the bounds of a node or other scene graph object. (Rectangle2D is still used to define the viewport of ImageView and MediaView.)

TABLE 4.11 Node Bounding Rectangles

Property	Type	Description
boundsInLocal	Bounds (Rectangle2D prior to JavaFX 1.2)	Rectangular bounds of Node in local coordinate space, including space for stroke, effect, clip. Not included is rotate, transforms, layout, translate, scale properties.
layoutBounds	Bounds (Rectangle2D prior to JavaFX 1.2)	Rectangular bounds of Node. Includes transforms, but not rotate, translate, layout, scale properties.
boundsInParent	Bounds (Rectangle2D prior to JavaFX 1.2)	Rectangular bounds of Node in parent coordinate system; includes effects of transforms, layout, translate, scale, and rotate.
boundsInScene	Bounds (Rectangle2D prior to JavaFX 1.2)	Rectangular bounds of Node in scene coordinate system; includes effects of transforms, layout, translate, scale, and rotate.

Bounding rectangle boundsInParent is relative to the parent node and responds to all transformations on the node, including those set in transforms, layoutX, layoutY, translateX, translateY, scaleX, scaleY, and rotate properties.

Bounding rectangle boundsInScene provides the same dimensions as boundsInParent. However, the bounding rectangle is defined in terms of the scene's coordinate system. This means coordinate values will change if the parent node has been adjusted with properties such as layoutX and layoutY.

Layout Tip

When doing layout, you almost always want to use layoutBounds *instead of* boundsInScene *and* boundsInParent *(*layoutBounds *is more efficient). Also, it is an error to bind properties such as* centerX *and* centerY *(for Circles) or* x *and* y *(for Rectangle or Text) to an expression that depends upon its own layoutBounds for the purpose of positioning the node.*

Positioning with Bounding Rectangles

Suppose you want to position a VBox layout component over a background Rectangle node. Figure 4.24 shows a vertical box (VBox) layout component containing three Text components ("Small," "Medium," and "Large"). The VBox is positioned (using layoutX and layoutY) so that it is on top of the background rectangle.

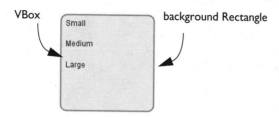

Figure 4.24 Using bounding rectangles to position two nodes

Listing 4.10 shows the code that renders the scene in Figure 4.24.

To align the VBox directly over the Rectangle, set the VBox properties layoutX and layoutY with the background rectangle's layoutBounds.minX and layoutBounds.minY, respectively. Read-only variable margin maintains spacing so that the three subnode Text components aren't directly at the top and left edges.

You must set Text property textOrigin to TextOrigin.TOP. Otherwise, the default placement of Text aligns the Text *baseline* with the top of VBox. With TextOrigin.TOP, the *top* of the Text aligns with the top of the VBox.

Note that you position the background Rectangle with properties x and y. The VBox component is positioned using layoutX and layoutY.

Listing 4.10 Using Bounding Rectangles for Layout

```
def controlWidth = 150;
def controlHeight = 150;
def offsetX = 20;
def offsetY = 20;

def background = Rectangle {
    width: controlWidth
    height: controlHeight
    x: offsetX y: offsetY
    arcWidth: 20 arcHeight: 20
    stroke: Color.SLATEBLUE
    strokeWidth: 2
    fill: Color.ANTIQUEWHITE
}

def margin = 10;
def vbox = VBox {
    spacing: 20
        // Use layoutX and layoutY (new to JavaFX 1.2) to position nodes
```

```
layoutX: background.layoutBounds.minX + margin
layoutY: background.layoutBounds.minX + margin
content: [
    Text {
        content: "Small"
        textOrigin: TextOrigin.TOP
    }
    Text {
        content: "Medium"
        textOrigin: TextOrigin.TOP
    }
    Text {
        content: "Large"
        textOrigin: TextOrigin.TOP
    }
]
}
```

Book Example

- "CarouselPhoto Scene Graph", Listing 8.15 on page 278, (Chapter 8). Uses bounding rectangles to position images and image titles.

5 User Interface Components

Graphical objects include user interface components, described in this chapter. JavaFX currently offers two flavors: Java Swing-based components that are wrapped for seamless integration into JavaFX and "native" JavaFX components. Recently, the native JavaFX UI component offerings have increased, and we briefly describe these new components in this chapter. We point you to examples throughout the book that use the described components, where possible.

You can apply CSS styles to graphical objects ("skin" them), which is especially useful for incorporating UI components with a uniform look and feel. You can also build your own "skinnable" UI components. (Skinnable components let you apply a uniform style to components through external CSS style sheets. By using different style sheets, you can change the entire look of your components.)

What You Will Learn

- JavaFX user interface components
- Swing-based user interface components
- Integrating UI controls into applications with binding
- Applying CSS styles to graphical objects
- Creating "skinnable" UI components

5.1 JavaFX UI Controls

JavaFX includes a native TextBox UI component which is discussed below. The JavaFX 1.2 release also includes additional UI components briefly described in Table 5.2.

TextBox

A TextBox obtains textual input from users. You specify the width with property `columns` and an event handler with property `action`. Boolean `editable` specifies whether or not the TextBox is editable by the user (`true` is the default). Property `rawText` reflects the text in the TextBox (updated as the user provides input) and text holds the input when the event handler is invoked. In addition, properties adjustingSelection, dot, and mark let you query user text selection. Figure 5.1 shows an example.

```
var textInput: TextBox;
    . . .
textInput = TextBox {
    columns: 20
    action: function(): Void {
        if (textInput.text != "") {
            processInput(textInput.text);
        }
    }
}
```

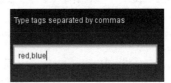

Figure 5.1 TextBox UI Component

Table 5.1 lists the TextBox properties.

TABLE 5.1   TextBox Properties

Property	Type	Description (Default)
action	function():Void	Function that is called when an action is fired on this TextBox (typically with <Enter>).
columns	Number	Horizontal size: approximate number of characters (default 10).
editable	Boolean	If true, text is editable by user (default true).
font	Font	Default font for text.
selectOnFocus	Boolean	If true, focus gain on this TextBox via keyboard or softkey navigation causes a selection of its text contents (default true).
text	String	Text contained in this TextBox, updated when user commits.
rawText	String	Raw text value (as user types).
promptText	String	Displayed when no text has been entered into the Control.
adjustingSelection	Boolean	Used to query state of text selection. Property dot is location of caret, mark is the anchor. If dot != mark then there is text selection.
dot	Integer	
mark	Integer	

Book Examples

- "FlickrTag (Main.fx)", Listing 9.20 on page 310, (Chapter 9). Provide a search tag for Flickr.

- "Scene Graph (FlickrUser)", Listing 9.24 on page 314, (Chapter 9). Provide a screen name for Flickr.

UI Components

Table 5.2 lists the UI components included with the JavaFX 1.2 release. With these components, developers will have a richer selection of built-in UI controls. Unlike the JavaFX Swing components (which only run in the desktop environment), these UI components are portable across all environments (desktop, mobile, and TV). See Figure 1.1, "JavaFX Platform," on page 2 for an overview of the JavaFX platform.

TABLE 5.2 UI Components

UI Component	Description
TextBox	Textual input with action event handler.
Button	Pressable component with action event handler.
Hyperlink	Alternative view of Button. Keeps track of whether it has been "visited" and optionally renders differently if it has.
ToggleButton	Similar to SwingToggleButton. If the component is part of a ToggleGroup, the group ensures that only one ToggleButton is selected at a time. Otherwise, toggles between selected and not selected states.
RadioButton	Extends ToggleButton and provides alternate view (the traditional radio button look).
ToggleGroup	Groups ToggleButtons or RadioButtons so that selection is mutually exclusive among all buttons in the same group.
CheckBox	Tri-state selection control typically skinned as a box with a checkmark or tick mark when checked.
ListView	Scrollable list of selectable items.
ComboBox	List of pre-defined Strings with the option of entering a custom string.
Label	Non-editable text and/or graphic control. Displayed text is modified to fit within a specific space using ellipses or truncation.
ScrollBar	Scrolling control.
Slider	Similar to SwingSlider.

TABLE 5.2 UI Components *(Continued)*

UI Component	Description
ProgressBar	Visual progress status indicator. Property `progress` (if between 0 and 1) indicates percentage complete, if >= 1 indicates done.
ProgressIndicator	Alternate view to ProgressBar. Provides a small, circular progress indicator.

Figure 5.2 shows many of these UI components and Listing 5.1 is the source code for the application shown.

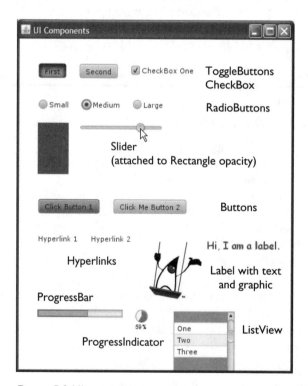

Figure 5.2 UI component menagerie

Listing 5.1 UI Component Menagerie

```
// Two ToggleButtons in a ToggleGroup and One CheckBox
var toggleGroup = ToggleGroup {}
def tg1 = ToggleButton { text: "First", toggleGroup: toggleGroup }
def tg2 = ToggleButton { text: "Second", toggleGroup: toggleGroup }
def tg3 = CheckBox { text: "CheckBox One" }
```

```
// Three RadioButtons in a ToggleGroup
def tb = ToggleGroup {}
def r1 = RadioButton { text: "Small", toggleGroup: tb }
def r2 = RadioButton { text: "Medium", toggleGroup: tb }
def r3 = RadioButton { text: "Large", toggleGroup: tb }

// Slider controls Rectangle's opacity
def slider = Slider {
    min: 0, max: 1
    vertical: false
    showTickMarks: true, showTickLabels: true
    value: 0.5
    majorTickUnit: .25, minorTickCount: 3
}
def rectangle = Rectangle {
    width: 50, height: 80
    opacity: bind slider.value, fill: Color.BLUE
}

// Two Buttons
def b1 = Button {
    text: "Click Button 1"
    strong: true
    action: function() { println("Button 1 clicked"); }
}
def b2 = Button {
    strong: false
    text: "Click Me Button 2"
    action: function() { println("Button 2 clicked"); }
}

// Two Hyperlinks and a Label
def h1 = Hyperlink { text: "Hyperlink 1" }
def h2: Hyperlink = Hyperlink { text: "Hyperlink 2" }
def l1 = Label { text: "Hi, I am a label." font: Font { ... }
    graphic: ImageView { image: Image { url: "{__DIR__}duke.gif" } }
    textFill: Color.CRIMSON
}

// ProgressBar and ProgressIndicator reporting on same variable n
var n: Number = 0;
var pb = ProgressBar {
    progress: bind ProgressBar.computeProgress(1000, n)
}
var pi = ProgressIndicator {
    progress: bind ProgressIndicator.computeProgress(1000, n)
}
def lv = ListView { items: ["One", "Two", "Three"] }
```

Popup Windows

JavaFX includes two external "windows" you can invoke from applications: Alert and Popup. Both components are not part of your main application's scene graph but have their own stage.

Alert provides a high-level, configurable popup dialog. There are three types: confirm, inform, and question, instantiated by invoking either Alert function `confirm`, `inform`, or `question`. The title is the optional first argument. Figure 5.3 shows a question alert with Yes/No buttons.

```
// action property in Button
action: function() {
    if (Alert.question (
            "Important Question???",
            "Do you want to continue?"))
        statusString = "We will continue!"
    else
        statusString = "We will stop!";
    }
}
```

Figure 5.3 Alert window (question)

Popup provides a general-purpose component that pops up on the user's screen. You can build a Popup with any scene graph structure that you'd like. Figure 5.4 shows a Popup rendered with a Rectangle and Text component.

```
def myPopUp = Popup {
    // put Popup contents here
    content: [ . . . ]
}
. . .
// action property in Button
action: function() {
    if (myPopUp.visible) myPopUp.hide()
    // use absolute screen coordinates
    else myPopUp.show(600, 400);
}
```

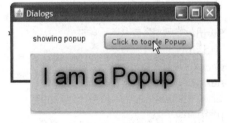

Figure 5.4 Popup window

5.2 Swing Components

JavaFX provides direct access to a subset of the Java Swing components. These Swing components have been wrapped so they are consistent with the JavaFX scene graph model and node behavior. Swing components only run in the desktop environment, which means you can't use them in mobile applications.

SwingButton

SwingButton provides a push button graphical UI component. You can adorn it with text, an icon, or both. Use property action for event handling, as shown in Figure 5.5.

```
SwingButton {
    text: "Group Rotate"
    action: function(): Void {
        shapeArea.rotate += 45;
    }
}
```

Figure 5.5 SwingButton example

Book Examples

- "Piano—Step 4: Add Swing buttons and note buffer—Part 3", Listing 6.12 on page 187, (Chapter 6). Uses SwingButton components to control a piano keyboard.

- "Photo4: Photo Study Scene Graph", Listing 8.7 on page 261, (Chapter 8). Uses SwingButton components to select effects to apply to a photo.

SwingCheckBox

SwingCheckBox is a "checkbox" component that lets users toggle between checked and unchecked to represent boolean values. Property selected is true when the box is checked. You can enforce the behavior of checking only one SwingCheckBox component in a group by assigning the same value for property toggleGroup to all Swing-CheckBox components in the group. (Figure 5.11 on page 140 shows how to use property toggleGroup and enforce mutual exclusion behavior.)

Figure 5.6 illustrates a SwingCheckBox component with an action event handler. A node (p) moves to the front of its container if the checkbox is selected. Otherwise, it moves to the back.

```
def frontCheck: SwingCheckBox = SwingCheckBox {
    text: "Polygon In Front"
    selected: true
    action: function(): Void {
        if (frontCheck.selected) { p.toFront(); }
        else { p.toBack(); }
    }
}
```

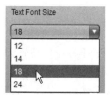

Figure 5.6 SwingCheckBox example

SwingComboBox

SwingComboBox provides a selection mechanism from a drop-down list. When you make the combo box editable, users can type values into an editable field. You populate the SwingComboBox with a sequence of SwingComboBoxItem components in property `items`. Figure 5.7 shows a SwingComboBox populated with four SwingComboBoxItem selection options.

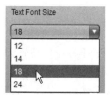

Figure 5.7 SwingComboBox and SwingComboBoxItems

SwingComboBoxItem

The items in a SwingComboBox are of type SwingComboBoxItem. Property `text` provides a text-based name for the item. You can construct an arbitrary object with property `value`. For example, Listing 5.2 builds a different sized Font object for each SwingComboBoxItem providing a convenient way to update an object's `font` property with binding. The Text object's `font` property bind expression is shown in bold.

Listing 5.2 SwingComboBox and SwingComboBoxItem

```
def fontbox = SwingComboBox {
    width: 100
    items: [
        SwingComboBoxItem {
            text: "12"
            value: Font { size: 12 }
            selected: true
        }
        SwingComboBoxItem {
            text: "14"
            value: Font { size: 14 }
        }
        SwingComboBoxItem {
            text: "18"
            value: Font { size: 18 }
        } ]
}
. . .
Text {
    x: 35, y: 30
    font: bind fontbox.selectedItem.value as Font
    content: "The quick brown fox jumps over the lazy yellow dog."
}
```

SwingIcon

SwingIcon is an image for decorating components. Use JavaFX Image to set the icon's image. Figure 5.8 shows how to create a button that includes both an icon and text.

```
SwingButton {
    text: "Duke says 'Hi!'"
    icon: SwingIcon {
        image: Image { url: "{__DIR__}duke.gif" } }
    action: function(): Void {
        // action code here
    }
}
```

Figure 5.8 SwingButton with SwingIcon Example

SwingLabel

SwingLabel components display a string, icon, or both. Use property icon (see Figure 5.8) to supply images. Figure 5.9 shows a text-only SwingLabel component associated with SwingSlider component fillOpacity (see "SwingSlider" on page 141).

Property labelFor lets you optionally associate a label with a swing component. (Property labelFor is null if this label is not associated with a component.)

```
SwingLabel {
    width: controlWidth - 20
    text: " Polygon Opacity"
    labelFor: fillOpacity
}
fillOpacity
```

Figure 5.9 SwingLabel Example

SwingScrollPane

SwingScrollPane is a container that allows its contents to be scrolled. Set property view to its scrollable contents. Figure 5.10 shows a SwingScrollPane component (with a SwingList) and Listing 5.3 shows the corresponding code that renders it.

SwingList

SwingList displays a list of SwingListItem objects and allows users to select one or more items. Property items holds a sequence of SwingListItem objects. Property selectedIndex returns the index of the selected item, and property selectedItem returns the selected item. When multiple items are selected, selectedIndex is the smallest selected index and returns -1 if there is no selection.

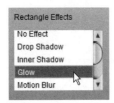

Figure 5.10 SwingScrollPane, SwingList, and SwingListItems

SwingListItem

SwingListItem represents a selectable item in a SwingList component. Property selected is true when this item has been selected. Property text contains the display text and property value is an object associated with this list item.

Listing 5.3 shows an example with a SwingListItem. Here, property value is an Effect object (DropShadow, InnerShadow, Glow, MotionBlur) that updates a Rectangle using binding. The Rectangle's effect property binding expression is in bold.

Listing 5.3 SwingScrollPane, SwingList, and SwingListItems

```
var effectList: SwingList;
SwingScrollPane {
    height: 100
    width: 150
    scrollable: true
    view: effectList = SwingList { items: [
            SwingListItem {
                text: "No Effect"
                selected: true
                value: null
            },
            SwingListItem {
                text: "Drop Shadow"
                value: DropShadow {
                }
            }
            SwingListItem {
                text: "Inner Shadow"
                value: InnerShadow {
                    offsetX: 4
                    offsetY: 4
                }
            }
            SwingListItem {
                text: "Glow"
                value: Glow {
                    level: 1
                }
            },
            SwingListItem {
                text: "Motion Blur"
                value: MotionBlur {
                    angle: 45
                    radius: 10
                }
            }
            . . .
        ]
    }
}
. . .
// Rectangle that receives effect from SwingList component selection
Rectangle {
    x: 30
    y: 10
```

```
        height: 100
        width: 80
        fill: defaultColor
        stroke: Color.BLACK
        effect: bind effectList.selectedItem.value as Effect
}
```

SwingRadioButton

SwingRadioButton renders a selectable radio button. If you have multiple SwingRadioButton components that share the same SwingToggleGroup (as set in property toggleGroup), the SwingToggleGroup enforces mutual exclusion selection. Figure 5.11 shows a radio button group that exhibits this behavior.

```
SwingRadioButton {
            toggleGroup: pizzaSizeGroup
            text: "Small"
            action: function(): Void {
                // action . . .
            }
        }
SwingRadioButton {
            toggleGroup: pizzaSizeGroup
            text: "Medium"
            action: function(): Void {
                // action . . .
            }
        }
SwingRadioButton {
            toggleGroup: pizzaSizeGroup
            selected: true
            text: "Large"
            action: function(): Void {
                // action . . .
            }
        }
```

Figure 5.11 SwingRadioButton example with mutual exclusion

SwingToggleButton

SwingToggleButton provides the same behavior as SwingRadioButton except that it looks like a regular button. A SwingToggleButton can be toggled between a pressed and released state to represent a boolean value to the user. If you assign multiple

SwingToggleButton components to the same SwingToggleGroup, the group enforces mutual exclusion selection.

SwingToggleGroup

SwingToggleGroup is a class used to enforce mutual exclusion selection for a set of buttons (either SwingToggleButton, SwingCheckBox, or SwingRadioButton). When buttons are in the same SwingToggleGroup, selecting one button deselects all the other buttons with the same `toggleGroup` setting.

SwingSlider

SwingSlider lets users graphically select a value by sliding a knob within a bounded interval. You provide properties `maximum` and `minimum` for the upper and lower bounds of the slider. Property `value` is the slider's current value, which is within the maximum and minimum range (inclusive). If property `vertical` is true, the slider is rendered vertically.

Figure 5.12 shows an example of SwingSlider that lets users set a node's opacity. The slider's value is in the range 0 to 100, but the binding expression divides by 100.0 to get the desired opacity range (0 to 1). Note that properties `minimum`, `maximum`, and `value` are all Integers.

```
def fillOpacity = SwingSlider {
    minimum: 0
    maximum: 100
    width: controlWidth - 20
    height: 20
    value: 50
}
. . .

var opacity = bind (fillOpacity.value / 100.0);
```

Figure 5.12 SwingSlider example with binding opacity

SwingTextField

SwingTextField allows the display and editing of a single line of text. If property `editable` is true, users can edit the text. Figure 5.13 shows an editable SwingTextField. Here, a Text component's `content` property is bound to the SwingTextField's `text` property. As the user types in text, the Text component reflects the new input.

```
def tf = SwingTextField {
    columns: 10
    editable: true
    text: "Now is the time"
}
. . .

Text {
    x: 35
    y: 30
    content: bind tf.text
    fill: Color.BLACK
}
```

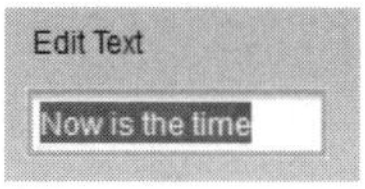

Edit Text

Now is the time

Figure 5.13 SwingTextField Example

5.3 Swing Example

Figure 5.14 shows two views from an application called Order Your Pizza. Unfortunately, this application doesn't really order pizza for you, but it does illustrate several Swing components. The application uses radio buttons with mutual exclusion selection and checkboxes that allow multiple selections. You'll also see how JavaFX bindings simplify the integration of UI components into your applications.

The example shows how easy it is to build *graphical* applications above and beyond one that simply uses radio buttons, checkboxes, and text components. Here, for example, you see visual pizzas and pizza toppings. As users select different sized pizzas, the pizza graphic changes size too. Furthermore, if the pizza includes one or more toppings, these toppings remain within the boundaries of the pizza.

Let's begin with the graphical objects first: pizza and pizza toppings.

Pizzas Are Circles

Listing 5.4 shows the code that builds the pizza. Our pizza comes in three sizes (small, medium, and large with radius 40, 55, and 70, respectively). Pizzas have a crust (strokeWidth is 8) and a drop shadow. Property radius is bound to the sequence pizzaSize via the variable pizzaSizeIndex.

Listing 5.4 also defines clipToppings, a circle that matches the three pizza sizes. The topping group (pepperoni, sausage, onions) uses this circle for its clip property so

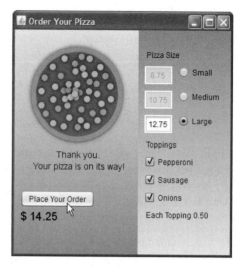

Figure 5.14 Order Your Pizza

that its size is adjusted appropriately when the user chooses a different sized pizza. Note that the node used for property clip is not inserted into the scene graph; it simply provides a geometric reference for clipping behavior.

Listing 5.4 Pizza and Clip Circles

```
def pizzaCenterX = 80;
def pizzaCenterY = 100;
def pizzaSize = [40, 55, 70];
var pizzaSizeIndex = 2;          // start with a "Large"
def pizzaArea = Group { layoutX: 20 }

// This is the Pizza
insert Circle {
    centerX: pizzaCenterX
    centerY: pizzaCenterY
    radius: bind pizzaSize[pizzaSizeIndex]
    fill: Color.web("#D72D02")
    stroke: Color.web("#CB7621")
    strokeWidth: 8
    effect: DropShadow { }
} into pizzaArea.content;
// This circle is used to provide clipping reference for the toppings
def clipToppings = Circle {
    centerX: pizzaCenterX
    centerY: pizzaCenterY
    radius: bind pizzaSize[pizzaSizeIndex];
}
```

Toppings Are Circles

Listing 5.5 displays the graphical objects that render pizza toppings. The toppings are in a group, with a `clip` property bound to the currently selected pizza size. The toppings themselves are small circles built at the coordinate values in sequence `toppingLocations`. Each pair of numbers initializes the `centerX` and `centerY` properties of a circle. The `for` loop builds the toppings and inserts them into the `topping` Group.

```
for (i in [0.. <sizeof toppingLocations step 6]) { . . . }
```

Each pizza topping has its own color and all have their `visible` property bound to the SwingCheckBox component that selects the topping.

Listing 5.5 Toppings

```
// x and y coordinate values for toppings
def toppingLocations = [
    88, 42, 101, 45, 118, 58, 126, 72, 134, 88, 135, 108,
    123, 128, 114, 141, 97, 150, 82, 152, 59, 151, 42, 146,
    30, 131, 23, 118, 23, 96, 28, 75, 41, 58, 60, 45
    77, 53, 90, 60, 109, 69, 112, 84, 113, 100, 120, 115,
    106, 130, 87, 141, 68, 137, 50, 123, 42, 109, 45, 89,
    54, 72, 78, 65, 93, 70, 101, 81, 100, 96, 97, 108,
    88, 124, 65, 118, 61, 108, 59, 95, 67, 85, 81, 85
    85, 98, 79, 105, 70, 105, 67, 94, 78, 94, 77, 100
];

// Group to hold the toppings, clipped to the current pizza size
def toppings = Group { clip: bind clipToppings }

// Build (small) circles for each kind of topping
for( i in [0.. <sizeof toppingLocations step 6]) {
    insert Circle {
        effect: DropShadow {}
        centerX: toppingLocations[i]
        centerY: toppingLocations[i + 1]
        radius: 5
        fill: Color.web("#D47F54");
        visible: bind checkPepperoni.selected
    } into toppings.content;
    insert Circle {
        effect: DropShadow {}
        centerX: toppingLocations[i + 2]
        centerY: toppingLocations[i + 3]
        radius: 5
        fill: Color.web("#FFAA00");
        visible: bind checkSausage.selected
    } into toppings.content;
    insert Circle {
        effect: DropShadow {}
        centerX: toppingLocations[i + 4]
```

```
        centerY: toppingLocations[i + 5]
        radius: 5
        fill: Color.BURLYWOOD;
        visible: bind checkOnions.selected
    } into toppings.content;
}
insert toppings into pizzaArea.content;
```

Selecting Pizza Size with SwingRadioButton

Listing 5.6 builds the components for pizza size selection. The selection mechanism is a SwingRadioButton that sets its toggleGroup property to pizzaSizeGroup. This enforces the desired mutual exclusion selection behavior (you can only select one size at a time). The SwingRadioButton and an associated SwingTextField are grouped into an HBox layout component so they appear side by side. Note that the SwingTextField component is only enabled when its associated SwingRadioButton is selected. The SwingTextField component displays the cost of its associated sized pizza.

The action event handler sets variable pizzaSizeIndex to the selected pizza size (0 for small, 1 for medium, and 2 for large). This change renders the correct pizza size and causes the bound clip properties in the toppings groups to update their size.

Listing 5.6 Selecting Pizza Size

```
def pizzaCost = [8.75, 10.75, 12.75];
def pizzaSizeGroup = SwingToggleGroup { }
def smPizza = HBox {
    spacing: 10
    content: [
        SwingTextField {
            columns: 3
            editable: false
            disable: bind not sbSmall.selected
            text: " {pizzaCost[0]}"
        }
        sbSmall = SwingRadioButton {
            toggleGroup: pizzaSizeGroup
            text: "Small"
            action: function() {
                pizzaSizeIndex = 0;
            }
        }
    ]
}
def medPizza = HBox {
    spacing: 10
    content: [
        SwingTextField {
```

```
                columns: 3
                editable: false
                disable: bind not sbMedium.selected
                text: "{pizzaCost[1]}"
            }
            sbMedium = SwingRadioButton {
                toggleGroup: pizzaSizeGroup
                text: "Medium"
                action: function() {
                    pizzaSizeIndex = 1;
                }
            }
        ]
    }
}
def lgPizza = HBox {
    spacing: 10
    content: [
        SwingTextField {
            columns: 3
            editable: false
            disable: bind not sbLarge.selected
            text: "{pizzaCost[2]}"
        }
        sbLarge = SwingRadioButton {
            toggleGroup: pizzaSizeGroup
            selected: true
            text: "Large"
            action: function() {
                pizzaSizeIndex = 2;
            }
        }
    ]
}
```

Selecting Toppings with SwingCheckBox

Listing 5.7 builds the object literals for the pizza topping checkboxes. Each checkbox
sets property text to the topping name and property selected to false. The visible
properties of all of the associated graphical "toppings" are bound to the appropriate
checkbox selected property (see Listing 5.5 on page 144). When the user selects a topping, the graphical representation of that topping appears on top of the pizza through
the binding. When the topping is deselected, the graphical representation disappears.

Listing 5.7 Selecting Toppings

```
def checkPepperoni = SwingCheckBox {
    text: "Pepperoni"
    selected: false
}
```

```
def checkSausage = SwingCheckBox {
    text: "Sausage"
    selected: false
}
def checkOnions = SwingCheckBox {
    text: "Onions"
    selected: false
}
```

Integrating with Bound Functions and Binding

Listing 5.8 shows the code that keeps the total price of the pizza order current with updates from the user's selections (pizza size and number of toppings). As the user changes selections, the total changes and the new amount is displayed. This happens with the aid of *bound* function getTotal.

A bound function is called whenever any variable in the function body changes. Function getTotal, then, is executed whenever property selected changes for components checkPepperoni, checkSausage, or checkOnions. In addition, getTotal is executed whenever pizzaSizeIndex changes. Each of these variables affects the total price.

Note that with bound functions, you cannot assign to local variables (here, add1, add2, add3, and total). Function getTotal returns a String, making it easy to update Text component finalOrder, which binds its content property to function getTotal's String return value.

Listing 5.8 Update Order Total

```
bound function getTotal(): String {
    def add1 = if (checkPepperoni.selected) .5 else 0;
    def add2 = if (checkSausage.selected) .5 else 0;
    def add3 = if (checkOnions.selected) .5 else 0;
    def total = pizzaCost[pizzaSizeIndex] + add1 + add2 + add3;
    return "$ {total}";
}

def finalOrder = Text {
    content: bind getTotal()
    font: Font {
        size: 18
    }
}
```

Listing 5.9 includes the order button (a SwingButton) with property text set to "Place Your Order" and property action makes Text component t visible. This displays the thank you message shown in the second view of Figure 5.14 on page 143.

Listing 5.9 Finish Ordering with SwingButton

```
def orderButton = SwingButton {
    text: "Place Your Order"
    action: function(): Void {
        t.visible = true;
    }
}

def t = Text {
    underline: true
    x: 10
    y: 200
    visible: false;
    font: Font { size: 14 }
    content: "Thank you. \nYour pizza is on its way!"
    textAlignment: TextAlignment.CENTER
    fill: Color.BLACK
}
```

5.4 Creating Skinnable Components

This section describes how to build custom UI components with "skins" (external style sheets to control their look). You can skip this section with no loss of continuity with material in the rest of the book. However, you may still want to customize components with CSS, which we discuss here.

JavaFX lets you create "skinnable" components—components that use CSS-type sheets for styling. Before we show you how to create skinnable components, let's discuss how to style JavaFX objects with CSS.

Cascading Style Sheets (CSS)

Cascading Style Sheets (CSS) help define the look of your objects. You can specify most properties with style elements and gather common styles into external style sheets. This helps separate an object's look from its behavior. With CSS, you can build style sheets that target a company-wide look, target an application, or target an individual object.

JavaFX has a built-in CSS parser that works with properties and styles. Most property names and style labels are obvious, but the syntax rules are different from JavaFX object literal declarations. Several types of errors are possible.

- If you leave off a terminating ; or commit a similar syntax error, you'll see a ParseException.

- If you name a property value that is not supported (for example, an unsupported color name), you'll see a StylesheetException.

- If you name an element that is not supported, the parser will let you know, but the application will still run.

Style Tip

*While JavaFX is very forgiving with terminating punctuation, CSS requires **;** to separate style elements. Fortunately, the JavaFX parser gives informative error messages when you break the rules. The behavior of your application after a ParseException or StylesheetException depends on any exception handling in place.*

CSS encourages cascading styles; that is, you write a general style for a "look" and then refine it for certain situations or specific types of objects. All styles that are defined will apply, with the "specialized styles" replacing the "general" styles only for the those specialized properties.

CSS style rules can appear in both external style sheets or embedded in object literals. Styles can apply to any node using properties `style` (specify CSS styles directly), `styleClass` (reference a style class in an external style sheet) and `id` (reference a node-specific style in an external style sheet). You specify external style sheets with a scene's `stylesheets` property (either a sequence of URLs or a single URL).

Let's use the JavaFX Rectangle class to show you the various ways to specify styles. Figure 5.15 shows four similar Rectangle objects with slight variations in style. First, all rectangles are the same size (properties `height` and `width` are both 80). Property `fill` is `Color.WHITESMOKE` for Rectangle A, `Color.YELLOW` for Rectangles B and C, and `Color.DARKRED` for Rectangle D. Properties `stroke` and `strokeWidth` also vary.

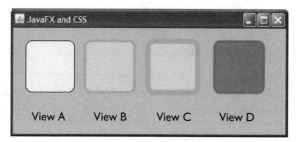

Figure 5.15 Using CSS with JavaFX objects

Listing 5.10 shows the external style sheet (**RectangleStyles.css**) used for the application in Figure 5.15. It includes three styles that apply to node type javafx.scene.shape.Rectangle (you must fully specify the class path). The first style applies to *all* Rectangle nodes, the second style apples to Rectangle nodes with property styleClass set to "basic," and the third style applies to Rectangle nodes with property id set to "special."

Listing 5.10 RectangleStyles.css

```
"javafx.scene.shape.Rectangle"
{
    fill: whitesmoke;
    stroke: black;
    height: 80;
    width: 80;
    arcWidth: 20;
    arcHeight: 20;
}

"javafx.scene.shape.Rectangle".basic
{
    fill: yellow;
    stroke: coral;
    strokeWidth: 4;
    opacity: 0.8;
}

"javafx.scene.shape.Rectangle"#special
{
    strokeWidth: 8;
}
```

Listing 5.11 shows the JavaFX program that creates the four Rectangles shown in Figure 5.15. Property stylesheets references the external style sheet (**Rectangle-**

Styles.css) in the local execution environment. Rectangle View A uses the default object literal, taking any initialized property values from the external style sheet (properties `fill`, `stroke`, `height`, `width`, `arcHeight`, and `arcWidth`).

Rectangles View B, C, and D show how cascading works. Rectangle View B uses the default property values, except those specified in style class "basic" (properties `fill`, `stroke`, `strokeWidth`, and `opacity`), which override any properties specified in the default style. Rectangle View C uses the default style, the "basic" style class, and the "special" id style. You can see that Rectangles B and C are identical, except that C has a wider outline stroke (`strokeWidth` is 8).

Finally, Rectangle D specifies inline styles with property `style`. It uses the default style settings and applies the inline styles on top of the default styles.

Style Tip

In practice, you probably won't use inline styles that often. With object literal notation, you can create Rectangles with the styles you want and get error messages at compile time.

Listing 5.11 Using CSS with Rectangles (Main.fx)

```
Stage {
    title: "JavaFX and CSS"
    width: 450
    height: 200
    scene: Scene {
        fill: Color.LIGHTSTEELBLUE
        stylesheets: "{__DIR__}RectangleStyles.css"
        content: HBox {
            layoutX: 20
            layoutY: 20
            spacing: 15
            content: [
                Rectangle {
                    // default style (View A)
                }
                Rectangle {
                    // default style "basic" style class (View B)
                    styleClass: "basic"
                }
                Rectangle {
                    // default style + "basic" style class + "special" ID
                    // (View C)
                    styleClass: "basic"
                    id: "special"
                }
                Rectangle {
                    // default style + inline style (View D)
```

```
                style: "fill: darkred;"
                    "stroke: blue;"
                    "strokeWidth: 4;"
                    "opacity: 0.5;"
            }
        ]
    }
  }
}
```

Skinnable TextButton Component

We'll now create a skinnable component. We'll start with a straightforward Text-Button. In the next section, we'll incorporate TextButton into a more complicated component, a skinnable ChoiceDialog.

Figure 5.16 shows an example application with three TextButton components skinned differently. The first button uses default settings and the second and third buttons provide external CSS styles to customize their look.

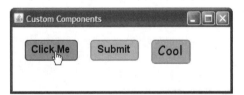

Figure 5.16 Skinnable TextButtons

A TextButton component has several important properties. Property `displayText` is the text to display, `action` is the function to call when the component is selected (clicked), and `disappearOnAction` (default is `true`) handles whether or not you want the button to fade after the function is invoked. Here are the TextButton object literals for the Submit and Cool buttons in Figure 5.16.

```
TextButton {
    disappearOnAction: false;
    displayText: "Submit"
    action: function(): Void {
        println("You pressed submit.");
    }
}

TextButton {
```

```
      displayText: "Cool"
      action: function(): Void {
         println("You pressed Cool.");
      }
   }
}
```

Each "skinnable" component requires two classes:[1] Control, which exposes properties users can define in object literals (or modify with JavaFX statements if the user has write permission), and Skin, the graphical representation of the component. Class Control is similar to CustomNode (indeed, it extends CustomNode) in that you get a specialized Node object that you can add to the scene graph. Control also includes property skin, the part of the component that can be styled. Class Skin includes property node, the parent of the graphical objects you build for your component, and control, the part of the component exposed to the user.

When building your own components, you create a class that extends Control and a class that extends Skin. You connect them through the respective class variables skin and control. Listing 5.12 shows **TextButton.fx** (the control). The create function initializes Control property skin and invokes create in class Control (using super).

Listing 5.12 TextButton.fx

```
public class TextButton extends Control {
    public var displayText: String;
    public var action: function(): Void;
    public var disappearOnAction = true;

    protected override function create(): Node {
        skin = TextButtonSkin { };
        super.create();
    }
}
```

Listing 5.13 shows a partial listing of TextButtonSkin (the skin).

Listing 5.13 TextButtonSkin.fx (partial)

```
public class TextButtonSkin extends Skin {
    def textButtonControl = bind control as TextButton;

        // public variables provide "skinnable" properties for component
        . . .
    init {
```

---

1. Class Skin is required only for skinnable components. A third class, Behavior, is required to implement behavior differences, especially specialized behaviors regarding key events. TextButton implements a specialized Skin class but does not implement a Behavior class.

```
        node = Group {
            content: [ . . . graphical objects that make up component . . .]
    }
}
```

Figure 5.17 illustrates the relationship between a component's Control class and its Skin class.

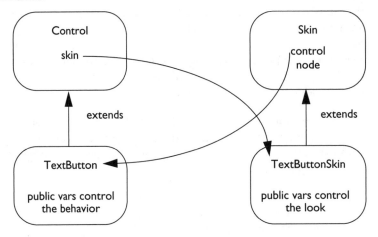

Figure 5.17 Control is the model; Skin is the view

Let's look at the complete TextButtonSkin class now, as shown in Listing 5.14. Through binding, object textButtonControl points to the Control object, TextButton. Next, we specify as public var all "skinnable" properties. Providing reasonable default values helps the user minimize the need to customize a component. Each of these properties (fillColor, outlineColor, etc.) is plugged into some aspect of the component's graphical makeup. For example, property fillColor defines the button's background fill. The various mouse event properties dictate the button's fill color associated with these events.

TextButton properties displayText, action, and disappearOnAction are referenced with object textButtonControl. For example, Text property content binds to text-ButtonControl.displayText to maintain the button's text, as shown here.

```
    def text = Text {
        x: 10
        y: 8
        font: bind buttonFont
        textOrigin: TextOrigin.TOP
        fill: bind textColor
        content: bind textButtonControl.displayText
```

```
    }
```

Note that class TextButtonSkin includes an `init` block (`init` blocks are invoked after a class's instance variables are initialized). The job of `init` is to build the graphical objects that make up the component and assign them to inherited Skin property `node` (using the public variables to style them). The TextButtonSkin scene graph includes a background Rectangle and a Text component to hold the label.

The TextButton action function (`textButtonControl.action`) is invoked in the `onMouse-Released` event handler. After calling `action`, the event handler sets up a fade transition, fading out the node (if `disappearOnAction` is true). Overridden functions `contains` and `intersects` are required for classes that extend Skin.

Listing 5.14 TextButtonSkin.fx

```
public class TextButtonSkin extends Skin {

    def textButtonControl = bind control as TextButton;

    // Skinnable properties with their default values
    public var fillColor: Paint = Color.LIGHTBLUE;
    public var outlineColor: Paint = Color.BLACK;
    public var mouseEnteredColor: Paint = Color.LIGHTSLATEGRAY;
    public var mouseExitedColor: Paint = Color.LIGHTBLUE;
    public var mousePressedColor: Paint = Color.GRAY;
    public var mouseReleasedColor: Paint = Color.GRAY;
    public var textColor: Paint = Color.BLACK;
    public var buttonFont: Font = Font { size: 16, name: "Arial Bold" }
    def button: Rectangle = Rectangle {
        fill: bind fillColor
        stroke: bind outlineColor
        height: bind text.layoutBounds.height + 16;
        width: bind text.layoutBounds.width + 20;
        arcWidth: 10, arcHeight: 10
    }
    def text = Text {
        x: 10, y: 8
        font: bind buttonFont
        textOrigin: TextOrigin.TOP
        fill: bind textColor
        content: bind textButtonControl.displayText
    }
    public override function contains(localX: Number, localY: Number)
            : Boolean {
        node.contains(localX, localY);
    }
    public override function intersects(localX: Number, localY: Number,
            localWidth: Number, localHeight: Number) : Boolean {
        node.intersects(localX, localY, localWidth, localHeight);
    }
```

```
    init {
        node = Group {
        //this Group represents a button that is pressed
            cursor: Cursor.HAND
            onMouseEntered: function (evt: MouseEvent): Void {
                fillColor = mouseEnteredColor;
            }
            onMouseExited: function (evt: MouseEvent): Void {
                fillColor = mouseExitedColor;
            }
            onMousePressed: function(evt: MouseEvent): Void {
                if(evt.button == MouseButton.PRIMARY){
                    fillColor = mousePressedColor;
                }
            }
            onMouseReleased: function(evt: MouseEvent): Void {
                if(evt.button == MouseButton.PRIMARY){
                    fillColor = mouseReleasedColor;
                    textButtonControl.action();        // invoke user action
                    def fade = FadeTransition {
                        node: node
                        duration: 1.5s
                        fromValue: 1
                        toValue: .0
                    }
                    if (textButtonControl.disappearOnAction) fade.play();
                }
            }
            content: [ button text ]
        }
    }
}
```

Listing 5.15 shows the CSS file that styles the TextButton components. It includes two styles (both labeled with an id selector). Note that each of the style elements corresponds to public variables in class TextButtonSkin.

Listing 5.15 ComponentStyle.css

```
"custom.TextButton"#submitID
{
    fillColor: orange;
    mouseEnteredColor: bisque;
    mouseExitedColor: orange;
    mousePressedColor: darkorange;
    mouseReleasedColor: orange;
    outlineColor: brown;
}
"custom.TextButton"#coolButton
```

```
{
    fillColor: coral;
    mouseEnteredColor: lightblue;
    mouseExitedColor: coral;
    mousePressedColor: darkred;
    mouseReleasedColor: crimson;
    outlineColor: brown;
    buttonFont: bold 20pt "comic sans ms";
}
```

Listing 5.16 shows the code for the three TextButton components in Figure 5.16 on page 152. The first component uses default styling, the second component is styled with id selector "submitID," and the third component is styled with id selector "cool-Button."

Listing 5.16 Test Program (Main.fx)

```
Stage {
    title: "Custom Components"
    scene: Scene {
        stylesheets: "{__DIR__}ComponentStyle.css"
        height: 100
        width: 355
        content: HBox {
            layoutX: 20
            layoutY: 20
            spacing: 20
            content: [
                TextButton {
                    // use default styling
                    disappearOnAction: false;            // don't disappear
                    displayText: "Click Me"
                    action: function(): Void {
                        println("You clicked me!");
                    }
                }
                TextButton {
                    // use id selector "submitID"
                    id: "submitID"
                    disappearOnAction: false;            // don't disappear
                    displayText: "Submit"
                    action: function(): Void {
                        println("You pressed submit.");
                    }
                }
                TextButton {
                    // use id selector "coolButton"
                    // disappears after action is called (default behavior)
                    id: "coolButton"
                    displayText: "Cool"
```

```
                     action: function(): Void { println("You pressed Cool."); }
              }
          ]
       }
    }
}
```

Skinnable ChoiceDialog Component

The ChoiceDialog component is a high level "pop-up" dialog with a title, display text, and two buttons: one to confirm or accept an action and a second button to cancel an action. Developers can configure the title, the display text, the text on each button, and the action functions associated with each button.

The ChoiceDialog can be styled by specifying a header fill color, the header text color, the background fill and display text color, and the button fill and text colors. The dialog itself is translucent, letting the obscured portion be (somewhat) visible through the component. Naturally, we'd like to reuse the TextButton component from the previous section when we build the ChoiceDialog component.

Figure 5.18 shows the Order Your Pizza application presented earlier in the chapter, using the ChoiceDialog component to confirm a pizza order.

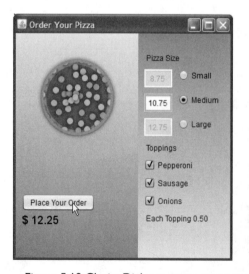 

Figure 5.18 ChoiceDialog custom component

Listing 5.17 shows how the ChoiceDialog is integrated into the Order Your Pizza application. The ChoiceDialog (`dialog`) is initially invisible but appears when you click the "Place Your Order" SwingButton. ChoiceDialog function `unFade` "pops up" the dialog.

The ChoiceDialog object literal sets properties `windowWidth`, `heading`, `displayText`, `buttonConfirm`, `buttonCancel`, and `onConfirm`. The object literal also includes node properties `layoutX`, `layoutY`, and `visible`.

Bound function `getOrderDescription` updates property `displayText`, which keeps track of the user's pizza choices.

Listing 5.17 Using the ChoiceDialog component

```
// Display the ChoiceDialog from the "Place Your Order" swing button
def orderButton = SwingButton {
    text: "Place Your Order"
    action: function(): Void {
        t.visible = false;
        dialog.unFade();
    }
}

def pizzaSizes: String[] = ["Small", "Medium", "Large"];

bound function getOrderDescription(): String {
    def s = pizzaSizes[pizzaSizeIndex];
    def top1 = if (checkPepperoni.selected) "Pepperoni" else "NO Pepperoni";
    def top2 = if (checkSausage.selected) "Sausage" else "NO Sausage";
    def top3 = if (checkOnions.selected) "Onions" else "NO Onions";
    return "{s} with {top1} and {top2} and {top3}";
}

def dialog = ChoiceDialog {
    layoutX: 20
    layoutY: 20
    visible: false
    windowWidth: 300
    heading: "Please confirm your pizza order"
    displayText: bind getOrderDescription()
    buttonConfirm: "Order"
    buttonCancel: "Make changes"
    onConfirm: function(): Void {
        // Display thank you message
        t.visible = true;
    }
}
```

Let's examine the Control portion of ChoiceDialog first, since that's the part exposed in the object literal. Listing 5.18 shows class ChoiceDialog. Note that the object literal in Listing 5.17 initializes each of the public variables (except Boolean `disappearOn-Action`, which defaults to `true`). Function `unFade` makes the node visible and reverses any fade transition that may have been applied, calling function `unFade` from class ChoiceDialogSkin. The `create` function initializes Control property `skin` (as shown earlier with class TextButton).

Listing 5.18 ChoiceDialog.fx (Control)

```
public class ChoiceDialog extends Control {
    public var windowWidth: Number = 150;
    public var heading: String;
    public var displayText: String;
    public var buttonConfirm: String;
    public var buttonCancel: String;
    public var onConfirm: function(): Void;
    public var onCancel: function(): Void;
    public var disappearOnAction = true;
    public function unFade() {
        visible = true;
        (skin as ChoiceDialogSkin).unFade();
    }
    protected override function create(): Node {
        skin = ChoiceDialogSkin { };
        super.create();
    }
}
```

Class ChoiceDialogSkin defines the component's graphical objects (Rectangle, Text, and TextButton) and installs them in the skin's scene graph. Figure 5.19 shows the ChoiceDialog with these underlying composite parts labeled.

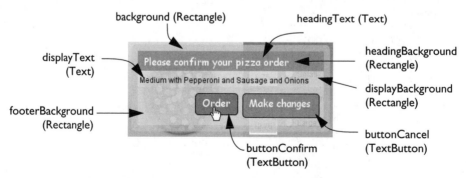

Figure 5.19 ChoiceDialog custom component and its composition

Listing 5.19 and Listing 5.20 show the code for class ChoiceDialogSkin. Listing 5.19 shows the graphical objects, the init block, and the initialization of Skin property choiceDialogControl with ChoiceDialog. Each of the graphical objects (background, headingBackground, etc.) is labeled in Figure 5.19. Note that most of the code is used to position the Text and Rectangle objects and calculates layout parameters. Most object literals use bind expressions with either properties in other graphical objects, properties of ChoiceDialog control (for example, choiceDialogControl.windowWidth), or public variables (that take on new values through CSS styles).

The parent Group component binds its opacity property to each of the two TextButton components using utility function fade. This makes the ChoiceDialog fade when either of the two TextButtons fade. (Function fade is in Listing 5.21 on page 164.)

Listing 5.19 ChoiceDialogSkin—Scene Graph

```
public class ChoiceDialogSkin extends Skin {
    def choiceDialogControl = bind control as ChoiceDialog;

    // Objects that go into the component scene graph:
    def background: Rectangle = Rectangle {
        fill: bind borderFill
        height: bind headingBackground.height
            + displayBackground.height + footerBackground.height + 20
        width: bind headingBackground.width + 20
        arcHeight: 15
        arcWidth: 15
        opacity: 0.7
    }

    def headingBackground: Rectangle = Rectangle {
        x: 10
        y: 10
        width: bind if (choiceDialogControl.windowWidth >
                        headingText.layoutBounds.width + 20)
                choiceDialogControl.windowWidth else
                headingText.layoutBounds.width + 20
        height: bind headingText.layoutBounds.height + 10
        fill: bind headingFill
        opacity: 0.9
    }
    def headingText: Text = Text{
        layoutY: bind headingBackground.layoutBounds.minY + 10
        font: bind dialogFont
        textOrigin: TextOrigin.TOP
        fill: bind headingTextColor
        content: bind choiceDialogControl.heading
        layoutX: bind headingBackground.layoutBounds.minX + 10
    }
    def displayBackground: Rectangle = Rectangle {
        x: 10
```

```
        layoutY: bind headingBackground.layoutBounds.maxY
        width: bind headingBackground.width
        height: bind displayText.layoutBounds.height + 10
        fill: bind displayFill
        opacity: 0.5
    }
    def displayText: Text = Text {
        wrappingWidth: bind displayBackground.width - 20
        layoutY: bind headingBackground.layoutBounds.maxY + 10
        font: Font {
            name: "Arial"
            size: 12
        }
        textOrigin: TextOrigin.TOP
        fill: bind displayTextColor
        content: bind choiceDialogControl.displayText
        layoutX: bind (displayBackground.layoutBounds.width -
                displayText.layoutBounds.width) / 2
    }
    def footerBackground: Rectangle = Rectangle {
        x: 10
        layoutY: bind headingBackground.layoutBounds.maxY +
                displayBackground.height
        width: bind background.layoutBounds.width - 20
        height: bind buttonCancel.layoutBounds.height + 20
        fill: footerFill
        opacity: 0.5
    }

    // Position buttonCancel on the right
    def buttonCancel: TextButton = TextButton {
        layoutX: bind background.layoutBounds.maxX -
                buttonCancel.layoutBounds.width - 15 ;
        layoutY: bind headingBackground.layoutBounds.maxY +
                displayBackground.height + 10
        displayText: bind choiceDialogControl.buttonCancel
        action: bind choiceDialogControl.onCancel
    }

    // Position buttonConfirm to the left of buttonCancel
    def buttonConfirm: TextButton = TextButton {
        layoutX: bind background.layoutBounds.maxX -
                buttonConfirm.layoutBounds.width -
                buttonCancel.layoutBounds.width - 20;
        layoutY: bind headingBackground.layoutBounds.maxY +
                displayBackground.height + 10
        displayText: bind choiceDialogControl.buttonConfirm
        action: bind choiceDialogControl.onConfirm
    }
    init {
        node = Group {
            content: [ background, headingBackground, headingText,
```

```
            displayBackground, displayText,
            footerBackground, buttonCancel, buttonConfirm ]
        opacity: bind fade(
            (buttonCancel.skin as TextButtonSkin).node.opacity,
            (buttonConfirm.skin as TextButtonSkin).node.opacity);
    }
  }
}
```

Listing 5.20 shows the ChoiceDialogSkin public variables (and public function unFade). The code after the first comment describes public properties for ChoiceDialog. The code after the second comment uses on replace to update the underlying TextButton components. Many of these properties have the same name, although some are renamed to be more descriptive in the ChoiceDialogSkin context (for example, TextButtonSkin property fillColor is renamed to buttonFill in ChoiceDialogSkin).

Listing 5.20 ChoiceDialogSkin—Public Variables

```
// Class ChoiceDialogSkin public variables

    public var borderFill: Paint = Color.LIGHTGRAY;
    public var headingFill: Paint = Color.CADETBLUE;
    public var displayFill: Paint = Color.WHITE;
    public var footerFill: Paint = Color.WHITESMOKE;
    public var headingTextColor: Paint = Color.WHITE;
    public var displayTextColor: Paint = Color.BLACK;

    public function unFade() {
        (buttonCancel.skin as TextButtonSkin).node.opacity = 1;
        (buttonConfirm.skin as TextButtonSkin).node.opacity = 1;
    }

    // hook into TextButton styles
    public var buttonFill: Paint on replace {
        (buttonConfirm.skin as TextButtonSkin).fillColor = buttonFill;
        (buttonCancel.skin as TextButtonSkin).fillColor = buttonFill;
    }
    public var mouseEnteredColor: Paint on replace {
        (buttonConfirm.skin as TextButtonSkin).mouseEnteredColor =
            mouseEnteredColor;
        (buttonCancel.skin as TextButtonSkin).mouseEnteredColor =
            mouseEnteredColor;
    }

    public var mouseExitedColor: Paint on replace {
        (buttonConfirm.skin as TextButtonSkin).mouseExitedColor =
            mouseExitedColor;
        (buttonCancel.skin as TextButtonSkin).mouseExitedColor =
            mouseExitedColor;
```

```
    }
    public var mousePressedColor: Paint on replace {
        (buttonConfirm.skin as TextButtonSkin).mousePressedColor =
            mousePressedColor;
        (buttonCancel.skin as TextButtonSkin).mousePressedColor =
            mousePressedColor;
    }
    public var buttonTextColor: Paint on replace {
        (buttonConfirm.skin as TextButtonSkin).textColor = buttonTextColor;
        (buttonCancel.skin as TextButtonSkin).textColor = buttonTextColor;
    }

    public var dialogFont = Font {size: 16 name: "Arial Bold"} on replace {
        (buttonConfirm.skin as TextButtonSkin).buttonFont = dialogFont;
        (buttonCancel.skin as TextButtonSkin).buttonFont = dialogFont;
    }
```

Listing 5.21 shows functions contains and intersects (required for classes that extend Skin) and function fade. Functions contains and intersects simply call these functions for the root node (property node).

Function fade (called from the init block in Listing 5.19) adjusts the node's visible property so that it is visible when both button's opacity is 1 and not visible if either button's opacity is 0. This ensures that the dialog does not receive mouse events or keyboard focus after the dialog disappears (fades).

Listing 5.21 Functions contains, intersects, and fade

```
public override function contains(localX: Number, localY: Number): Boolean {
    node.contains(localX, localY);
}
public override function intersects(localX: Number, localY: Number, localWidth:
        Number, localHeight: Number) : Boolean {
    node.intersects(localX, localY, localWidth, localHeight);
}

function fade(o1: Number, o2: Number): Number {
    if (o1 == 1 and o2 == 1) {
        choiceDialogControl.visible = true;
        return 1;
    }
    if (o1 == 0 or o2 == 0) {
        choiceDialogControl.visible = false;
        return 0;
    }
    if (o1 < 1) return o1 else return o2
}
```

With these "skinnable" properties exposed, we can now style the ChoiceDialog with CSS. Listing 5.22 shows the external CSS file (**ComponentStyle.css**) included with the updated Order Your Pizza application. The selector ("`choice.ChoiceDialog`") includes the component name only. This makes these styles apply to any Choice-Dialog object in the application, assuring a uniform look.

Listing 5.22 ComponentStyle.css

```
"choice.ChoiceDialog"
{
    headingTextColor: white;
    headingFill: cadetblue;
    buttonFill: cadetblue;
    mouseEnteredColor: slategray;
    mouseExitedColor: cadetblue;
    mousePressedColor: lightslategray;
    buttonTextColor: white;
    dialogFont: 16pt "comic sans ms";
}
```

6 Anatomy of a JavaFX Application

JavaFX applications with graphical elements have a certain structure. The main program defines a Stage and a Scene that holds the graphical objects. In a simple application, you declare the graphical objects and the application just runs. Now, however, you'll learn about an application (project Piano) that's a bit more involved. You'll see how object oriented design principles help describe custom objects. This application also lets you explore additional JavaFX features that help build rich applications. In this chapter, you'll see how to use GUI components, layout components, gradients and effects, and custom graphical components. You'll also learn how to apply timelines and transitions (animation) to control your application.

The source code for application Piano appears at the end of the chapter (see "Source Code for Project Piano" on page 194.

What You Will Learn

- Using inheritance to create well-designed custom graphical objects
- Creating graphical objects with gradients and effects
- Using drop shadow effects with Text objects
- Applying animation to show and hide components
- Using timelines to execute code
- Using GUI components
- Building sequences of objects and event handlers to manipulate them
- Using layout components and dynamic centering to achieve effective rendering

6.1 Project Piano

Project Piano displays a virtual piano keyboard. When you move the mouse over a key, that key displays a circle indicator. When you click a key, you'll hear the synthesized note corresponding to the selected key. A drop shadow also appears around the "pressed" key. The letter (note) corresponding to the piano key appears below the keyboard and the note is saved in a note buffer. Figure 6.1 shows this application running.

When the program starts, a Help window appears. You can hide this Help window by clicking the Hide Help button. Clicking the Show Help button brings it back.

The Play button plays the notes currently in the note buffer. By default, you will hear a predefined sequence of notes.[1] As you play new notes on the keyboard, the program adds them to the note buffer. You can clear the note buffer with button Clear Notes. The Stop button stops play. Project Piano uses the Java `javax.sound.midi` API to generate sound.

Figure 6.1 JavaFX application Piano

Before we examine the scene graph and JavaFX code for the Piano application, you'll see how to build this application from the ground up. You'll first examine the WhiteKey and BlackKey custom nodes that together compose the keyboard. Then you'll build the keyboard, examine the layout of the scene, and add the buttons that

---

1. The opening phrase of 1761 French melody 'Ah! Vous dirai-je, Maman' (also known as 'Twinkle, Twinkle, Little Star').

let you play notes, clear the note buffer, and stop playing. By building this application gradually, you'll see how a stepwise approach helps you create well-designed applications. Furthermore, understanding the component pieces lets you see how the complete application works.

6.2 PianoKey Components

The Piano application has a keyboard made up of keys. The keys work as individual components; that is, each key operates independently. When you press a key, you hear a note and see a visual effect that lets you know the key is selected. All keys exhibit the same behavior (black keys and white keys). This abstraction of behavior lets you create abstract class PianoKey, encapsulating the common traits piano keys share.

However, since white keys and black keys look significantly different from each other, we also create two subclasses that specialize the different graphical structure of each piano key type.

Custom graphical components extend JavaFX class CustomNode so that the customized component fits seamlessly into a JavaFX scene graph. Figure 6.2 shows the Piano application's class hierarchy consisting of class CustomNode, class PianoKey, and two subclasses: WhiteKey and BlackKey.

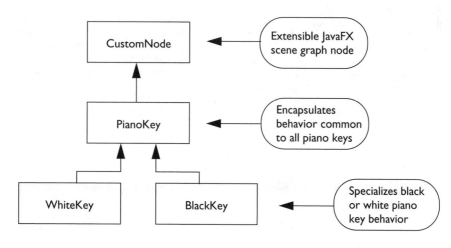

Figure 6.2 PianoKey Class Hierarchy

Class PianoKey

In the Piano application, class PianoKey extends CustomNode and provides all the behaviors that are common between white and black piano keys on the virtual keyboard.

Listing 6.1 shows the code for class PianoKey. Class PianoKey is abstract (you'll see why when we look at the code for classes WhiteKey and BlackKey). This class implements the piano key behaviors that are common to all piano keys. Note that PianoKey has no graphical objects defined; defining the "look" of a piano key is relegated to the specialized classes, WhiteKey and BlackKey.

Recall that public-init variables in JavaFX are read-only, but the user provides initial values when constructing the object literal that builds the key. In class PianoKey, these initial values determine where the key is drawn, the letter associated with the key, and the note it emits when played. It also includes a handle to the synthesizer object responsible for actually producing sound (synthNote). Variable showKeyPress is protected so that the subclasses WhiteKey and BlackKey can access it.

Listing 6.1 Class PianoKey

```
package piano;

import javafx.scene.CustomNode;
import noteplayer.SingleNote;

public abstract class PianoKey extends CustomNode {
    public-init var xOffset: Number;          // position x coordinate
    public-init var yOffset: Number;          // position y coordinate
    public-init var note: Integer;            // numeric value of note
    public-init var keyText: String;          // letter equivalent of note
    public-init var synthNote: SingleNote;    // synthesizer object
    protected var showKeyPress = false;       // toggle to visualize events

    // turn the note on
    public function noteOn(): String {
        showPress();
        synthNote.noteOn(note);
        return keyText;
    }

    // turn the note off
    public function noteOff(): Void {
        synthNote.noteOff(note);
        clearPress();
    }

    // turn on key press visualization
    public function showPress(): Void {
```

```
        showKeyPress = true;
    }
    // turn off key press visualization
    public function clearPress(): Void {
        showKeyPress = false;
    }
}
```

Subclass WhiteKey

When you extend a class from CustomNode, you must provide function create or tag the extended class with keyword abstract. Since class PianoKey does not define function create it must be abstract. The subclasses (WhiteKey and BlackKey) provide implementations for create, which includes the graphical structure of the key. These classes also specify mouse detection event handlers for onMouseEntered and onMouseExited. White keys display a blue circle for event onMouseEntered and black keys display an orange circle.

Note that to modify the display in a scene graph, you simply manipulate its objects' properties and the JavaFX engine redraws the display for you. So, to make the WhiteKey circle visible for a mouse entered event, you set the circle's visible property to true. To make it disappear, set it to false. You can apply this principle to any number of properties, such as those that manipulate an object's size, orientation, location, or fill.

Listing 6.2 shows the first part of class WhiteKey. It includes the gradients that fill the rectangular key and the circular key press indicator. The linear gradient helps give a key depth for a more realistic look. The WhiteKey's linear gradient changes in the x direction (only startX and endX have different values) and the gradient affects only the right half of the key (property startX is .5). The key is white on the left half and changes to Color.LIGHTGRAY on the right side. Property stops is a sequence of Stop objects containing an offset and a color. The offset is a value between 0 and 1 inclusive; each succeeding offset must have a higher value than the preceding one.

The Circle's radial gradient is centered and covers half of the Circle's radius, changing from white to blue.

Listing 6.2 Class WhiteKey—Part I

```
public class WhiteKey extends PianoKey {
    // linear gradient to fill the "white" key
    def keyFill = LinearGradient {
        startX: .5
        startY: 1
        endX: 1
        endY: 1
```

```
      stops: [
          Stop {
              offset: 0
              color: Color.WHITE }
          Stop {
              offset: 1
              color: Color.LIGHTGREY }
      ]
  };

// radial gradient to fill the "key press" circle indicator
def circleFill = RadialGradient {
    centerX: 0.5        // 0.5 centers the gradient along the x axis
    centerY: 0.5        // 0.5 centers the gradient along the y axis
    radius: 0.5         // the radius of the gradient
    stops: [
        Stop {
            offset: 0
            color: Color.WHITE }
        Stop {
            offset: 1
            color: Color.DODGERBLUE }
    ]
};
```

Listing 6.3 shows the second part of class WhiteKey. Here you see the all-important create function, which returns a Group node customized for WhiteKey. Using Group here gives you the flexibility of adding multiple objects to a CustomNode's scene graph, since a Group object includes a content sequence for holding multiple graphical objects. Here, class WhiteKey's content sequence includes a Rectangle (to render the key) and a Circle (to render the play/press indicator).

Group also lets you define properties that apply to the Node as a whole. Here you see several Group-level properties: cursor, effect, onMouseEntered, and onMouseExited.

Class WhiteKey uses shape Rectangle to render a white key. Rectangles have x, y positions and height and width. You give the Rectangle rounded corners by specifying values for properties arcWidth and arcHeight. Property stroke specifies the shape's outline color, strokeWidth specifies the width of the outline, and property fill is the keyFill LinearGradient.

You define a Circle with a center point (centerX and centerY) and a radius. The Circle also includes a radial gradient for the fill property (circleFill).

Listing 6.3 Class WhiteKey—Part 2

```
// required CustomNode function create that builds the scene graph
protected override function create(): Node {
```

```
        return Group {
            // Group-level properties
            cursor: Cursor.HAND
            effect: DropShadow { }
            onMouseEntered: function(e: MouseEvent): Void {
                showPress();
            }
            onMouseExited: function(e: MouseEvent): Void {
                clearPress();
            }

            content: [
                // White Key Rectangle
                Rectangle {
                    x: xOffset
                    y: yOffset
                    width: 35
                    height: 112.5
                    arcWidth: 10
                    arcHeight: 10
                    stroke: Color.BLACK
                    strokeWidth: 1
                    fill: keyFill
                }, // Rectangle
                Circle {
                    radius: 10
                    centerX: xOffset + 18
                    centerY: yOffset + 90
                    // control circle's visibility with bind
                    visible: bind showKeyPress
                    fill: circleFill
                } // Circle
            ]

        } // Group
    }
}
```

Take a moment to examine the Circle node more closely in Listing 6.3. The Circle's visible property binds with Boolean variable showKeyPress (showKeyPress is a protected class variable defined in PianoKey). By using bind, the Circle dynamically appears and disappears as variable showKeyPress changes. (Boolean showKeyPress is true when the mouse is over the key or when the key's note is "played.") This is how the application controls the key's indicator circle.

Single Key Application

Let's back off a bit from our grand Piano application and build a simple starter application with a single white key that plays the key's note and displays its letter. This

way, you'll see how to use a custom node in the scene graph defined in the main program. This application doesn't address layout issues other than defining a scene
graph that includes one key and a Text object to display the note. Figure 6.3 shows the
simplified application running.

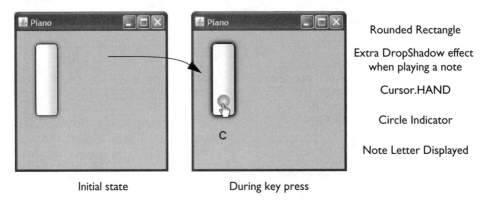

| Initial state | During key press |

Figure 6.3 Piano with a single white key shown before and during a key press

Listing 6.4 shows the code for the Single Key application. Variable `singleNote` initializes the synthesizer object that plays the notes. String variable `notesPlayed` holds the
letter associated with the note played. Note that the Stage object includes property
`onClose` to provide a function with "end of life" code. This includes invoking `single-
Note.close`, which shuts down the synthesizer channels. The scene's `content` sequence
holds a WhiteKey object and a Text object.

Listing 6.4 Piano—Step 1: Single Key

```
var singleNote =  SingleNote { };
var notesPlayed: String;
Stage {
   title: "Piano"
   onClose: function() {
       singleNote.close();    // close the synthesizer
       FX.exit();
   }
   width: 250
   height: 250
   scene: Scene {
      fill: Color.LIGHTSTEELBLUE
      content: [
           WhiteKey {
           // provide required initialization values
               xOffset: 30
```

```
                    yOffset: 20
                    synthNote: singleNote
                    note: 60      // middle "C"
                    keyText: "C"
                    onMousePressed: function (e: MouseEvent): Void {
                      // add a drop shadow effect and play the note
                        e.node.effect = DropShadow { };
                        notesPlayed = (e.node as PianoKey).noteOn();
                    }
                    onMouseReleased: function(e: MouseEvent): Void {
                      // stop playing the note and remove drop shadow
                        e.node.effect = null;
                        (e.node as PianoKey).noteOff();
                    }
                },
                // Text object to display the letter associated with each note
                Text {
                    x: 40
                    y: 170
                    font: Font {
                        size: 18
                    }
                    content: bind notesPlayed
                }
            ]
        }
    }
}
```

The WhiteKey object literal specifies a value for the keyText property to display the note's letter (C). It also includes event handlers to play the note (adding a drop shadow effect) or stop playing the note (removing the drop shadow). Here you see the advantage of the scene graph and how easily you can update it.

```
        onMousePressed: function (e: MouseEvent): Void {
            // add a drop shadow effect and play the note
            e.node.effect = DropShadow { };
            notesPlayed = (e.node as PianoKey).noteOn();
        }
```

What's going on here? Object e is a MouseEvent containing event information accessible within the event handler. One of the MouseEvent properties is node, which is the graphical object that triggered the event. In this case, e.node is the WhiteKey object defined in the scene. So, applying a drop shadow effect to e.node here dynamically updates the WhiteKey object.

Similarly, the statement

```
    notesPlayed = (e.node as PianoKey).noteOn();
```

"plays" the WhiteKey's note. The casting expression (`e.node as PianoKey`) is necessary here; otherwise the compiler complains that function `noteOn` is not defined within class Node. The casting expression tells the static type system that `e.node` is really a PianoKey, making the call to function `noteOn` with `e.node` type-safe and legal. As shown in Listing 6.1 on page 170, class PianoKey defines function `noteOn`.

The Text object literal includes a binding expression for its `content` property.

```
Text {
    x: 40
    y: 170
    font: Font {
        size: 18
    }
    content: bind notesPlayed
}
```

When the WhiteKey object's `onMousePressed` event handler updates String `notesPlayed`, the Text object's contents (and scene graph) are simultaneously updated.

Subclass BlackKey

Class BlackKey provides essentially the same code as class WhiteKey except that its Rectangle and Circle components are sized differently and have different fill values. Listing 6.5 shows the first part of class BlackKey where the gradients are defined. The BlackKey's linear gradient changes in the x direction (only `startX` and `endX` have different values) and the gradient affects only the left half of the key (property `endX` is .5). The key is solid black on the right half.

Listing 6.5 Class BlackKey—Part I

```
public class BlackKey extends PianoKey {
    def keyFill = LinearGradient {
        startX: 0
        startY: 1
        endX: .5
        endY: 1
        stops: [
         Stop {
            offset: 0
            color: Color.BURLYWOOD }
          Stop {
            offset: 1
            color: Color.BLACK }
          ]
    };
    def circleFill = RadialGradient {
        centerX: 0.5
        centerY: 0.5
```

```
        radius: 0.5
        stops: [
            Stop {
                offset: 0
                color: Color.WHITESMOKE }
            Stop {
                offset: 1
                color: Color.ORANGE }
        ]
    };
```

Listing 6.6 shows the second part of class BlackKey. It includes function create, which builds the custom node's scene graph. Like WhiteKey, this class consists of a Rectangle for the key's graphical structure and a Circle object for the key press indicator and other mouse events. The Circle object's visible property is bound to PianoKey class variable showKeyPress, providing the same dynamic behavior you saw with class WhiteKey.

Listing 6.6 Class BlackKey—Part 2

```
    protected override function create(): Node {
        return Group {
            cursor: Cursor.HAND
            onMouseEntered: function(e: MouseEvent): Void {
                showPress();
            }
            onMouseExited: function(e: MouseEvent): Void {
                clearPress();
            }
            content: [
                Rectangle {
                    x: 20 + xOffset
                    y: yOffset
                    width: 22
                    height: 65
                    arcWidth: 10
                    arcHeight: 10
                    stroke: Color.BLACK
                    strokeWidth: 1
                    fill: keyFill
                }, // Rectangle
                // Circle shows up when a key is pressed or a note is played
                Circle {
                    radius: 7
                    centerX: xOffset + 31
                    centerY: yOffset + 43
                    visible: bind showKeyPress
                    fill: circleFill
                } // Circle
            ]
```

```
        } // Group
    }
}
```

Two Key Application

Now let's return to the partially built Piano application and add a BlackKey to the scene graph. Figure 6.4 shows this modified application running. The black key fill also has a linear gradient, but its colors are obviously darker. The circle indicator is smaller and the note letter includes both the musical sharp (#) and flat (b) notation. Its note "value" is set to 61, which is a half-step higher than the value used for the white key.

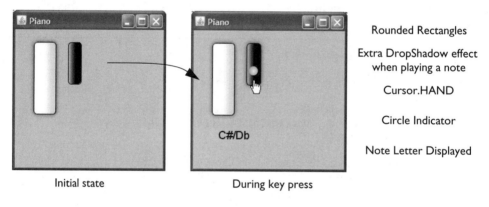

Figure 6.4 Single white and black key shown before and during a key press

Figure 6.5 shows the scene node diagram for the simplified Piano application. The scene now includes a WhiteKey, BlackKey, and Text component.

Listing 6.7 shows the code for the BlackKey node in the Piano scene graph (in bold). The mouse event handlers are the same as those defined for the WhiteKey node.

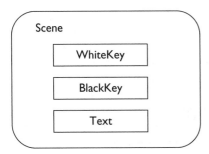

Figure 6.5 Scene Node Diagram for simplified Piano application

Listing 6.7 Piano—Step 2: Two Key

```
var singleNote = SingleNote { };
var notesPlayed: String;
Stage {
    title: "Piano"
    onClose: function() {
        singleNote.close();    // close the synthesizer
        FX.exit();
    }
    width: 250, height: 250
    scene: Scene {
        fill: Color.LIGHTSTEELBLUE
        content: [
            WhiteKey { . . . (unchanged) . . . }
            BlackKey {
                xOffset: 65
                yOffset: 20
                note: 61
                keyText: "C#/Db"
                synthNote: singleNote
                onMousePressed: function (e: MouseEvent): Void {
                    e.node.effect = DropShadow { };
                    notesPlayed = (e.node as PianoKey).noteOn();
                }
                onMouseReleased: function(e: MouseEvent): Void {
                    e.node.effect = null;
                    (e.node as PianoKey).noteOff();
                }
            }
            Text { . . . (unchanged) . . . }
        ]
    }
}
```

6.3 Building the Keyboard

Now that you've seen how to add WhiteKey and BlackKey custom nodes to the application's scene graph, the next step is to build a piano keyboard with white and black keys. Figure 6.6 shows this enhanced yet still simple application running. The keys are positioned to look like a keyboard and each note you play appears in the Text component positioned under the keyboard. The keyboard spans two octaves—there are fourteen white keys and ten black keys. The black keys are "on top of" the white keys. The application builds the white keys first and then adds a black key relative to the position of certain white keys to achieve the realistic look of a keyboard.

Figure 6.6 Piano application enhanced to include the keyboard

This version of the application introduces a layout component to help position the keyboard and text components. Since the keyboard should be treated as a single entity, you'll place the sequence of keys in its own Group. That way, you can position the keyboard on the scene without worrying about re-adjusting the placement of the individual keys. A VBox layout component positions the keyboard above the Text node. Figure 6.7 shows the scene graph diagram of the application with these added graphical objects.

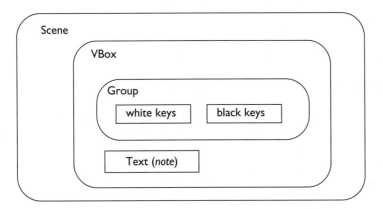

Figure 6.7 Scene Node Diagram for updated Piano application

Listing 6.8 shows the first part of the code that implements this enhanced application. The added code is in bold.

Let's examine the keyboard first. The String sequence `pianoNotes` holds the letter notes for two octaves of white keys and the Integer sequence `noteValues` contains their corresponding values. The program also has a PianoKey sequence to hold piano keys called `pianoKeys`. The Integer sequence `blackKeyIndex` holds the index values of the white keys that have black keys after them. This is how the black keys are positioned relative to the white keys.

You build the keyboard with two for loops (that return sequences); the first for loop builds the WhiteKey nodes and the second one builds the BlackKey nodes. Order is important here, because if the BlackKeys are placed in the scene graph first, they will be obscured by the WhiteKeys drawn over them.

The sequences are then combined (or flattened) with the following assignment.

```
// Add the blackKeys to pianoKeys sequence
pianoKeys = [pianoKeys, blackKeys];
```

Building the keys within a for loop also lets you specify PianoKey properties `note` and `keyText` with the associated value in the `noteValues` and `pianoNotes` sequences. The keyText property for WhiteKey and BlackKey objects is shown here.

```
keyText: "{pianoNotes[i]} "                      // WhiteKey
keyText: "{pianoNotes[i]}#/{pianoNotes[i+1]}b " // BlackKey
```

The BlackKey text is based on the WhiteKey letter with the sharp (#) and flat (b) notation added. Similarly, the BlackKey's note property is based on the WhiteKey note
value as shown here.

```
note: noteValues[i]                    // WhiteKey
note: noteValues[i] + 1                // BlackKey
```

The BlackKey must also specify a value for Node property blocksMouse. Because the
BlackKey overlaps the same coordinate space as two WhiteKeys, mouse events triggered inside BlackKey objects will propagate to the underlying WhiteKey object. To
prevent this interference, set the BlackKey blocksMouse property to true. This ensures
that mouse events inside BlackKey components trigger only BlackKey mouse event
handlers. Setting blocksMouse was not necessary in the previous version of the application (as shown in Figure 6.4 on page 178) since the keys did not overlap.

Listing 6.8 Piano—Step 3: Add the keyboard—Part I

```
var singleNote =  SingleNote { };
var notesPlayed: String;

def pianoNotes = ["F","G","A","B","C","D","E","F","G","A","B","C","D","E"];
def noteValues = [53,55,57,59,60,62,64,65,67,69,71,72,74,76];
// put a black key after these white key index numbers
def blackKeyIndex = [0, 1, 2, 4, 5, 7, 8, 9, 11, 12];

var pianoKeys: PianoKey[] = for (i in [0..<sizeof pianoNotes])
    WhiteKey {
        xOffset: i * 35 + 30
        yOffset: 25
        note: noteValues[i]
        keyText: "{pianoNotes[i]} "
        synthNote: singleNote
        . . . keyboard events unchanged . . .
    }
def blackKeys = for (i in blackKeyIndex)
    BlackKey {
        xOffset: i * 35 + 30
        yOffset: 25
        note: noteValues[i] + 1
        keyText: "{pianoNotes[i]}#/{pianoNotes[i+1]}b "
        synthNote: singleNote
        blocksMouse: true
        . . . keyboard events unchanged . . .
    }

// Add the blackKeys to pianoKeys sequence
pianoKeys = [pianoKeys, blackKeys];
```

Listing 6.9 is the code that defines the enhanced Stage and scene graph. The height and width of the stage have increased to hold the keyboard. The scene's `content` sequence includes the VBox layout component at the top level. Its `spacing` property (set to 30) provides space between the keyboard and the Text node. Note that the keyboard (sequence `pianoKeys`) is in its own Group so VBox doesn't affect the layout of the individual keys.

Listing 6.9 Piano—Step 3: Add the keyboard—Part 2

```
Stage {
    title: "Piano"
    onClose: function() {
        singleNote.close();    // close the synthesizer
        FX.exit();
    }
    width: 560
    height: 250
    scene: Scene {
        fill: Color.LIGHTSTEELBLUE
        content: [
            VBox {
                layoutX: 30
                layoutY: 25
                spacing: 30
                content: [
                    Group {
                        content: pianoKeys
                    }
                    Text {
                        x: 40
                        font: Font {
                            size: 18
                        }
                        content: bind notesPlayed
                    }
                ]
            }
        ]
    }
}
```

6.4 SwingButtons and Animation

To enhance the Piano application even more, you'll want to give it more "things" to do. The next version has three buttons that manage stored notes in a note buffer. Button Play plays the stored notes, Stop stops playing the notes, and Clear Notes clears the note buffer. Figure 6.8 shows this application after selecting the Play button. As each note plays, a circle indicator shows you which key is playing and the letter appears in the Text component below the keyboard. Each key that you click plays a note which is also added to the note buffer.

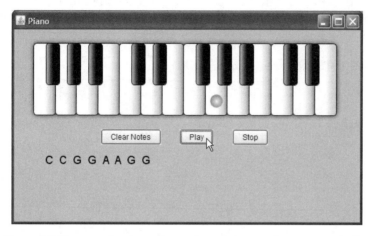

Figure 6.8 Piano application enhanced to play notes from a note buffer

Figure 6.9 shows the scene graph for this version of the application. The top-level node is now a Flow layout component with two child nodes: the Group containing the keyboard and a horizontal layout component (HBox) to hold the SwingButtons. The Flow layout component positions its contents in a vertical flow (property vertical is true) and centers the contents of each cell horizontally (property hPos is HPos.CENTER). The Text object that displays the notes is outside of the Flow layout component.

Listing 6.10 through Listing 6.12 show the modifications required to implement the behavior of the Play, Clear Notes, and Stop buttons.

Listing 6.10 shows the new code that lets a user play the notes saved in the note buffer. First, you define a sequence variable of PianoKey objects (noteSeq) with related index variable (noteSeqIndex). This sequence is the note buffer. Next, you initialize noteSeq to hold PianoKey objects that play a short musical phrase. A timeline (notes-Timeline) plays the notes. The timeline consists of two KeyFrame objects, one invoked at time 0s (0 seconds) and the second KeyFrame object invoked after a half second (.5s). Property action lets you specify a function to invoke at that time. Here, the first function plays the note (from the note buffer) and concatenates the note's letter with those already in the Text component's content. The second function turns off the current PianoKey note and moves the index to the next slot in the note buffer. Property repeatCount is bound to the note buffer's size, so that when the timeline plays, it repeats for each note saved in the note buffer.

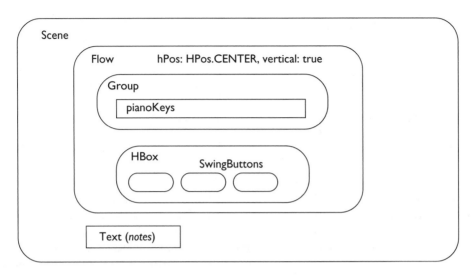

Figure 6.9 Scene Node Diagram updated to include GUI buttons

Function stopPlay stops the timeline and makes sure all associated variables are properly reset when the timeline stops.

Listing 6.10 Piano—Step 4: Add Swing buttons and note buffer—Part I

```
// Code to save the notes in a note buffer
// and to play the notes in the note buffer
// setup to play some notes
var noteSeq: PianoKey[];
var noteSeqIndex = 0;

// "Twinkle, Twinkle, Litter Star"
noteSeq = for (i in [4,4,8,8,9,9,8,8,7,7,6,6,5,5,4]) pianoKeys[i];

var notesTimeline = Timeline {
    repeatCount: bind sizeof noteSeq
    keyFrames: [
        KeyFrame {
            time: 0s
            action: function(): Void {
                notesPlayed = "{notesPlayed}{noteSeq[noteSeqIndex].noteOn()} ";
            }
        }
        KeyFrame {
            time: .5s
            action: function(): Void {
                noteSeq[noteSeqIndex].noteOff();
                noteSeqIndex++;
```

```
            }
         }
      ]
}

function stopPlay(): Void {
    notesPlayed = "";
    notesTimeline.stop();
    if (noteSeqIndex < sizeof noteSeq)
        noteSeq[noteSeqIndex].noteOff();
    noteSeqIndex = 0;
}
```

Listing 6.11 shows the modified code for the WhiteKey and BlackKey onMousePressed
event handlers (in bold). As a user plays each key, the event handler concatenates the
note's letter to the String displayed by the Text component (rather than overwrite it
with each note). The handler inserts the specific piano key object (e.node) into a
sequence, so it can be retrieved later. You must use a casting expression here (e.node
as PianoKey), since you can only insert PianoKey objects into sequence noteSeq.

Listing 6.11 Piano—Step 4: Add Swing buttons and note buffer—Part 2

```
var pianoKeys: PianoKey[] = for (i in [0..<sizeof pianoNotes])
    WhiteKey {
       . . .
       onMousePressed: function (e: MouseEvent): Void {
           e.node.effect = DropShadow{};
           // concatenate new note played with buffer
           notesPlayed = "{notesPlayed}{(e.node as PianoKey).noteOn()}";
           // remember which piano key was played
           insert (e.node as PianoKey) into noteSeq;
       }
       . . .
    }

def blackKeys = for (i in blackKeyIndex)
    BlackKey {
       . . .
       onMousePressed: function (e: MouseEvent): Void {
           e.node.effect = DropShadow{};
           // concatenate new note played with buffer
           notesPlayed = "{notesPlayed}{(e.node as PianoKey).noteOn()}";
           // remember which piano key was played
           insert (e.node as PianoKey) into noteSeq;
       }
       . . .
    }
```

Listing 6.12 shows the modifications needed to add SwingButton components to the scene graph. The added nodes in the scene graph require a larger scene height (300). There are three buttons labeled "Clear Notes," "Play," and "Stop." SwingButton property text holds the button label and action specifies a function to invoke when the button is clicked. All three SwingButtons stop the timeline by calling function stop-Play. SwingButton "Clear Notes" also removes the PianoKey objects from the note buffer sequence. SwingButton "Play" starts the timeline again from the beginning (timeline function playFromStart).

Layout component Flow specifies vertical mode (property vertical is true) with the vertical gap set to 20 (property vGap). It centers its contents horizontally (property hPos is HPos.CENTER).

Layout component HBox lets you arrange components horizontally in the scene. Here, HBox groups the SwingButton nodes together to achieve the layout shown in Figure 6.8 on page 184. Property spacing lets you define spacing between each node.

The Text component that displays the note buffer sets property wrappingWidth so that long note sequences are not clipped. Its layoutX and layoutY properties position it under the SwingButton nodes.

Listing 6.12 Piano—Step 4: Add Swing buttons and note buffer—Part 3

```
Stage {
    title: "Piano"
    onClose: function() {
        singleNote.close();    // close the synthesizer
        FX.exit();
    }
    scene: Scene {
        width: 560
        height: 300
        fill: Color.LIGHTSTEELBLUE
        content: [
            Flow {
                layoutX: 30
                layoutY: 20
                vertical: true
                vGap: 20
                hPos: HPos.CENTER
                height: 300
                content: [
                    Group {
                        content: pianoKeys
                    }
                    HBox { // Layout for the buttons
                        spacing: 30
                        content: [
                            SwingButton {
```

```
                        text: "Clear Notes"
                        action: function() {
                            stopPlay();
                            delete noteSeq;
                        }
                    }  // SwingButton
                    SwingButton {
                        text: "Play"
                        action: function() {
                            stopPlay();
                            notesTimeline.playFromStart();
                        }
                    }  // SwingButton
                    SwingButton {
                        text: "Stop"
                        action: function() {
                            stopPlay();
                        }
                    }  // SwingButton
                ]
            }// HBox
        ]
    }
    Text {
        layoutY: 210
        layoutX: 50
        font: Font {
            size: 18
        }
        wrappingWidth: 460
        content: bind notesPlayed;
    }
    ]
  }
}
```

6.5 Adding Help and Improving Visual Effects

Figure 6.10 shows the final version of the JavaFX Piano application. You'll note the addition of a title Text component, a Help window, and a Hide Help button in this version. Both the title and Help window text have drop shadows. The application background now has a linear gradient as does the Help window background. Additionally, the title, keyboard, buttons, and Help window are all centered horizontally in the scene.

Figure 6.10 JavaFX application Piano—the final version

The most obvious enhancement to this final version of the Piano application is a Help window, which appears when the application first comes up. Since this window takes up a large portion of the scene, the user can hide it by clicking the Hide Help button.

Figure 6.11 depicts the updated scene graph for the final version of this application. A Text component for the title is now inside the Flow layout component. The Text component for the notes and the new Help window appear outside the Flow layout component. The Help window is a Group, consisting of a Rectangle (for the background) and a Text component.

Listing 6.13 through Listing 6.15 show the added and updated code to implement the final version.

Listing 6.13 includes new variables, a fade transition to show and hide the Help window, and a SwingButton the user clicks to show or hide the Help window. Read-only variable helpText contains the text displayed by the Help window.

The listing includes a variable declaration for the Scene (scene) that lets you use scene in calculations to center components (and re-center them when a user resizes the window and the Scene's width property changes).

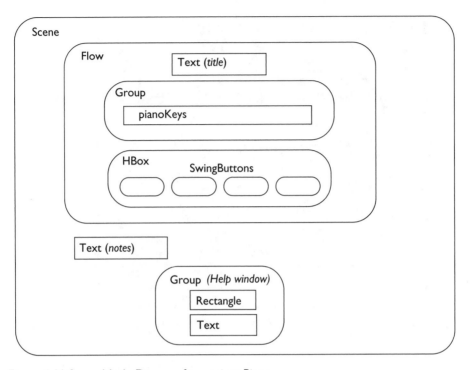

Figure 6.11 Scene Node Diagram for project Piano

A FadeTransition[2] is a specialized Timeline that fades the object specified in property node by gradually changing the node's opacity (1 is fully opaque and 0 is fully translucent). Although you can construct a Timeline object that is equivalent, using Fade-Transition (variable fadeHelp) is a convenient shortcut. Note that property rate is -1. (The normal rate value for timelines and transitions is 1.) If you increase the rate to 2, this makes the transition (or timeline) go twice as fast; rate .5 means twice as slow. Negative values make transitions go in reverse. Thus, a rate of -1 is at normal speed, but in reverse. We set the rate to reverse since the Help window is visible initially. Reversing the transition will make the Help window disappear (fully translucent).

A SwingButton object literal implements the Hide Help/Show Help button. Property text is bound to variable helpLabel, which toggles between Hide Help and Show Help. Property action provides the statements to show or hide the Help Window. The function toggles the transition's rate, plays fadeHelp, and toggles the button's text property.

---

2. See Section 7.3 ("Transitions") beginning on page 225 for more details on JavaFX Transitions.

Listing 6.13 Piano—Step 5: Final Build—Part I

```
def helpText = "Play: You will hear a short tune which you can Stop."
"\nYou can also play arbitrary notes using the mouse."
"\nYour notes will be added to the play buffer."
"\nClear Notes: clears the play buffer.";
var helpLabel = " Hide Help ";

var scene: Scene;
var pianoHelp: Group;

def fadeHelp = FadeTransition {
    duration: 1.5s
    node: pianoHelp
    fromValue: 1.0
    toValue: 0.0
    rate: -1
}
    . . .

    HBox {          // Layout for the buttons
        spacing: 30
        content: [
            . . . (original SwingButtons go here) . . .
            // SwingButton object literal added to HBox layout component
            SwingButton {
                text: bind helpLabel
                action: function(): Void {
                    fadeHelp.rate = (fadeHelp.rate * - 1.0);
                    fadeHelp.play();
                    helpLabel = if (helpLabel == "Show Help") " Hide Help "
                        else "Show Help";
                }
            } // SwingButton
        ]
    } // HBox
    . . .
```

Listing 6.14 shows the graphical element that makes up the Help window: a Rectangle and a Text node grouped together. The Group (pianoHelp) binds property translateX to a value based on the width of the scene (scene.width) and its own width (piano-Help.layoutBounds.width). Property layoutBounds defines the rectangular dimensions of a node.

The Help window has rounded corners (arcWidth and arcHeight), a drop shadow, and a linear gradient. The Help window's Text component has center alignment, a drop shadow, and property wrappingWidth defined. The content property is set to helpText.

Listing 6.14 Piano—Step 5: Final Build—Part 2

```
// the Help window scene graph nodes
pianoHelp = Group {
    // center the group horizontally
    layoutY: 290
    translateX: bind (scene.width - pianoHelp.layoutBounds.width) / 2
    content: [
        Rectangle {
            width: 500
            height: 130
            arcWidth: 10
            arcHeight: 10
            fill: LinearGradient {
                startX: 1
                startY: 0
                endX: 1
                endY: 1
                stops: [
                    Stop {
                        offset: 0
                        color: Color.LIGHTSLATEGREY }
                    Stop {
                        offset: 1
                        color: Color.DARKGRAY }
                ]
            }
            effect: DropShadow { }
        },
        Text {
            wrappingWidth: 495
            fill: Color.YELLOW
            textAlignment: TextAlignment.CENTER
            font: Font {
                name: "Serif"
                size: 20
            }
            effect: DropShadow {
                offsetX: 2
                offsetY: 2
                radius: 6
                color: Color.BLACK
            }
            x: 40
            y: 45
            content: helpText
        } // Text
    ]
}
```

Listing 6.15 shows the updated Stage and scene graph for the Piano application. The scene now has a linear gradient (from `Color.LIGHTSLATEGRAY` to `Color.LIGHTSTEELBLUE`) and the Flow layout component includes the title Text node. The Flow layout component centers its contents by setting property hPos to `HPos.CENTER`.

Listing 6.15 Piano—Step 5: Final Build—Part 3

```
Stage {
    . . .
    scene: scene = Scene {
        width: 560
        height: 450
        fill: LinearGradient {
            startX: 1
            startY: 0
            endX: 1
            endY: 1
            stops: [
                Stop {
                    offset: 0
                    color: Color.LIGHTSLATEGRAY
                },
                Stop {
                    offset: 1
                    color: Color.LIGHTSTEELBLUE
                }
            ]
        }
        content: [
            Flow {
                translateX: bind (scene.width-pianoHelp.layoutBounds.width)/2+ 3
                layoutY: 20
                vertical: true
                vGap: 20
                hPos: HPos.CENTER
                height: 420
                content: [
                    Text {
                        fill: Color.YELLOW
                        textAlignment: TextAlignment.CENTER
                        font: Font {
                            name: "Serif"
                            size: 24
                        }
                        effect: DropShadow {
                            offsetX: 2
                            offsetY: 2
                            radius: 6
                            color: Color.BLACK
                        }
                        content: "Welcome to the Piano"
```

```
                        } // Text
                        Group {
                            content: pianoKeys
                        }
                        HBox { // Layout for the buttons
                            spacing: 30
                            content: [ . . . (4 SwingButton components) . . . ]
                        }// HBox
                    ]
                } // Flow
                Text { // Display the notes
                    layoutY: 250
                    wrappingWidth: bind scene.width - 100
                    . . .
                }
                pianoHelp
            ]
        }
}
```

6.6 Source Code for Project Piano

Listing 6.16 through Listing 6.19 shows the complete code for the final version of Project Piano.

Listing 6.16 shows the source code for class PianoKey, which extends CustomNode. Recall that the JavaFX CustomNode class enables programmers to insert custom nodes into the scene graph. Note that class PianoKey is abstract, since it does not provide an implementation of function create (subclasses BlackKey and WhiteKey provide their own versions).

Listing 6.16 PianoKey.fx

```
package piano;

import javafx.scene.CustomNode;
import noteplayer.SingleNote;

public abstract class PianoKey extends CustomNode {
    public-init var xOffset: Number;
    public-init var yOffset: Number;
    public-init var note: Integer;
    public-init var keyText: String;
    public-init var synthNote: SingleNote;
    protected var showKeyPress = false;

    public function noteOn(): String {
```

```
            showPress();
            synthNote.noteOn(note);
            return keyText;
        }
        public function noteOff(): Void {
            synthNote.noteOff(note);
            clearPress();
        }

        public function showPress(): Void {
            showKeyPress = true;
        }
        public function clearPress(): Void {
            showKeyPress = false;
        }
}
```

Listing 6.17 shows the source code for class WhiteKey, a subclass of PianoKey. WhiteKey consists of a Rectangle and an overlaying Circle that is visible with certain mouse events. It uses color gradients for its fill attribute and a drop shadow effect around the node.

Listing 6.17 WhiteKey.fx

```
package piano;

import javafx.scene.Cursor;
import javafx.scene.effect.DropShadow;
import javafx.scene.Group;
import javafx.scene.input.MouseEvent;
import javafx.scene.Node;
import javafx.scene.paint.*;
import javafx.scene.shape.Circle;
import javafx.scene.shape.Rectangle;

public class WhiteKey extends PianoKey {
    def keyFill = LinearGradient {
        startX: .5
        startY: 1
        endX: 1
        endY: 1
        stops: [
            Stop {
                offset: 0
                color: Color.WHITE }
            Stop {
                offset: 1
                color: Color.LIGHTGREY }
        ]
    };
```

```
def circleFill = RadialGradient {
    centerX: 0.5        // 0.5 centers the gradient along the x axis
    centerY: 0.5        // 0.5 centers the gradient along the y axis
    radius: 0.5         // the radius of the gradient
    stops: [
        Stop {
            offset: 0
            color: Color.WHITE }
        Stop {
            offset: 1
            color: Color.DODGERBLUE }
    ]
};

protected override function create(): Node {
    return Group {
        cursor: Cursor.HAND
        effect: DropShadow { }
        onMouseEntered: function(e: MouseEvent): Void {
            showPress();
        }
        onMouseExited: function(e: MouseEvent): Void {
            clearPress();
        }
        content: [
            // White Key Rectangle
            Rectangle {
                x: xOffset
                y: yOffset
                width: 35
                height: 112.5
                arcWidth: 10
                arcHeight: 10
                stroke: Color.BLACK
                strokeWidth: 1
                fill: keyFill
            }, // Rectangle
            Circle {
                radius: 10
                centerX: xOffset + 18
                centerY: yOffset + 90
                visible: bind showKeyPress
                fill: circleFill
            } // Circle
        ]
    } // Group
}
}
```

Listing 6.18 shows the source code for class BlackKey, also a subclass of PianoKey. BlackKey consists of a Rectangle and an overlaying Circle visible with certain mouse events. It uses color gradients for its `fill` attribute.

Listing 6.18 BlackKey.fx

```
package piano;

import javafx.scene.Cursor;
import javafx.scene.Group;
import javafx.scene.input.MouseEvent;
import javafx.scene.Node;
import javafx.scene.paint.*;
import javafx.scene.shape.Circle;
import javafx.scene.shape.Rectangle;

public class BlackKey extends PianoKey {
    def keyFill = LinearGradient {
        startX: 0
        startY: 1
        endX: .5
        endY: 1
        stops: [
         Stop {
            offset: 0
            color: Color.BURLYWOOD }
          Stop {
            offset: 1
            color: Color.BLACK }
        ]
    };
    def circleFill = RadialGradient {
        centerX: 0.5
        centerY: 0.5
        radius: 0.5
        stops: [
            Stop {
                offset: 0
                color: Color.WHITESMOKE }
            Stop {
                offset: 1
                color: Color.ORANGE }
        ]
    };

    protected override function create(): Node {
        return Group {
            cursor: Cursor.HAND
            onMouseEntered: function(e: MouseEvent): Void {
                showPress();
            }
```

```
                onMouseExited: function(e: MouseEvent): Void {
                    clearPress();
                }
                content: [
                    Rectangle {
                        x: 20 + xOffset
                        y: yOffset
                        width: 22
                        height: 65
                        arcWidth: 10
                        arcHeight: 10
                        stroke: Color.BLACK
                        strokeWidth: 1
                        fill: keyFill
                    }, // Rectangle
                    // Circle shows up when a key is pressed or a note is played
                    Circle {
                        radius: 7
                        centerX: xOffset + 31
                        centerY: yOffset + 43
                        visible: bind showKeyPress
                        fill: circleFill
                    } // Circle
                ]
            } // Group
        }
    }
```

Listing 6.19 shows the code for **Piano.fx**, the main program in the Piano application.

Listing 6.19 Piano.fx (Main Program)

```
package piano;

import javafx.animation.KeyFrame;
import javafx.animation.Timeline;
import javafx.animation.transition.FadeTransition;
import javafx.ext.swing.SwingButton;
import javafx.geometry.HPos;
import javafx.lang.FX;
import javafx.scene.effect.DropShadow;
import javafx.scene.Group;
import javafx.scene.input.MouseEvent;
import javafx.scene.layout.Flow;
import javafx.scene.layout.HBox;
import javafx.scene.paint.Color;
import javafx.scene.paint.LinearGradient;
import javafx.scene.paint.Stop;
import javafx.scene.Scene;
import javafx.scene.shape.Rectangle;
import javafx.scene.text.Font;
```

```
import javafx.scene.text.Text;
import javafx.scene.text.TextAlignment;
import javafx.stage.Stage;
import noteplayer.SingleNote;
import piano.BlackKey;
import piano.PianoKey;
import piano.WhiteKey;

 // Application with a two-octave keyboard, Text component,
 // and buttons that let you play notes stored in the note buffer
 // Additional code added to implement Help window,
 // center components, add gradients, add title

var singleNote = SingleNote {
};
var notesPlayed: String;

def pianoNotes = ["F","G","A","B","C","D","E","F","G","A","B","C","D","E"];
def noteValues = [53,55,57,59,60,62,64,65,67,69,71,72,74,76];

// put a black key after these white key index numbers
def blackKeyIndex = [0, 1, 2, 4, 5, 7, 8, 9, 11, 12];

def helpText = "Play: You will hear a short tune which you can Stop."
"\nYou can also play arbitrary notes using the mouse."
"\nYour notes will be added to the play buffer."
"\nClear Notes: clears the play buffer.";
var helpLabel = " Hide Help ";
var scene: Scene;
var pianoHelp: Group;
var pianoKeys: PianoKey[] = for (i in [0..<sizeof pianoNotes])
    WhiteKey {
        xOffset: i * 35 + 30
        yOffset: 25
        note: noteValues[i]
        keyText: "{pianoNotes[i]} "
        synthNote: singleNote
        onMousePressed: function (e: MouseEvent): Void {
            // concatenate new note played with buffer
            notesPlayed = "{notesPlayed}{(e.node as PianoKey).noteOn()}";
            // remember which piano key was played
            insert (e.node as PianoKey) into noteSeq;
        }
        onMouseReleased: function(e: MouseEvent): Void {
            (e.node as PianoKey).noteOff();
        }
    }

def blackKeys = for (i in blackKeyIndex)
    BlackKey {
        xOffset: i * 35 + 30
        yOffset: 25
```

```
            note: noteValues[i] + 1
            keyText: "{pianoNotes[i]}#/{pianoNotes[i+1]}b "
            synthNote: singleNote
            blocksMouse: true
            onMousePressed: function (e: MouseEvent): Void {
                e.node.effect = DropShadow { };
                // concatenate new note played with buffer
                notesPlayed = "{notesPlayed}{(e.node as PianoKey).noteOn()}";
                // remember which piano key was played
                insert (e.node as PianoKey) into noteSeq;
            }
            onMouseReleased: function(e: MouseEvent): Void {
                e.node.effect = null;
                (e.node as PianoKey).noteOff();
            }
        }
    }
//Add the blackKeys to the PianoKeys
pianoKeys = [pianoKeys, blackKeys];

// Code to save the notes in a note buffer
// and to play the notes in the note buffer
// setup to play some notes
var noteSeq: PianoKey[];
var noteSeqIndex = 0;

// "Twinkle, Twinkle, Litter Star"
noteSeq = for (i in [4,4,8,8,9,9,8,8,7,7,6,6,5,5,4]) pianoKeys[i];

var notesTimeline = Timeline {
    repeatCount: bind sizeof noteSeq
    keyFrames: [
        KeyFrame {
            time: 0s
            action: function(): Void {
                notesPlayed = "{notesPlayed}{noteSeq[noteSeqIndex].noteOn()} ";
            }
        }
        KeyFrame {
            time: .5s
            action: function(): Void {
                noteSeq[noteSeqIndex].noteOff();
                noteSeqIndex++;
            }
        }
    ]
}

function stopPlay(): Void {
    notesPlayed = "";
    notesTimeline.stop();
    if (noteSeqIndex < sizeof noteSeq)
    noteSeq[noteSeqIndex].noteOff();
```

```
        noteSeqIndex = 0;
}

// the Help window scene graph nodes
pianoHelp = Group {
    // center the group horizontally
    layoutY: 290
    translateX: bind (scene.width - pianoHelp.layoutBounds.width) / 2
    content: [
        Rectangle {
            width: 500
            height: 130
            arcWidth: 10
            arcHeight: 10
            fill: LinearGradient {
                startX: 1
                startY: 0
                endX: 1
                endY: 1
                stops: [
                    Stop {
                        offset: 0
                        color: Color.LIGHTSLATEGREY
                    },
                    Stop {
                        offset: 1
                        color: Color.DARKGRAY
                    }
                ]
            }
            effect: DropShadow{
            };
        },
        Text {
            wrappingWidth: 495
            fill: Color.YELLOW
            textAlignment: TextAlignment.CENTER
            font: Font {
                name: "Serif"
                size: 20
            }
            effect: DropShadow {
                offsetX: 2
                offsetY: 2
                radius: 6
                color: Color.BLACK
            }
            x: 40
            y: 25
            content: helpText
        } // Text
    ]
```

```
}

def fadeHelp = FadeTransition {
    duration: 1.5s
    node: pianoHelp
    fromValue: 1.0
    toValue: 0.0
    repeatCount: 1
    rate: -1
}

Stage {
    title: "Piano"
    onClose: function() {
        singleNote.close();    // close the synthesizer
        FX.exit();
    }
    scene:
    scene = Scene {
        width: 560
        height: 450
        fill: LinearGradient {
            startX: 1
            startY: 0
            endX: 1
            endY: 1
            stops: [
                Stop {
                    offset: 0
                    color: Color.LIGHTSLATEGRAY
                },
                Stop {
                    offset: 1
                    color: Color.LIGHTSTEELBLUE
                }
            ]
        }
        content: [
            Flow {
                translateX: bind (scene.width-pianoHelp.layoutBounds.width)/2+ 3
                layoutY: 20
                vertical: true
                vGap: 20
                hPos: HPos.CENTER
                height: 420
                content: [
                    Text {
                        fill: Color.YELLOW
                        textAlignment: TextAlignment.CENTER
                        font: Font {
                            name: "Serif"
                            size: 24
```

```
                }
            effect: DropShadow {
                offsetX: 2
                offsetY: 2
                radius: 6
                color: Color.BLACK
            }
            content: "Welcome to the Piano"
        }  // Text
        Group {
            content: pianoKeys
        }
        HBox { // Layout for the buttons
            spacing: 30
            content: [
                SwingButton {
                    text: "Clear Notes"
                    action: function() {
                        stopPlay();
                        delete noteSeq;
                    }
                }  // SwingButton
                SwingButton {
                    text: "Play"
                    action: function() {
                        stopPlay();
                        notesTimeline.playFromStart();
                    }
                }  // SwingButton
                SwingButton {
                    text: "Stop"
                    action: function() {
                        stopPlay();
                    }
                }  // SwingButton
                SwingButton {
                    text: bind helpLabel
                    action: function() {
                        fadeHelp.rate = (fadeHelp.rate * - 1);
                        fadeHelp.play();
                        helpLabel = if (helpLabel == "Show Help")
                                " Hide Help " else "Show Help";
                    }
                }  // SwingButton
            ]
        }// HBox

    ]
}
Text { // Display the notes
    layoutY: 250
    layoutX: 50
```

```
                wrappingWidth: bind scene.width - 100
                font: Font {
                    size: 18
                }
                content: bind notesPlayed
            }
            pianoHelp
        ]
    }
}
```

7 Animation

If the scene graph is the central metaphor in JavaFX for specifying graphical objects, then animation is its metaphor for doing things. Animation is the heart and soul of JavaFX. Simply, it brings objects to life. With animation, you give motion to the JavaFX scene graph.

JavaFX provides a rich palette for animation. With Timelines, you can build just about any animation you need. Timelines provide a range of properties that let you specify how an object's properties might change over time. With binding, you can manipulate script-level variables that consequently change an object's bound properties. Timelines also let you specify interpolators, rate, time, repeat count, new values, and actions. You can even nest timelines and create recursive timeline calls.

With all this flexibility, you might conclude that timelines are complicated to use—especially if you simply want to fade, rotate, or scale an object. To address the more common animations that apply to graphical objects, JavaFX offers specialized time-lines called transitions. These specialized animations use timelines, making it easy to apply common transition-based animations to graphical objects. It's also possible to combine transitions either sequentially or in parallel.

In this chapter, you'll first look at Timeline objects (the basis for all JavaFX anima-tions). Next, you'll see how to build simple animations that change an object's prop-erty. You'll then explore commonly used Timeline properties to build more intricate animations. Finally, you'll see how transitions let you build animations easily.

What You Will Learn

- Using Timelines for animation and code execution
- Using KeyFrame objects to define effective Timelines
- Manipulating node variables within KeyFrame objects
- Controlling animation with interpolators
- Using basic Timeline properties such as `repeatCount` and `autoReverse`
- Animating target variables independently

- Animating composite scene graph nodes (Groups)
- Using Timeline actions
- Using Transitions to move, scale, fade, and rotate scene graph nodes
- Animating graphical nodes along a path with PathTransitions
- Building compound transitions with ParallelTransition and SequentialTransition

7.1 Timelines

JavaFX Node property variables, when changed, automatically update the scene graph. Therefore, if you change a property's value, the scene automatically reflects the transformed node. Common node properties for animation are `translateX` and `translateY` to move a node in the x or y direction, `scaleX` and `scaleY` to scale a node in the x or y direction, and `rotate`, to rotate a node about its center to a new orientation. However, you can animate any writable node property. To animate objects, then, you simply manipulate property values with timelines.

You can also animate properties of a node by binding target properties to script-level variables. You then manipulate these script-level variables with timelines, too.

A Timeline is a sequence of KeyFrame objects that the timeline processes. Each KeyFrame specifies a time offset (property `time`) within the timeline that animations should take place. KeyFrames contain a sequence of KeyValue objects (property `values`) or a function (property `action`) or both. Table 7.1 lists the KeyFrame properties.

TABLE 7.1 KeyFrame Properties

Property	Type	Description
time	Duration	The time offset within a single cycle of a Timeline at which the associated `values` will be set and at which the `action` function will be called.
values	KeyValue[]	The list of target variables and the desired values they should interpolate at the time offset of this KeyFrame. `Interpolator.LINEAR` is default.
action	function():Void	A function that is called when the time cursor passes the specified time offset of this KeyFrame.

TABLE 7.1 KeyFrame Properties *(Continued)*

Property	Type	Description
canSkip	Boolean	Defines whether or not the action function can be skipped if the master timer gets behind and more than one Timeline cycles are skipped between time pulses.
timelines	Timeline[]	A list of sub-timelines that will be started when the time cursor passes the specified time offset of this KeyFrame.

Timeline objects are meant to be flexible to fit different animation scenarios with properties and functions that let you manipulate their behavior. For example, property rate controls the basic timing. When rate is 1 (this is the default), the timeline runs at normal speed forward through the sequence of KeyFrames. If rate is -1, it runs at normal speed in reverse. A rate of 2 runs the timeline twice as fast. Table 7.2 lists some of the more common Timeline properties.

TABLE 7.2 Common Timeline Properties

Property	Type	Description
autoReverse	Boolean	If true, timeline reverses direction on alternating cycles
repeatCount	Integer	Number of cycles in this timeline
keyFrames	KeyFrame[]	The sequence of KeyFrames in this animation
paused	Boolean	Read-only variable that is true when timeline is paused
running	Boolean	Read-only variable that is true when timeline is running (even if paused)
rate	Number	The direction/speed at which timeline is expected to play (negative rate reverses direction)
currentRate	Number	Read-only variable that indicates current direction/speed that the timeline is playing
time	Duration	The current value of this timeline's time cursor

Table 7.3 shows the JavaFX timeline functions. Function play starts the animation at its current position. You can pause an animation (function pause) and play will restart the animation at the point in the cycle it was paused. Function stop stops the timeline and resets its position to the beginning. Function playFromStart starts the timeline at the beginning of the timeline cycle.

TABLE 7.3 Timeline Functions

Function	Description
play	Start or resume the timeline. If the timeline is running and paused, play resumes at the place in the timeline cycle where it was paused. If the timeline was previously stopped, play resumes at the beginning of the timeline cycle. Timeline property running is true.
playFromStart	Start the timeline from the beginning of the timeline cycle. Timeline property running is true.
pause	Pause the timeline. Timeline property running is true and property paused is true.
stop	Stop the timeline. Timeline property running is false.

Animation Basics—Moving an Object

Let's show you a simple animation that moves a circle across the scene, as shown in Figure 7.1. When the application first comes up, the circle is on the left and immediately begins moving slowly to the right. After three seconds, animation stops and the circle remains on the right side.

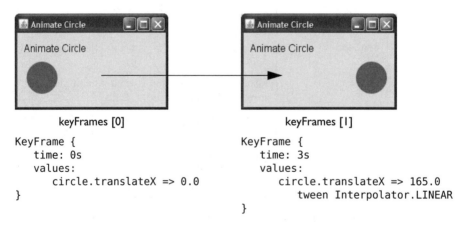

```
        keyFrames [0]                           keyFrames [1]
KeyFrame {                              KeyFrame {
    time: 0s                               time: 3s
    values:                                values:
        circle.translateX => 0.0               circle.translateX => 165.0
}                                                  tween Interpolator.LINEAR
                                       }
```

Figure 7.1 Timelines consists of a sequence of KeyFrame objects

For this example, the timeline includes two KeyFrame objects. The first (keyFrames[0]) specifies time offset 0s (0 seconds). Property values sets target variable circle.translateX to 0. This is the starting point.

JavaFX Node Properties

JavaFX nodes include properties that let you apply transformations to the node. Property translateX *specifies how far you move a node in the x direction within the scene. Thus, target variable* circle.translateX *controls x-direction movement for object* circle.

The second KeyFrame object (keyFrames[1]) specifies time offset 3s (three seconds into the timeline cycle). At this time offset, target variable circle.translateX will be 165.0. Operator tween specifies the type of interpolator. With linear interpolation (Interpolator.LINEAR), target variable circle.translateX takes on succeeding values (between 0 and 165.0) with a constant rate of increase. (See Table 7.4 on page 211 for the JavaFX built-in interpolators.)

Interpolation

Interpolation is used to calculate intermediary values between two known end points. In JavaFX animation, interpolation provides the intermediary values between a value in one Key-Frame and a value in the next KeyFrame. The actual intermediary values depend on the interpolator used. JavaFX default interpolation is linear, providing a set of intermediary values with a constant rate of increase (or decrease).

Listing 7.1 shows the timeline that provides the animation shown in Figure 7.1. Object circle includes property translateX, a property common to all graphical nodes. Property translateX lets you move an object in the x direction (it represents the x-direction *change* of the object from its original position). The Circle's position changes in the scene as translateX changes. Note that circle property translateX's default value is 0.0; it's not necessary to provide an initial value in circle's declaration.

The timeline is an object literal and is invoked with Timeline function play. This starts the timeline as soon as the application is fully initialized. Two KeyFrames specify how target variable circle.translateX should change.

Listing 7.1 Using Timeline to animate a Circle

```
def circle: Circle = Circle {
    centerX: 40
    centerY: 70
    radius: 25
    fill: Color.SEAGREEN
}

Timeline {
    keyFrames: [
        KeyFrame {
            time: 0s
```

```
                values: circle.translateX => 0.0
            }
        KeyFrame {
            time: 3s
                values: circle.translateX => 165.0 tween Interpolator.LINEAR
        }
    ]
}.play();

. . .
scene: Scene {
    . . .
    content: circle
}
. . .
```

Our initial animation example moves the circle across the scene and stops. We can have the circle return to its original location by including property autoReverse (set to true) and repeatCount (set to 2). Property autoReverse makes the timeline run in reverse automatically. Property repeatCount specifies how many times the timeline should play. Note that a play in reverse counts as one cycle, so repeatCount must be at least 2 for autoReverse to have an effect.

```
Timeline {
    autoReverse: true
    repeatCount: 2
        . . .
}
```

With this modification, the circle moves to the position on the right, returns to its original position, and stops. To move the circle back and forth indefinitely, set repeatCount to Timeline.INDEFINITE. A second modification that makes the animation more realistic is to specify Interpolator.EASEBOTH. This starts the animation slowly, ramps up to "normal" speed, then eases up at the end of the cycle. Listing 7.2 shows the new timeline, with these changes in bold.

Listing 7.2 Moving the Circle back and forth indefinitely

```
Timeline {
    autoReverse: true
    repeatCount: Timeline.INDEFINITE
     keyFrames: [
        KeyFrame {
            time: 0s
                values: circle.translateX => 0.0
        }
        KeyFrame {
            time: 3s
                values: circle.translateX => 165.0 tween Interpolator.EASEBOTH
```

```
       }
    ]
}.play();
```

Table 7.4 shows the JavaFX built-in timeline interpolators.

TABLE 7.4 Built-In JavaFX Timeline Interpolators

Interpolator	Description
DISCRETE	Provides discrete (no intermediary values are used) behavior
LINEAR	Provides intermediary values that are linear (constant rate of change)
EASEIN	Starts out slowly and ramps up to the "normal" rate
EASEOUT	Constant (linear rate of change) but slows down near the end of the frame
EASEBOTH	Eases at both the beginning and end of the frame

Animating Multiple Targets

You can animate more than one target variable in a KeyFrame by using sequence notation [ ] for multiple target variables. In this next example, we grow the circle as it moves by animating Node properties scaleX and scaleY. The circle grows in both x and y directions by a scale factor of 2. By using the same KeyFrame objects, both animations complete at the same time. Listing 7.3 shows the updated code.

Listing 7.3 Animate Multiple Targets

```
def circle: Circle = Circle {
    centerX: 40
    centerY: 70
    radius: 25
    fill: Color.SEAGREEN
}

Timeline {
    autoReverse: true
    repeatCount: Timeline.INDEFINITE
    keyFrames: [
        KeyFrame {
            time: 0s
            values: [circle.translateX => 0.0, circle.scaleX => 1,
                    circle.scaleY => 1]
        }
        KeyFrame {
            time: 3s
            values: [circle.translateX => 165.0 tween Interpolator.EASEBOTH,
```

```
                circle.scaleX => 2 tween Interpolator.EASEBOTH,
                circle.scaleY => 2 tween Interpolator.EASEBOTH]
        }
    ]
}.play();
```

Animation Tip

Use a single timeline when you want to specify changes that complete their cycles at the same time with the same basic timeline properties (`rate`*, *`autoReverse`*, *`repeatCount`*).*

Animating Multiple Targets Independently

Sometimes you want to animate properties of the same object, but you want the properties to change independently. In this case, use separate timelines. This lets you define KeyFrames that give a different time cycle to each animation. Separate timelines also let you define Timeline properties, such as `repeatCount`, independently.

To illustrate animating multiple targets independently, let's use three timelines: one to animate the circle in the x direction, one to animate it in the y direction, and a third to grow and shrink the circle. Figure 7.2 shows two frames from this example. The circle moves in both directions and also grows and shrinks, all with different cycle times.

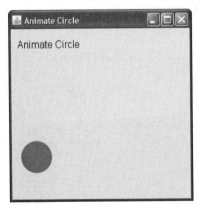 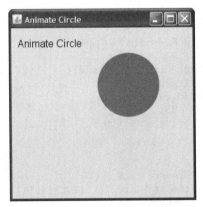

Figure 7.2 Moving the circle in both directions while growing and shrinking

Listing 7.4 shows the Circle animation code with three timelines. As the circle grows, it appears to move closer to the viewer. As it shrinks, it appears to move away. This gives the application a three-dimensional effect.

Here, we also use a shorthand notation to define the KeyFrame objects. Since defining KeyFrame object literals with target variables is common, JavaFX accepts a shorter form using keyword at. This shorthand notation is equivalent to the more verbose KeyFrame object literals shown in Listing 7.1 through Listing 7.3.

Listing 7.4 Independent Animations

```
def circle = Circle { . . . (unchanged) . . . }

// Move the circle in the x direction
Timeline {
    autoReverse: true
    repeatCount: Timeline.INDEFINITE
    keyFrames: [
        at (0s) { circle.translateX => 0.0 }
        at (3s) { circle.translateX => 165.0 tween Interpolator.EASEBOTH }
    ]
}.play();

// Move the circle in the y direction
Timeline {
    autoReverse: true
    repeatCount: Timeline.INDEFINITE
    keyFrames: [
        at (0s) { circle.translateY => 0.0 }
        at (2s) { circle.translateY => 130.0 tween Interpolator.EASEBOTH }
    ]
}.play();

// Grow and shrink (scale) the circle
Timeline {
    autoReverse: true
    repeatCount: Timeline.INDEFINITE
    keyFrames: [
        at (0s) { circle.scaleX => 1 }
        at (0s) { circle.scaleY => 1 }
        at (2.5s) { circle.scaleX => 2 tween Interpolator.EASEBOTH }
        at (2.5s) { circle.scaleY => 2 tween Interpolator.EASEBOTH }
    ]
}.play();
```

Animation Tip

Use separate timelines when you want to animate target variables independently. Usually animating objects in two dimensions (both x and y directions) requires two timelines unless both dimensions are equal and you want the rate of change to be exactly the same.

Animating Groups

You can learn much about how JavaFX shapes behave by grouping nodes together and animating the group. This next example does just that. You'll build on the last example and add a rotation to the circle. In order to see the effect, you'll add a Text component to the scene graph and bundle the Circle and Text components together in a Group. You want both the Circle and Text components to rotate together. In addition, you'll apply a radial gradient to the Circle. As the "group" rotates, both the Circle and Text spin together. You'll also maintain the previous animations. In order for both the Circle and Text to transform uniformly, you'll apply all animations to the parent Group node.

Figure 7.3 shows two frames from this example. Note that as the Circle moves, grows, and rotates, the Text component is likewise moving, growing and rotating.

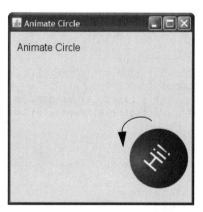

Figure 7.3 Rotating both the Text and Circle requires an enclosing Group node

Listing 7.5 shows the modified scene graph to implement this animated Group. First, the Circle fill property includes a radial gradient so that you can see rotation effects on the Circle. Next, we define Group group, which includes both the previously defined Circle and a Text object literal.

The Text component is centered within the Circle. Because the Text is part of the same enclosing group, it will also move, rotate, and grow with the Circle.

Listing 7.5 Modified Scene Graph for the Animating Group

```
def circle: Circle = Circle {
    centerX: 40
    centerY: 70
```

```
        radius: 25
        fill: RadialGradient {
            centerX: 0.25
            centerY: 0.25
            radius: 1                   // the radius of the gradient
            stops: [
                Stop {
                    offset: 0
                    color: Color.SEAGREEN
                }
                Stop {
                    offset: 1
                    color: Color.BLACK
                }
            ]
        }
    }

    def group: Group = Group {
        content: [
            circle,                     // defined above
            Text {
                fill: Color.WHITE
                font: Font {
                    size: 18
                }
                x: 28
                y: 75
                content: "Hi!"
            }
        ]
    }
```

Listing 7.6 shows the modified timelines. The timelines that control both the x and y direction movement now specify variables group.translateX and group.translateY to reflect the new animation target. This is the only change required to implement moving the group instead of the circle.

The timeline that controls scaling of the Group component manipulates Node properties group.scaleX and group.scaleY. These variables are 1 (no change from the original size) at startup and become 2 (doubling the node's size in both directions) using Interpolator.EASEBOTH. The same timeline animates rotation by manipulating Node variable group.rotate, starting at value 0 (no rotation) and becoming 360 (full circle rotation).

This timeline plays in reverse automatically and repeats indefinitely. This means the Circle first rotates clockwise as the Circle grows, then counter-clockwise as the Circle shrinks. (Note that to make the rotation continuously clockwise without reversing, you must create a separate timeline for the rotation and set autoReverse to false.)

Listing 7.6 Modified Timelines for the Animating Group

```
// Move the group in the x direction
Timeline {
    autoReverse: true
    repeatCount: Timeline.INDEFINITE
    keyFrames: [
        at (0s) { group.translateX => 0.0 }
        at (3s) { group.translateX => 165.0 tween Interpolator.EASEBOTH }
    ]
}.play();

// Move the group in the y direction
Timeline {
    autoReverse: true
    repeatCount: Timeline.INDEFINITE
    keyFrames: [
        at (0s) { group.translateY => 0.0 }
        at (2s) { group.translateY => 130.0 tween Interpolator.EASEBOTH }
    ]
}.play();

// Modified timeline to both scale and rotate the Group
Timeline {
    autoReverse: true
    repeatCount: Timeline.INDEFINITE
    keyFrames: [
        at (0s) { group.scaleX => 1 }
        at (0s) { group.scaleY => 1 }
        at (0s) { group.rotate => 0 }
        at (2.5s) { group.scaleX =>2.0 tween Interpolator.EASEBOTH }
        at (2.5s) { group.scaleY => 2.0 tween Interpolator.EASEBOTH }
        at (2.5s) { group.rotate => 360 tween Interpolator.EASEBOTH }
    ]
}.play();
```

Animation and Binding

The examples you've seen so far include Timelines that animate a single node. You can easily construct KeyFrame objects that directly manipulate properties of that node such as scaleX or rotate. Let's now build a timeline that simultaneously animates multiple nodes. To do this, you construct script-level variables that become the target for KeyFrame animations and bind their node properties to these script-level variables.

For this example, you'll animate two circles. The first circle (circle1) changes its fill color to several target colors defined in separate KeyFrame objects. The second circle (circle2) changes its stroke color using the same timeline. Both circles fade out as the final KeyFrame manipulation. Figure 7.4 shows two frames in this animation sequence.

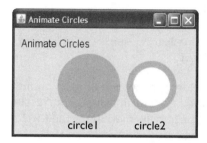 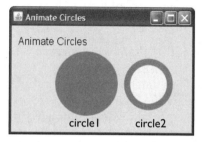

Figure 7.4 Binding variables lets you easily animate multiple objects

Listing 7.7 shows the script-level target variables (circleColor, circleOpacity) controlled by the timeline and the circles with properties that bind to these target variables. Circle circle1 binds property fill to circleColor and opacity to circleOpacity. Circle circle2 binds property stroke to circleColor and opacity to circleOpacity.

Listing 7.7 Binding node properties to script-level variables

```
var circleColor: Color = Color.YELLOW;
var circleOpacity = 1.0;

def circle1: Circle = Circle {
    centerX: 120
    centerY: 90
    radius: 50
    fill: bind circleColor
    opacity: bind circleOpacity
}

def circle2: Circle = Circle {
    centerX: 220
    centerY: 90
    radius: 35
    stroke: bind circleColor
    strokeWidth: 10
    fill: Color.WHITE
    opacity: bind circleOpacity
}

. . .
    scene: Scene {
        content: [ Text { . . . }, circle1, circle2 ]
```

```
    }
. . .
```

Listing 7.8 shows the timeline that manipulates the Circle nodes. This timeline uses the shorthand notation to specify target variables. Variable `circleColor` starts at `Color.Yellow`, becomes `Color.ORANGE` at four seconds, `Color.RED` at eight seconds, and finishes at `Color.BLACK` at ten seconds. Variable `circleOpacity` starts out at 1.0 and diminishes to 0.0 between time slices (`10s`) and (`14s`).

Note that this timeline includes multiple KeyFrame objects (not just two). Without the intermediary KeyFrames, variable `circleColor` would transform from `Color.YELLOW` to `Color.BLACK`, resulting in a completely different color transformation for the Circle nodes.

This timeline is different than the previous examples because it manipulates script-level variables instead of node properties directly. With this approach, you apply animation to objects by binding their properties to the script-level variables.

Listing 7.8 Timeline that targets script-level variables

```
Timeline {
    autoReverse: true
    repeatCount: Timeline.INDEFINITE
    keyFrames: [
        at (0s) { circleColor => Color.YELLOW tween Interpolator.EASEBOTH }
        at (4s) { circleColor => Color.ORANGE tween Interpolator.EASEBOTH }
        at (8s) { circleColor => Color.RED tween Interpolator.EASEBOTH }
        at (10s) { circleOpacity => 1.0 }
        at (10s) { circleColor => Color.BLACK tween Interpolator.EASEBOTH }
        at (14s) { circleOpacity => 0.0 tween Interpolator.EASEBOTH }
    ]
}.play();
```

7.2 Timeline Actions

The previous animation examples all involve manipulating scene graph node properties (directly or with binding) to achieve change. You can also use timelines to execute code with the Timeline `action` property.

Using action with a Digital Clock Display

This example creates a timeline that calls a function every second. The function in turn uses the JavaFX DateTime class (new with JavaFX 1.2) to update a script-level String variable. The Text component's `content` property is bound to the String variable, updating a digital clock display every second. `Timeline.INDEFINITE` for the Timeline's `repeatCount` property keeps the clock running indefinitely. Figure 7.5 shows the digital clock running.

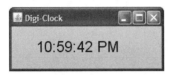

Figure 7.5 Timelines providing periodic updates

Listing 7.9 shows the timeline and function `updateTime`. The function you specify with property `action` must return Void and have no arguments. You can either name the function (as shown in Listing 7.9) or specify an anonymous function as follows.

```
action: function() {
    // statements here
}
```

Function `updateTime` instantiates a DateTime object (variable `temp`). DateTime property `instant` holds the time at which it was created. A call to `java.text.DateFormat` formats the time as `hh:mm:ss AM/PM` (`DateFormat.MEDIUM`). `DateFormat` returns the formatted String, which is stored in script-level variable `dTime`.

This timeline needs only one KeyFrame object with `time` set to `1s` and property `action` set to the function name `updateTime`. The `canSkip` property (set to `true`) permits the runtime to skip a call to the action function (`updateTime`) if the master timer gets behind. In this case, only one call to `updateTime` is made for each time pulse, regardless of how many cycles have occurred since the last time pulse was processed.

The Text object `content` property binds to variable `dTime` to dynamically update the digital clock display.

Listing 7.9 Digital Clock Timeline

```
var dTime: String;

function updateTime(): Void {
    var temp = DateTime { }
    dTime = DateFormat.getTimeInstance(DateFormat.MEDIUM).format(temp.instant);
}

Timeline {
    repeatCount: Timeline.INDEFINITE
    keyFrames: [
        KeyFrame {
```

```
            time: 1s
            canSkip: true
            action: updateTime
        }
    ]
}.play();
. . .

    Text {
        font: Font {
            size: 24
        }
        x: 40
        y: 40
        content: bind dTime
    }
. . .
```

Using action with a Progress Bar

Another common use for periodic updates is a progress bar.[1] Progress bars provide a visual display reflecting the progress of a running task. This example includes a progress bar that is hidden at startup (property opacity is 0), as shown in scenario 1 of Figure 7.6. To begin, the user clicks the rectangle area. The progress bar fades in and the timeline starts (scenario 2). The user can toggle the timeline status to pause and resume progress bar updates (scenario 3). Finally, when the progress bar reaches 100% completion, the timeline stops and the progress bar fades out (scenario 4). In reality, you would tie a progress bar to some lengthy task; here, progress is simply tied to an incrementing counter variable.

---

1. JavaFX includes two different progress bar components (see Listing 5.1 on page 132 for an example using both components). It is nevertheless instructive to see how these might be implemented.

(1) At startup: Progress Bar is hidden

(2) Starting: Progress Bar is updating

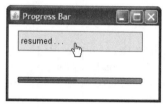

(3) Resumed: Progress Bar is updating
again after a pause

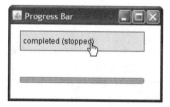

(4) At completion: Progress Bar is fading

Figure 7.6 Progress Bar reflects periodic updating

Listing 7.10 shows the ProgressBar custom node. The progress bar consists of two overlaying rectangles: a red indicator rectangle (progressIndicator), which reflects progress as its width increases (or decreases on "backward" progress), and a gray foundation rectangle (progressFoundation), which is slightly larger than the red indicator rectangle. The indicator's width is bound to public class variable progress which can be changed by code outside of the class. As the progress variable changes, the indicator bar takes on a new width (a percentage of the width of the foundation bar).

Listing 7.10 Progress Bar

```
public class ProgressBar extends CustomNode {

    public var progress: Number = 0.0;                    // updated externally
    public-init var width = 150.0;

    var progressFoundation: Rectangle = Rectangle {
        width: width
        height: 8
        fill: Color.GRAY
        stroke: Color.BLACK
        arcWidth: 5
        arcHeight: 5
    }
```

```
    var progressIndicator: Rectangle = Rectangle {
        y: 2
        height: 4
        arcWidth: 5
        arcHeight: 5
        width: bind ((width * progress) / 100.0)      // changes with progress
        fill: Color.CRIMSON
    }

    override function create(): Node {
        return Group { content: [ progressFoundation, progressIndicator ] }
    }
}
```

Listing 7.11 shows the scene graph for the main program. A Rectangle node handles
mouse click events by calling function toggleProgress (which starts and stops the
progress bar timeline). The Text node content property is bound to String variable
status and variable progressbar is the ProgressBar custom node.

Listing 7.11 Progress Bar Scene Graph

```
var clicker = 0;                    // arbitrary variable used to control progress
var status = "Progress Bar: Click Me to Start";
// Instantiate a ProgressBar custom node
var progressBar = ProgressBar {
    opacity: 0
    width: 200
};

// 'Progress' means variable clicker increments
function getProgress() {
    return clicker++;
}
. . .
Scene {
. . .
   content: [
      Rectangle {
         width: 200
         height: 30
         fill: Color.BISQUE
         stroke: Color.DARKSLATEGRAY
         cursor: Cursor.HAND
         onMouseClicked: toggleProgress      // See Listing 7.12
      }
      Text {
         font: Font {
            size: 12
         }
```

```
        x: 5
        y: 20
        content: bind status
    }
    progressBar
]
. . .
```

Listing 7.12 consists of two timelines and an event handler that controls them. Timeline progressTimeline is the main timeline for this program. The progress timeline has one KeyFrame with property time set to 100ms (100 milliseconds). Property action consists of an anonymous function and property repeatCount is set to Timeline.INDEFINITE. This means that every 100 milliseconds the function in property action executes.

First, the function updates the progress bar's progress property. If its value is 100 (100 percent progress), the timeline stops itself and variable clicker is reset to zero. The progress bar fades by calling Timeline opacityTimeline.playFromStart. Timeline opacityTimeline changes the progress bar's opacity to 0, causing it to gradually disappear.

JavaFX Tip

It's perfectly legal for a timeline to "stop" itself (or pause, play, or playFromStart). However, JavaFX requires an explicit Timeline type along with the object literal, as shown here and in Listing 7.12.

```
var progressTimeline: Timeline = Timeline {        // object literal
    if (progressBar.progress == 100.0) {
        progressTimeline.stop();
        . . .
    }
    . . .
};
```

Function toggleProgress is the event handler for the Rectangle node's mouse click. This function pauses and resumes the progress bar timeline (with Timeline functions pause and play) and updates String variable status. If the progress bar timeline is stopped (either because it hasn't run yet or it has completed), then function toggleProgress starts it up.

Timeline Tip

To see if a timeline is playing, you must check to make sure running *is true and* paused *is false, as follows.*

```
var t1: Timeline = Timeline {
    . . .
};
. . .
if (t1.running and not t1.paused) {
    // Timeline t1 is running and not paused
}
```

Listing 7.12 Progress Bar Timelines and Controls

```
// Check status every 100 milliseconds
var progressTimeline: Timeline = Timeline {
    repeatCount: Timeline.INDEFINITE
    keyFrames: [
        KeyFrame {
            time: 100ms
            action: function(): Void {
                // update progress variable and stop if progress is 100
                progressBar.progress = getProgress();
                // stop this timeline, update status display,
                // and fade out the progress bar
                if (progressBar.progress == 100.0) {
                    progressTimeline.stop();
                    status = "completed (stopped)";
                    clicker = 0;
                    opacityTimeline.rate = 1;
                    opacityTimeline.playFromStart();
                }
            }
        }
    ]
};

// fade in or fade out progress bar
var opacityTimeline: Timeline = Timeline {
    keyFrames: [
        KeyFrame {
            time: 0s
            values: progressBar.opacity => 1.0
        }
        KeyFrame {
            time: 1s
            values: progressBar.opacity => 0.0 tween Interpolator.EASEBOTH
        }
    ]
```

```
};

// pause the progress time line if it's running
// resume play if it's paused
// start it up if it's stopped (not running)
function toggleProgress (e: MouseEvent): Void {
    if (progressTimeline.running and not progressTimeline.paused) {
        progressTimeline.pause();
        status = "paused . . .";
    }
    else if (progressTimeline.paused) {
        progressTimeline.play();
        status = "resumed . . .";
    }
    else if (not progressTimeline.running) {
        opacityTimeline.rate = -1;      // toggle the direction of the timeline
        opacityTimeline.play();
        clicker = 0;
        progressTimeline.playFromStart();
        status = "start . . .";
    }
}
```

7.3 Transitions

JavaFX transitions are specialized timelines that simplify common animations of graphical objects. JavaFX transitions include animations for movement, scaling, rotating, and fading. Transitions for movement include TranslateTransition (a transition to move an object in the x-direction, y-direction, or both) and PathAnimation (a transition to animate an object along a path).

Transitions operate on nodes, which can be simple graphical objects, or compound nodes such as Groups. Transition properties include node (the target graphical object), duration (the length of the transition), interpolator (the transition's interpolator), repeatCount, and autoReverse as well as functions and properties you've already seen with timelines.

Table 7.5 lists the JavaFX simple transitions.

TABLE 7.5 JavaFX Simple Transitions

Transition	Description
TranslateTransition	Creates a move/translate animation that spans its duration by updating the translateX and translateY properties of node.
ScaleTransition	Creates a scale animation that spans its duration by updating the scaleX and scaleY properties of node.
RotateTransition	Creates a rotation animation that spans its duration by updating the rotate property of node. The rotation angle is specified in degrees.
FadeTransition	Creates a fade effect animation that spans its duration by updating the opacity property of node.
PathTransition	Creates a path animation that spans its duration by updating the translateX and translateY properties of node. It updates the node's rotate property if orientation is set to OrientationType.ORTHOGONAL_TO_TANGENT.
PauseTransition	Executes an action at the end of its duration.

Table 7.6 lists the JavaFX compound transitions. Compound transitions include property content, a sequence of sub-transitions.

TABLE 7.6 JavaFX Compound Transitions

Compound Transition	Description
ParallelTransition	Builds a composite transition that includes all transitions (sub-transitions) in its content property and starts them in parallel. Sub-transitions inherit node if their node property is not specified. Properties duration, repeatCount, and autoReverse variables have no effect on ParallelTransition.
SequentialTransition	Builds a composite transition that includes all transitions (sub-transitions) in its content property and starts them sequentially. Sub-transitions inherit node if their node property is not specified. Properties duration, repeatCount, and autoReverse variables have no effect on Sequential-Transition.

Transition Basics—Simple Movement

The example we presented earlier in this chapter (see Figure 7.1 on page 208 and Listing 7.2 on page 210 for the code) depicts a Circle moving back and forth across the scene. Let's redo this example now using a TranslateTransition instead of a Timeline.

To use a Transition (see Listing 7.13), you specify the node (here, variable `circle`), a duration, and optionally, repeatCount, autoReverse, and interpolator. (The default interpolator for Transition is `Interpolator.EASEBOTH`.)

For a TranslateTransition you specify `fromX` and `toX` (to move in the x-direction) and `fromY` and `toY` (to move in the y-direction). You do not need to specify properties `translateX` or `translateY` in the target node; the transition automatically updates these properties for you.

Listing 7.13 TranslateTransition—Simple Movement

```
def circle: Circle = Circle {
    centerX: 40
    centerY: 70
    radius: 25
    fill: Color.SEAGREEN
};

TranslateTransition {
    node: circle
    duration: 3s
    fromX: 0
    toX: 165.0
    repeatCount: Timeline.INDEFINITE
    autoReverse: true
}.play();       // Use play, playFromStart, pause, stop just like Timelines

. . .
Scene {
   content: circle
. . .
}
```

Animation Tip

Transitions are often easier to use than timelines. As you see in this example, you don't have to bind variables, specify node properties (such as `translateX`), or define KeyFrame objects.

ScaleTransition

Let's use a scale transition now to grow and shrink the circle. ScaleTransition grows or shrinks its named node by the multiplier specified in byX (x-direction growth) and byY (y-direction growth). For multiplier 1, the node is unchanged from its original size, multiplier 2 doubles the size of the node, and so forth. ScaleTransition manipulates the scaleX and scaleY properties of the named node.

The program in Listing 7.14 moves the circle back and forth across the scene and grows and shrinks the circle at the same time. It mimics the behavior shown in Listing 7.3 on page 211 using transitions for the animation instead of timelines.

Listing 7.14 ScaleTransition and TranslateTransition

```
def circle: Circle = Circle {
    centerX: 40
    centerY: 70
    radius: 25
    fill: Color.SEAGREEN
};

// manipulates node property translateX
TranslateTransition {
    node: circle
    duration: 3s
    fromX: 0
    toX: 165.0
    repeatCount: Timeline.INDEFINITE
    autoReverse: true
}.play();        // Use play, playFromStart, pause, stop just like Timelines

// manipulates node property scaleX and scaleY
ScaleTransition {
    node: circle
    duration: 3s
    byX: 2
    byY: 2
    repeatCount: Timeline.INDEFINITE
    autoReverse: true
}.play();


. . .
Scene {
    content: circle
. . .
}
```

Rotate and Fade Transitions

Let's add two more transitions to the program, and at the same time create a Group component with the Circle and Text node to better show rotation (similar to the example in Listing 7.5 on page 214 and Listing 7.6 on page 216). In this example, we'll also add a Fade transition.

RotateTransition rotates a node. You specify byAngle, with 0 (degrees) being unchanged from the original orientation, 90 is a quarter turn, and 360 a full rotation.

FadeTransition manipulates the node's `opacity` property, with 1 being fully opaque and 0 being fully translucent.

Figure 7.7 shows this program running. Here, the circle on the left shows the starting position. The circle on the right is not quite fully opaque, rotated about 45 degrees, moved from its original location, and larger than its original size.

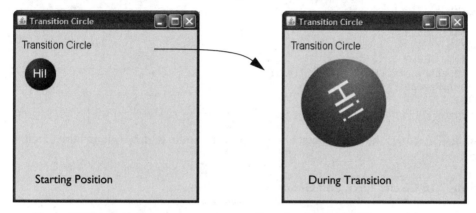

Figure 7.7 Four simultaneous transitions effect the Circle and Text group

Listing 7.15 shows the code to define these four transitions.

Listing 7.15 Transitions to Scale, Rotate, Fade, and Translate

```
ScaleTransition {
    node: group
    duration: 3s
    byX: 2
    byY: 2
    repeatCount: Timeline.INDEFINITE
    autoReverse: true
}.play();

RotateTransition {
    node: group
    duration: 2.5s
    byAngle: 360
    repeatCount: Timeline.INDEFINITE
    autoReverse: true
}.play();

FadeTransition {
    node: group
    duration: 6s
    fromValue: 1
```

```
        toValue: .3
        repeatCount: Timeline.INDEFINITE
        autoReverse: true
}.play();

TranslateTransition {
    node: group
    duration: 1.5s
    fromX: 0
    toX: 165.0
    fromY: 0
    toY: 130.0
    repeatCount: Timeline.INDEFINITE
    autoReverse: true
}.play();
```

Listing 7.16 shows the Circle object and the Group node, which contains the Circle and Text objects.

Listing 7.16 Circle, Text, and Group

```
def circle: Circle = Circle {
    centerX: 40
    centerY: 70
    radius: 25
    fill: RadialGradient {
        centerX: 0.25
        centerY: 0.25
        radius: 1
        stops: [
            Stop {
                offset: 0
                color: Color.SEAGREEN
            }
            Stop {
                offset: 1
                color: Color.BLACK
            }
        ]
    }
};

def group: Group = Group {
    content: [
        circle,
        Text {
            fill: Color.WHITE
            font: Font {
                size: 18
            }
            x: 28
```

```
            y: 75
            content: "Hi!"
        }
    ]
}
. . .
Scene {
    content: group
. . .
}
```

Compound Transitions

You can combine transitions and have them execute ("play") in parallel or sequentially. In Listing 7.15 you see four transitions created and invoked one after the other in the script. This provides parallel execution by default. However, coding becomes clearer if you group such transitions together into a ParallelTransition, specifying simultaneous execution. Using ParallelTransition becomes especially convenient when manipulating transitions from an event handler, for example.

Figure 7.8 shows a program that pauses and restarts the animation when you click the text title. The event handler code simply pauses and plays the ParallelTransition, without having to individually manipulate the sub-transitions.

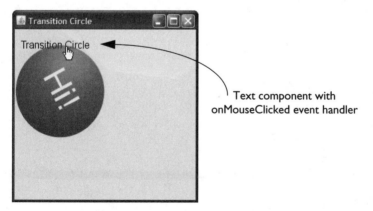

Figure 7.8 Compound transitions make coding easier with multiple transitions

JavaFX provides both ParallelTransition and SequentialTransition. These transitions are essentially the same, except that their sub-transitions are executed either in parallel (with ParallelTransition) or sequentially (with SequentialTransition). These compound transitions consist of a node (the target of the transitions) and property content (a sequence of sub-transitions). If the sub-transitions do not specify a node, they manipulate the target node specified in the parent transition.

Properties duration, repeatCount, and autoReverse have no effect on ParallelTransition and SequentialTransition. You specify these properties in sub-transitions.

Listing 7.17 shows the code for ParallelTransition par, which contains four sub-transitions. These are the same transitions used in the previous example.

Listing 7.17 ParallelTransition

```
var par = ParallelTransition {
    node: group
    content: [
        ScaleTransition {
            duration: 3s
            byX: 2
            byY: 2
            repeatCount: Timeline.INDEFINITE
            autoReverse: true
        }

        RotateTransition {
            duration: 2.5s
            byAngle: 360
            repeatCount: Timeline.INDEFINITE
            autoReverse: true
        }

        FadeTransition {
            duration: 6s
            fromValue: 1
            toValue: .3
            repeatCount: Timeline.INDEFINITE
            autoReverse: true
        }

        TranslateTransition {
            duration: 1.5s
            fromX: 0
            toX: 165.0
            fromY: 0
            toY: 130.0
            repeatCount: Timeline.INDEFINITE
            autoReverse: true
        }
    ]
}
par.play();
```

Listing 7.18 shows the onMouseClicked event handler for the Text component (as shown in Figure 7.8 on page 231). Note how simple the mouse click event handler is, since you only need to manipulate the parent ParallelTransition par.

Listing 7.18 Scene Graph and Mouse Event Handler

```
. . .
Scene {
    content: [
            Text {
                cursor: Cursor.HAND
                onMouseClicked: function(e: MouseEvent): Void {
                    if (par.paused) {
                        par.play();
                    }
                    else {
                        par.pause();
                    }
                }
                font: Font {
                    size: 16
                }
                x: 10
                y: 30
                content: "Transition Circle"
            }
            group
    ]
}
```

7.4 Path Animation

Path animation lets you move shapes along pre-defined paths. A path is a sequence of path elements, where each path element can be any one of several geometric objects, such as line to, arc to, quadratic curve to, and cubic curve to. Once you define a path, you can animate a node along the path using a PathTransition.

Creating a Path

Let's build a path animation example with a Rectangle as the target node and a simple oval-shaped path. The first step is to construct a path.

Figure 7.9 shows an example path. You always begin a Path with PathElement MoveTo. This is the required starting point, here point (30,120). To create the oval shape, the first PathElement shape is ArcTo, which draws an arc-shaped line to point (300,120). Next, the Path includes PathElement LineTo, which draws a line to point

(300,170). A second ArcTo draws another arc segment to point (30,170). Finally, the path is closed with PathElement ClosePath, which draws a line from the current location to the starting point. (You could use a LineTo here instead of ClosePath to complete the path.)

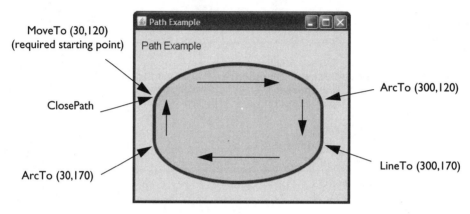

Figure 7.9 A Path connects PathElements

Path as Shape

You can also use Path to create custom shapes when you want something other than the standard JavaFX Shapes: Arc, Circle, CubicCurve, Ellipse, Line, Polygon, Polyline, QuadCurve, Rectangle, ShapeIntersection, ShapeSubtraction, and SVGPath. (See "Shapes" on page 103.)

Listing 7.19 is the code that builds the path shown in Figure 7.9. Since Path is a Shape, you can specify values for Shape properties such as strokeWidth, stroke, and fill. To build a Path, you provide multiple PathElements in property elements. PathElement MoveTo is always the first PathElement. Each succeeding PathElement starts at the current location, continuing the path according to the rules of its shape. The ArcTo sweepFlag property is set to true so that when the arc is drawn clockwise, the curve is correct for the oval shape. If sweepFlag is false, the orientation of the curve is opposite, and the shape is no longer an oval.

Listing 7.19 Path Example

```
def path: Path = Path {
    strokeWidth: 5
    stroke: Color.DARKSLATEGRAY
    fill: Color.AQUAMARINE
```

```
    elements: [
        MoveTo {                    // required starting point
            x: 30
            y: 120
        }
        ArcTo {
            x: 300
            y: 120
            radiusX: 100
            radiusY: 50
            sweepFlag: true
        }
        LineTo {
            x: 300
            y: 170
        }
        ArcTo {
            x: 30
            y: 170
            radiusX: 100
            radiusY: 50
            sweepFlag: true
        }
        ClosePath {                 // finish with a line to the starting point
        }
    ]
}
. . .
scene: Scene {
    . . .
    content: path
}
. . .
```

PathTransition

Once you have constructed a path, the hard part of path animation is done. Transition PathTransition lets you animate a node along your path. You can use a Path that you've already built, or you can provide PathElements when you construct the Path-Transition.

Figure 7.10 shows path animation with a "car" rectangular-shaped node and the Path constructed in the previous example. Increasing the Path property strokeWidth to 15 emphasizes the oval animation path.

Note that as the rectangle shape travels along the path, its orientation changes as the path goes from vertical to horizontal. PathTransition property orientation set to Ori-entationType.ORTHOGONAL_TO_TANGENT keeps the shape's orientation relative to the path.

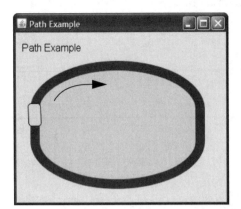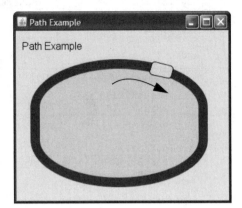

Figure 7.10 Animating a shape along a path

Listing 7.20 is the code that implements the PathTransition in Figure 7.10. The PathElements are unchanged; only property strokeWidth is increased.

Shape rectangle is wider than it is high so that when its orientation is changed, it has the correct look of a "car" (well, sort of).

The PathTransition is similar to other transitions you've seen with properties node, interpolator, duration, and repeatCount. PathTransition takes an AnimationPath object (constructed from a Path object) using function createFromPath. You can alternatively provide an SVGPath object instead of Path or use helper function createFromShape with a Shape object.

This PathTransition specifies Interpolator.LINEAR for property interpolator. Otherwise, the "car" would slow down at the beginning and end of each transition cycle.

Note that node rectangle is added to the scene graph after node path, so that the rectangle appears on top of the path.

Listing 7.20 PathTransition Example

```
def path: Path = Path {
    strokeWidth: 15
    stroke: Color.DARKSLATEGRAY
    fill: Color.AQUAMARINE
    elements: [ . . . unchanged . . . ]
}
```

```
def rectangle: Rectangle = Rectangle {
    x: 30
    y: 120
    width: 35
    height: 20
    arcWidth: 10
    arcHeight: 10
    fill: Color.YELLOW
    stroke: Color.BLACK
}

PathTransition {
    node: rectangle
    path: AnimationPath.createFromPath(path)
    orientation: OrientationType.ORTHOGONAL_TO_TANGENT
    interpolator: Interpolator.LINEAR
    duration: 6s
    repeatCount: Timeline.INDEFINITE
}.play();

scene: Scene {
    . . .
    content: [ path, rectangle ]
}
. . .
```

7.5 Chutes and Ladders

In this final section, we'll put several animation concepts to work to create a JavaFX widget that animates a set of "path balls" along a three-part path consisting of a chute, the ground, and a ladder. The user animates one or more of the path balls by clicking buttons (labeled and color-coded to match the target ball). Figure 7.11 shows the widget in its startup configuration with four path balls lined up along the top. The second frame shows the widget after all the path balls are moving at various spots along the path. Each path ball has a slightly different path that it follows, since a path ball journey begins at its own starting point and returns to the same location.

The path for each path ball begins at a specific location along the top line (its origin) and proceeds to the top of the chute. The chute consists of three consecutive CubicCurveTo lines strung together. The ground is simply a straight line and the ladder strings together consecutive lines at 90-degree angles. The final line stops at each path ball's origin. You'll see that when a path ball is initialized, it takes on a unique set of path elements that define its path. These path elements build the individual PathTransition objects that animate each ball.

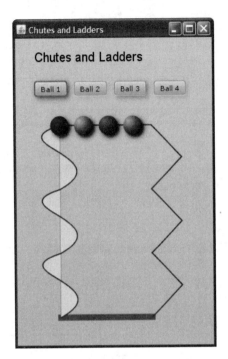 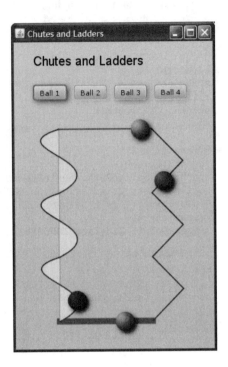

Figure 7.11 JavaFX application Chutes and Ladders

Class PathBall (PathBall.fx)

Figure 7.12 is a class diagram for class PathBall. Class PathBall extends CustomNode and implements the behavior to animate the path ball with function play. The encapsulated behavior includes three PathTransitions (for each portion of the path) and a SequentialTransition to animate the path ball throughout the complete path.

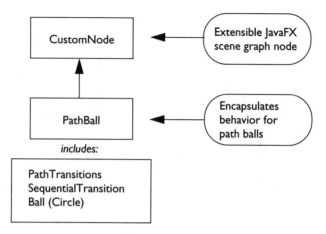

Figure 7.12 Chutes and Ladders PathBall class

Listing 7.21 through Listing 7.23 is the code that implements class PathBall. Listing 7.21 shows the class-level variables for PathBall. Each path ball has its own color (ballColor), an x-direction origin (centerX), and three sequences of PathElements (chute, ground, and ladder).

The ball itself is a Circle. Its radius, centerY, and effect properties have standard settings. Property fill is a radial gradient using the class-level variable ballColor with Color.BLACK.

Listing 7.21 PathBall

```
public class PathBall extends CustomNode {
    public-init var ballColor: Color;
    public-init var centerX: Number;
    public-init var chute: PathElement[];
    public-init var ground: PathElement[];
    public-init var ladder: PathElement[];

    def theBall = Circle {
        translateX: centerX
        radius: 15
        effect: DropShadow {
            offsetX: 4
            offsetY: 4
            spread: 0
            color: Color.BLACK
```

```
    }

    fill: RadialGradient {
        centerX: 0.25
        centerY: 0.25
        radius: 1
        stops: [
            Stop {
                offset: 0
                color: ballColor
            }
            Stop {
                offset: 1
                color: Color.BLACK
            }
        ]
    }
}
```

Listing 7.22 includes the transitions defined for each path ball, constructed using the class-level PathElement sequences (chute, ground, and ladder). The PathTransition for the chute (animChute) and the ladder (animLadder) have adjustments depending on class-level variable centerX. This makes the path ball starting and ending locations unique.

Note that, although the duration properties will be consistent for each path ball created, the paths themselves will be slightly unequal because of the different starting locations of each path ball. Thus, if you start Ball 4 and then immediately start Ball 1, you'll see Ball 1 overtake Ball 4 on the last portion (the ladder) of the path because Ball 1 has further to go within the same time frame.

Also, note that each PathTransition has its own value for property duration. Thus, the speed for travel in the chute is faster than the speed for the ground or the ladder (the ladder has the slowest speed, taking a full 12 seconds to climb).

Finally, the three PathTransitions are combined into a compound SequentialTransition (ballSeqTransition). This connects the three PathTransitions together into a single path animation with different speeds for the different segments.

Listing 7.22 PathBall Transitions

```
def animChute = PathTransition {
    node: theBall
    path: AnimationPath.createFromPath(Path { elements: [
        MoveTo {
            x: centerX
            y: 0
        }
```

```
                LineTo {
                    x: 0
                    y: 0
                }
            chute]
        })
        interpolator: Interpolator.LINEAR
        duration: 2.5s
    };
    def animGround = PathTransition {
        node: theBall
        path: AnimationPath.createFromPath(Path { elements: ground })
        interpolator: Interpolator.LINEAR
        duration: 3s
    };
    def animLadder = PathTransition {
        node: theBall
        path: AnimationPath.createFromPath(Path { elements: [
                ladder,
                LineTo {
                    x: centerX
                    y: 0
            } ]
        })
        interpolator: Interpolator.EASEOUT
        duration: 12s
    };

    def ballSeqTransition = SequentialTransition {
        node: theBall
        content: [ animChute, animGround, animLadder ]
    }
```

Listing 7.23 implements functions play and create for class PathBall. Function play starts the path ball's SequentialTransition from the start. Function create is the overridden CustomNode function so a PathBall object can be inserted into the scene graph. Group theGroup holds the path ball Circle object. (You could alternatively return the Circle object (theBall) here, but in a subsequent version we add a second object to the class scene graph, requiring a Group for the returned Node. See Listing 10.11 on page 335.)

Listing 7.23 PathBall Behavior

```
    public function play(): Void {
        ballSeqTransition.playFromStart();
    }

    def theGroup = Group {
        content: [ theBall ]
    };
```

```
    protected override function create(): Node {
        return theGroup;
    }
}
```

Main Program (Main.fx)

Listing 7.24 through Listing 7.27 is the code for **Main.fx**. The main program builds the
sequence of PathElements to implement the visible Path objects. (It also supplies these
PathElements to each PathBall object literal.) In addition to the Path and PathBall
objects, the scene graph includes a Text component and four JavaFX Button components to control the animation.

Listing 7.24 includes the PathElements for sequences chute, ground, and ladder. Note
that each sequence begins with required path element MoveTo.

Listing 7.24 Main PathElements

```
// PathElements for the chute
def chute = [
    MoveTo {
        x: 0
        y: 0
    },
    CubicCurveTo {
        controlX1: -100
        controlY1: 30
        controlX2: 100
        controlY2: 50
        x: 0
        y: 100
    }
    CubicCurveTo {
        controlX1: -100
        controlY1: 130
        controlX2: 100
        controlY2: 150
        x: 0
        y: 200
    }
    CubicCurveTo {
        controlX1: -100
        controlY1: 230
        controlX2: 100
        controlY2: 250
        x: 0
        y: 300
    }
```

```
];

// PathElements for the ground
def ground = [
    MoveTo {
        x: 0
        y: 300
    }
    LineTo {
        x: 150
        y: 300
    }
];

// PathElements for the ladder
def ladder = [
    MoveTo {
        x: 150
        y: 300
    }
    LineTo {
        x: 200
        y: 250
    }
    LineTo {
        x: 150
        y: 200
    }
    LineTo {
        x: 200
        y: 150
    }
    LineTo {
        x: 150
        y: 100
    }
    LineTo {
        x: 200
        y: 50
    }
    LineTo {
        x: 150
        y: 0
    }
];
```

Listing 7.25 contains the code to create the four Path objects (chute, ground, ladder, and a "pole" that appears down the center of the chute). Note that a Path is a type of Shape, and as such, can be inserted into the scene graph like any other shape. (In contrast, a sequence of PathElements is a collection of points and geometry rules and cannot be inserted into a scene graph.)

Listing 7.25 Create Path Objects

```
def chutePath = Path {
    fill: Color.YELLOW
    stroke: Color.DARKSLATEGRAY
    strokeWidth: 2
    elements: chute
};

def ladderPath = Path {
    stroke: Color.DARKSLATEGRAY
    strokeWidth: 2
    elements: [ladder,
        LineTo {
            x: 0
            y: 0
        }]
};

def chutePole = Path {
    stroke: Color.GRAY
    strokeWidth: 2
    elements: [
        MoveTo {
            x: 00
            y: 0
        }
        LineTo {
            x: 00
            y: 300
        }
    ]
};

def groundPath = Path {
    stroke: Color.DARKOLIVEGREEN
    strokeWidth: 10
    elements: ground
};
```

Listing 7.26 contains the script-level variables that define and create the four path balls. Note that as each path ball is created, PathBall properties chute, ground, and ladder are set to the PathElement sequences built in Listing 7.24.

Listing 7.26 Script-level Variables to Create the PathBalls

```
def numberBalls = 4;
def ballColors = [ Color.CRIMSON, Color.CHARTREUSE,
                   Color.DODGERBLUE, Color.ORANGE ];

def theBalls = for (i in [0..<numberBalls])
    PathBall {
        centerX: i * 40
        ballColor: ballColors[i]
        chute: chute
        ground: ground
        ladder: ladder
    }
```

Figure 7.13 shows the Chutes and Ladders Scene Graph. A VBox layout component positions the Text component and the JavaFX Button components above the Path objects. The Button components appear in their own HBox layout component. The Path nodes and four PathBall nodes appear in their own Group. The PathBall nodes are added last, so they are displayed on top of the Path objects.

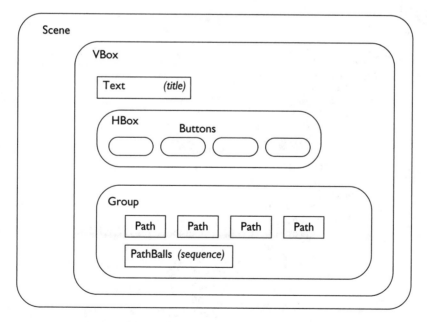

Figure 7.13 Chutes and Ladders nested Scene Graph

Finally, Listing 7.27 contains the Chutes and Ladders Scene Graph.

Listing 7.27 Chutes and Ladders Scene Graph

```
Stage {
    title: "Chutes and Ladders"
    scene: Scene {
        width: 320
        height: 480
        fill: LinearGradient {
            startX: 1
            startY: 0
            endX: 1
            endY: 1
            stops: [
                Stop {
                    offset: 0,
                    color: Color.LIGHTGRAY
                },
                Stop {
                    offset: 1,
                    color: Color.LIGHTSTEELBLUE
                }
            ]
        }
        content: [
            VBox {
                layoutY: 20
                layoutX: 30
                spacing: 20
                content: [
                    Text {
                        font: Font {
                            size: 20
                        }
                        content: "Chutes and Ladders"
                    }
                    HBox {
                        spacing: 10
                        content: [
                            for (i in [0 .. <numberBalls])
                                Button {
                                    effect: DropShadow {
                                        offsetX: 3
                                        offsetY: 3
                                        spread: 0
                                        color: ballColors[
                                        i mod (sizeof ballColors)]
                                    }
                                    text: "Ball {i+1}"
                                    action: function() {
                                        theBalls[i].play();
```

```
                        }
                    }
                ]
            }
            Group {
                translateX: -60
                translateY: 20
                content: [
                    groundPath, chutePole, chutePath, ladderPath,
                    theBalls
                ]
            }
        ]
    }
  ]
 }
}
```

8 Working with Images

There's no substitute for an evocative picture. Images enhance web sites, widgets, and applications. So, it follows that applications that manipulate images give you great choices for creating that killer widget or web application.

In this chapter you'll learn how to use images in your JavaFX applications. JavaFX provides flexibility for loading and scaling images, as well as choices in how to display images using the ImageView component. The ImageView component is a node, and as such, you can provide transformations, animations, and effects to enhance both the image and your application.

What You Will Learn

- All about Image and ImageView components

- Options for loading images

- Scaling an image during loading

- Scaling an image for display options

- Applying transformations, animations, and effects

- Photo layout examples

- Implementing a mouse dragging application

- Designing a modular application to handle image loading efficiently

- Implementing a "3D-like" animated photo carousel application

8.1 Using Image

JavaFX provides two main classes for manipulating images: class Image lets you define an image from a URL and class ImageView lets you display an Image object. Because ImageView is a JavaFX node, you can apply any of the scene graph manipulations such as animation, scaling, effects, and opacity changes to ImageView nodes.

Before we delve into the fun of image manipulation, let's look at the workhorse, class Image.

Class Image

You *load* an image by specifying its URL. (Load means read the file that contains the bit representation of the image. Images are *displayed* with scene graph node Image-View, which includes property image, the Image object.) Here is the code to load a JPG image found in the local environment (__DIR__ is a built-in JavaFX variable that holds your script file directory location).

```
def myImage = Image {
    url: "{__DIR__}MaasRiver.jpg"
}
```

The Image class has properties that let you manipulate the loading and scaling of images. Table 8.1 lists the common properties of class Image.

TABLE 8.1 Image Properties

Property	Type	Description
url	String	URL used to fetch the image's pixel data.
backgroundLoading	Boolean	If true, loads the image in the background and uses a placeholder image.
placeholder	Image	Displayed while image is loading if background-Loading is true.
smooth	Boolean	If true (default), a better quality filtering is used. If false, a faster but lesser quality filtering is used.
progress	Number	The approximate percentage of image loading that is complete.
error	Boolean	Indicates whether an error was detected while loading an image.
height	Number	Resize source image to fit within height. Affected by preserveRatio.
width	Number	Resize source image to fit within width. Affected by preserveRatio.
preserveRatio	Boolean	If true, preserves the aspect ratio of the original image when scaling to fit using width and height.

Loading images can be an I/O intensive operation. To help ease the burden when you have many images to load (or possibly a few, large images), set property background-Loading to true. This lets you load images in the background. When you do this, a placeholder image is displayed in its place. Listing 8.1 shows an example of how to load a large image in the background. Note that property placeHolder is also an

Image, but the assumption is that the place holder image is small and the same place holder can be used with any number of Image objects.

Listing 8.1 Using backgroundLoading with Image

```
def myBigImage = Image {
   url: "http://url_of_some_large_image.jpg"
   backgroundLoading: true
   placeholder: Image {
      url: "{__DIR__}placeHolderImage.jpg"
   }
}
```

If you use background loading, the image size won't be accurate until the loading is complete. You can monitor the progress of an image's loading with property progress. Listing 8.2 shows a timeline that monitors property progress every 100 milliseconds. When the image is loaded, the timeline stops. (See "Using action with a Progress Bar" on page 220 for an example of a visual progress bar.)

Listing 8.2 Monitoring Image Loading with Property progress

```
var progressTimeline: Timeline = Timeline {
      repeatCount: Timeline.INDEFINITE
      keyFrames: [
         KeyFrame {
            time: 100ms
            action: function(): Void {
               if (image.progress > 99.9) then progressTimeline.stop();
               if (image.progress > 75.0) then
                        println("loading status: {image.progress}%")
            }
         }
      ]

   }

   def image:Image = Image {
      url: "http://url_of_some_large_image.jpg"
      backgroundLoading: true
      placeholder: Image {
         url: "{__DIR__}placeHolderImage.jpg"
      }
   }
   progressTimeline.play();
```

Image properties width, height, and preserveRatio help you scale images as they load. Using these properties to reduce image size helps limit the memory consumed by the

Image object. Property preserveRatio keeps the aspect ratio of the Image object consistent with the source image.

If preserveRatio is true and you specify property width only, the image is resized to the specified width *and* the height is adjusted to preserve the aspect ratio. Specifying property width with preserveRatio set to false uses the specified width with the original height.

If you specify both properties width and height and preserveRatio is false, the image is scaled to these dimensions. When preserveRatio is true, however, the height and width act as limits and the aspect ratio is consistent with the original image.

8.2 Using ImageView

Class ImageView displays an image. ImageView is a JavaFX node and can be inserted into a scene graph and manipulated like any other node. Figure 8.1 shows a simple program that displays an image with a black border.

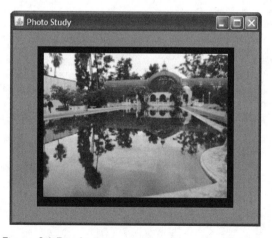

Figure 8.1 Displaying an image

Before we show you the code for this program, lets look at some ImageView properties. Table 8.2 lists the common properties of class ImageView.

TABLE 8.2 ImageView Properties

Property	Type	Description
fitHeight	Number	Resize image to fit height. If <= 0, use original height of source image.
fitWidth	Number	Resize image to fit width. If <= 0, use original width of source image.
preserveRatio	Boolean	If true, preserves the aspect ratio of original source image when scaling to fit using fitWidth and fitHeight.
image	Image	The displayed image.
viewport	Rectangle2D (does not change with JavaFX 1.2)	If viewport is non-null, only the portion of the image which falls within the viewport will be displayed.
x	Number	The x coordinate origin.
y	Number	The y coordinate origin.
smooth	Boolean	If true (default), a better quality filtering is used. If false, a faster but lesser quality filtering is used.

Properties fitHeight, fitWidth, and preserveRatio are similar to properties height, width, and preserveRatio of class Image. However, there are differences. In general, you will see better performance if you specify Image scaling with the width, height, and preserveRatio properties of Image. Image scaling is calculated just once as the image is loaded, thereby reducing the image's memory footprint. With ImageView, however, scaling is recalculated whenever you apply a transformation. Consequently, there isn't any permanent image size reduction.

Note that you can display the same Image instance with multiple ImageView objects. In this case, you can use ImageView scaling, especially if you need different sizes of the same image with different ImageView objects.

Property image holds the Image object that is rendered. Property viewport lets you specify a Rectangle2D area where only the portions of the image that fall within the viewport area will be displayed.

Listing 8.3 shows the JavaFX code that displays the image shown in Figure 8.1. The scene graph includes a Rectangle and an ImageView bundled together in a Group. The Rectangle is slightly larger than the ImageView component and positioned so that the ImageView is centered on top of it. This creates the frame border.

You position the ImageView with properties x and y and specify its contained Image with property image. Image property width sets the width to 300 and image property preserveRatio (set to true) sets the height to preserve the image's aspect ratio.

Listing 8.3 Photo1: Displaying an image

```
Stage {
    title: "Photo Study"
    visible: true
    scene: Scene {
        width: 400
        height: 300
        fill: Color.GRAY
        content: [
            Group {
                content: [
                    Rectangle {
                        x: 40
                        y: 25
                        width: 320
                        height: 250
                        fill: Color.BLACK
                    }
                    ImageView {
                        x: 50
                        y: 35
                        image: Image {
                            url: "{__DIR__}BalboaPark.jpg"
                            preserveRatio: true
                            width: 300
                        }
                    }
                ]
            }
        ]
    }
}
```

Listing 8.3 centers the ImageView over the Rectangle, but the size of the ImageView component is known beforehand and the location of the components is fixed. A big part of manipulating images is dealing with various-sized images. You don't always know an image's size before loading it into the Image component. Image properties width, height, and preserveRatio help you prioritize decisions regarding image sizing. You can also use binding and JavaFX layout geometry to center an ImageView component within a framing Rectangle.

Listing 8.4 is a rewrite of the previous example that centers the ImageView component over the Rectangle and makes the Rectangle slightly larger than the ImageView.
The listing includes other important changes, discussed below.

Listing 8.4 defines read-only variables that determine centering. The Rectangle binds
its dimensions to those of the ImageView. By using bind, the Rectangle will resize
itself after the ImageView node is fully initialized. Without bind, Rectangle properties
height and width are set with an empty ImageView component (and results in a small
20 by 20 rectangle).

The ImageView and Rectangle both depend on read-only variables (originX and
originY) for their initial positioning (properties x and y), which do not change, so
binding is not necessary here.

Besides implementing dynamic sizing with binding and variables, Listing 8.4 also
includes code to load the image in the background. When target images are large,
you'll notice a delay before an image appears. With this new version, a placeholder
image appears before the target image is displayed (as shown in Figure 8.2). Although
this hardly affects our small example, background loading can improve performance
dramatically with applications that have a large number of images.

Listing 8.4 Photo2: Centering an ImageView Component

```
def sceneWidth = 400;
def sceneHeight = 300;
def imageWidth = 300;
def originX = sceneWidth/2 - imageWidth/2 - 10;
def originY = 20;
def PlaceHolderImage = Image {
    url: "{__DIR__}placeholder.jpg"
}
def rect = Rectangle {
    x: originX
    y: originY
    width: bind iv.layoutBounds.width + 20
    height: bind iv.layoutBounds.height + 20
    fill: Color.BLACK
}
def iv = ImageView {
    x: originX + 10
    y: originY + 10
    image: Image {
        url: "{__DIR__}BalboaPark.jpg"
        preserveRatio: true
        width: imageWidth
        backgroundLoading: true
        placeholder: PlaceHolderImage
    }
}
```

```
def group = Group {
    content: [ rect, iv ]
}

var scene: Scene;
Stage {
    title: "Photo Study"
    visible: true
    scene: scene = Scene {
        width: sceneWidth
        height: sceneHeight
        fill: Color.GRAY
        content: group
    }
}
```

Programming Tip

Note that it is necessary to bind image size calculations with background loading, since the component's size won't be finalized until after the image has finished loading.

Figure 8.2 shows the placeholder image displayed while the target image is loading.

Figure 8.2 Using a placeholder image with background loading

Scaling

Let's take the basic example you've already seen and apply some transformations to the image. The first transformation is scaling. Scaling is interesting because if you scale an object along one axis only (centered), you get the illusion of rotation about that axis. As the image shrinks from both sides inward, it appears to present its side view. If you continue scaling to factor -1, the image then grows outward and is flipped. (Note that this is different than a rotate transformation.) Each time you click the image in this example, the timeline that controls the scaling changes direction. This allows you to flip back and forth between the two views.

Figure 8.3 shows two snap shot views of a scaled image as it's shrinking. (The effect is somewhat lost here with snap shot views, but print media have these constraints).

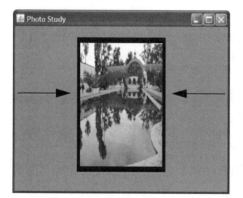 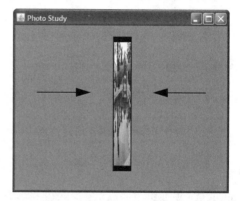

Figure 8.3 Scaling an image along one axis provides the illusion of rotation

Listing 8.5 shows the added code (in bold) that implements this image scaling. There are no changes to the variables, Rectangle, or ImageView. The group that holds the rectangular frame and the image (read-only variable group) now defines property cursor (to indicate an active mouse event handler) and a Scale transformation. The Scale object leaves the y-direction scaling unchanged; scaling only occurs in the x-direction. Scale property x binds to variable scale; variable scale is controlled by the animation. Property pivotX controls how the scaling proceeds. By setting pivotX to a point centered in the x-direction for the image, shrinking proceeds equally from the edges. Conversely, growing proceeds outwards equally towards the edges.

The group's mouse event handler initiates animation with timeline.play. Each time you click the mouse, the timeline direction is reversed. Note that if you click the mouse before the timeline completes, it simply reverses direction in place. It's necessary to use function play here instead of playFromStart to implement this behavior.

Timeline object `timeline` controls the scaling. It changes variable `scale` from 1 (normal scaling) to -1 (normal size but the object is flipped) and uses interpolator `EASEBOTH`.

Listing 8.5 Photo3: Scaling an ImageView Component

```
def sceneWidth = 400;
. . . (unchanged from Listing 8.4) . . .
def rect = Rectangle { . . . }
def iv = ImageView { . . . }

def group = Group {
    cursor: Cursor.HAND
    transforms: Scale{
        x: bind scale
        y: 1
        pivotX: sceneWidth / 2
        pivotY: 0
    } // Scale
    onMouseClicked: function(e: MouseEvent): Void {
        // when rate is -1 it plays the timeline in reverse
        // at regular speed
        timeline.rate *= -1.0;
        timeline.play();
    }
    content: [ rect, iv ]
}

var scale = 1.0;
def timeline = Timeline {
    rate: -1
    keyFrames: [
        at (0s) {scale => 1.0},
        at (6s) {scale => -1.0 tween Interpolator.EASEBOTH}
    ]
};
Stage {
    . . . (unchanged from Listing 8.4) . . .
}
```

Transformation and Effects Menagerie

JavaFX offers numerous transformations and effects that you can apply to nodes. Let's enhance our photo study example and create animations, transformations, and effects and apply them to the group that holds the ImageView and Rectangle components. The code for this appears in Listing 8.6 and Listing 8.7. Figure 8.4 shows this new version running. The application has two rows of buttons that let you select a transformation or effect to apply to the image and rectangle as a group below.

Button Scale applies the animation demonstrated in the previous program. Button Rotate applies successive 45 degree rotations to the group. Button Fade begins a fade-out transition, which toggles the animation by alternating between fade-in and fade-out transitions. The remaining buttons all update the group's effect property. Only one effect is applied at a time, but any transformation (rotate, fade, and scale) can be applied simultaneously with a single effect.

Button Perspective applies a perspective transformation effect, button Sepia Tone applies a sepia tone effect (sepia tone makes the image look like an antique photograph), and button Reflection applies a reflection effect (pictured in Figure 8.4). Finally, button No Effect removes any effect that may have been previously applied. (These effects all use the default values provided when you drag the specific effect into the JavaFX code editor from the NetBeans JavaFX Effects palette.)

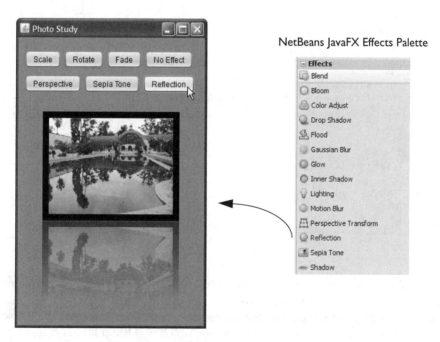

Figure 8.4 Applying various effects and transformations to components

Listing 8.6 includes the nodes for the Rectangle and ImageView components (unchanged from Listing 8.4) and the Group that contains them. The listing also includes a timeline that controls scaling and fading. These animations are initiated with SwingButtons (shown in Listing 8.7).

Listing 8.6 Photo4: Applying Transformations and Effects

```
def sceneWidth = 400;
. . . (unchanged from Listing 8.4) . . .
def rect = Rectangle { . . . }
def iv = ImageView { . . . }

def group = Group {
    layoutY: 85
    transforms: Scale {
        x: bind scale
        y: 1
        pivotX: sceneWidth / 2
        pivotY: 0
    } // Scale
    content: [ rect, iv ]
}

// Control scaling
var scale = 1.0;
def timeline = Timeline {
    rate: -1
    keyFrames: [
        at (0s) {scale => 1.0},
        at (6s) {scale => -1.0 tween Interpolator.EASEBOTH}
    ]
}

// Control fading
def fade = FadeTransition {
    rate: -1
    node: group
    duration: 3s
    fromValue: 1.0
    toValue: 0.2
}
```

Listing 8.7 shows the scene graph code for this application. The top level layout node is a vertical box (VBox) that holds two rows of SwingButtons. The Group that contains the Rectangle frame and the ImageView component is positioned below the VBox. Each row of buttons is contained within a horizontal box (HBox) layout component.

SwingButtons specify property text (the button's label) and property action (code to execute when the button is clicked). Property action initiates or applies the specified transformation or effect. The SwingButton action code is bold so you can easily identify each transformation. The Scale and Fade actions are animations initiated by function play. Scale uses a Timeline and Fade uses a FadeTransition. The effects buttons (Reflection, Perspective, and Sepia Tone) modify the group's effect property. Button No Effect sets the effect property to null.

Listing 8.7 Photo4: Photo Study Scene Graph

```
Stage {
    title: "Photo Study"
    visible: true
    scene: Scene {
        width: sceneWidth
        height: sceneHeight
        fill: Color.GRAY
        content: [
            VBox {
                layoutX: 10
                layoutY: 20
                spacing: 10
                content: [
                    HBox {
                        spacing: 5
                        content: [
                            SwingButton {
                                text: "Scale"
                                action: function() {
                                    timeline.rate *= -1.0;
                                    timeline.play();
                                }
                            }
                            SwingButton {
                                text: "Rotate"
                                action: function() {
                                    group.rotate += 45.0;
                                }
                            }
                            SwingButton {
                                text: "Fade"
                                action: function() {
                                    fade.rate = *= -1.0;
                                    fade.play();
                                }
                            }
                            SwingButton {
                                text: "No Effect"
                                action: function() {
                                    group.effect = null;
                                }
                            }
                        ]
                    }
                    HBox {
                        spacing: 5
                        content: [
                            SwingButton {
                                text: "Perspective"
                                action: function() {
```

```
                                group.effect = PerspectiveTransform {
                                    llx: 13.4,
                                    lly: 210.0,
                                    lrx: 186.6,
                                    lry: 190.0,
                                    ulx: 13.4,
                                    uly: -10.0,
                                    urx: 186.6,
                                    ury: 10.0
                                }
                            }
                        }
                        SwingButton {
                            text: "Sepia Tone"
                            action: function() {
                                group.effect = SepiaTone {
                                    level: 0.5
                                }
                            }
                        }
                        SwingButton {
                            text: "Reflection"
                            action: function() {
                                group.effect = Reflection {
                                    fraction: 0.75
                                    topOffset: 0.0
                                    topOpacity: 0.5
                                    bottomOpacity: 0.0
                                }
                            }
                        }
                    ]
                }
            ]
        }, group
    ]
}
}
```

Table 8.3 lists common JavaFX effects you can apply to nodes in a scene graph. Note that some effects apply more commonly to images, some to text objects, and some are common for both. You can, however, apply any effect to any node.

Effects Tip

Effects cannot be applied to applications in the mobile environment.

TABLE 8.3 Common JavaFX Node Effects

Effect	Description
Blend	Blend two nodes together specifying mode and node input.
Bloom	Makes brighter portions of the input node appear to glow, based on a configurable threshold.
ColorAdjust	Provides per-pixel adjustments of hue, saturation, brightness, and contrast.
DropShadow	Renders a shadow behind the node with the specified color, radius, and offset.
Flood	Renders a rectangular region filled with the given Paint.
GaussianBlur	Blur Gaussian convolution kernel, with a configurable radius.
Glow	Makes the input image appear to glow, based on a configurable threshold.
InnerShadow	Renders a shadow inside the edges of the given node with the specified color, radius, and offset.
Lighting	Simulates a light source shining on the given content, which can be used to give flat objects a more realistic, three-dimensional appearance. Lighting types are DistantLight, SpotLight, or PointLight.
MotionBlur	Motion blur using a Gaussian convolution kernel with a configurable radius and angle.
PerspectiveTransform	Provides non-affine transformation of the input content used to provide a "faux" three-dimensional effect for otherwise two-dimensional content.
Reflection	Renders a reflected version of the input below the actual input content. (The reflected portion does not respond to mouse events.)
SepiaTone	Produces a sepia tone effect similar to antique photographs.

8.3 Building a Wall of Photos

As you can see, there are many ways to manipulate images. Let's branch out now and create an application that formats a wall of images stored in the local environment. Figure 8.5 shows this application running in a browser.

Figure 8.5 Creating a wall of photos

The Wall of Photos application displays nine images arranged in three categories (city, animal, and flower) on a grid. Each image is a standard width, set into a rectangular area with a photo title displayed under the image. The category headings appear above the associated row in a Text component. Each row consists of an HBox layout node. A VBox layout component holds the category title Text nodes and associated row of photos. The Photo node is a custom node class. Figure 8.6 shows the scene graph diagram for the Wall of Photos application.

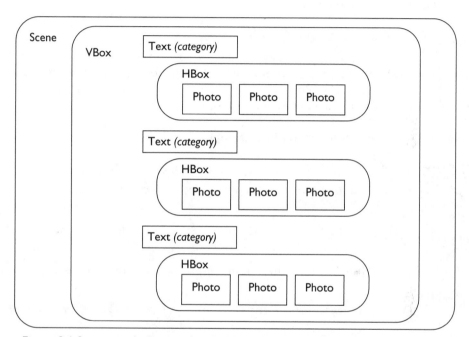

Figure 8.6 Scene graph diagram for the Wall of Photos application

Each image has a title, category, and filename. To hold the data for each image, we create a convenience class, PhotoData.

Listing 8.8 shows the class for PhotoData. It includes three `public-init` variables that are initialized with an object literal, as shown here.

```
PhotoData {
    filename: "paris"
    title: "Eiffel Tower, Paris"
    category: "city"
}
```

Note that class PhotoData does not extend CustomNode and cannot be used in a scene graph. It is a convenience class to encapsulate the data associated with each photo.

Listing 8.8 PhotoData.fx

```
public class PhotoData {
    public-init var title: String;
    public-init var category: String;
    public-init var filename: String;
}
```

The first part of the main program (see Listing 8.9) initializes each PhotoData object
with an object literal, creating a sequence of PhotoData objects. The program loops
through this sequence and builds HBox layout components that contain three custom
Photo nodes, displaying the images in the category's row.

Listing 8.9 Initializing Sequence PhotoData[]

```
def photoData: PhotoData[] = [
    PhotoData {
        filename: "paris", title: "Eiffel Tower, Paris", category: "city"
    }
    PhotoData {
        filename: "london", title: "Trafalgar Square, London", category: "city"
    }
    PhotoData {
        filename: "newyork", title: "Brooklyn Bridge, New York",category: "city"
    }
    PhotoData {
        filename: "kitty", title: "Playing Hide and Seek", category: "animal"
    }
    PhotoData {
        filename: "caterpillar", title: "Caterpillar in the Desert",
            category: "animal"
    }
    PhotoData {
        filename: "butterfly", title: "Butterfly in Kauai", category: "animal"
    }
    PhotoData {
        filename: "gladiolus", title: "Gladiolus", category: "flower"
    }
    PhotoData {
        filename: "artichoke", title: "Artichoke Flower", category: "flower"
    }
    PhotoData {
        filename: "brittlebush", title: "BrittleBush Flower",
            category: "flower"
    }
];
```

Listing 8.10 shows the application's main script that builds the scene graph with the
custom Photo nodes, the HBox nodes for each row, and the parent VBox node.

Listing 8.10 Wall of Photos (Main.fx)

```
def boxIndent = 20;
def boxSpace = 10;

def categoryFont = Font {
    size: 20
}
var xOffset = 0.0;
// Each category has its own HBox component that
// includes the category title Text node
// and the custom node Photo that displays
// the image
var cityList = HBox {
    layoutX: boxIndent
    spacing: boxSpace
}
var animalList = HBox {
    layoutX: boxIndent
    spacing: boxSpace
}
var flowerList = HBox {
    layoutX: boxIndent
    spacing: boxSpace
}
// VBox photoList holds all three HBox components
var photoList = VBox {
    spacing: 10
    layoutX: 40
}
var categoryName: String;
var targetList: HBox;

// Create the category title's Text node and set the
// correct category HBox component
function setTargetList(target: HBox, categoryTitle: String): Void {
    insert Text {
        layoutY: 20
        font: categoryFont
        fill: Color.WHITE
        content: categoryTitle
    } into photoList.content;
    targetList = target;
    insert target into photoList.content;
    xOffset = 0;
}

def photoData: PhotoData[] = [ . . . see Listing 8.9 . . . ];

function loadImages() {
    var citySetupDone = false;
    var animalSetupDone = false;
```

```
        var flowerSetupDone = false;

    for (data in photoData) {
        categoryName = data.category;
        // city
        if (categoryName.equals("city") and not citySetupDone) {
            setTargetList(cityList, "City Photos");
            citySetupDone = true;
        }
        // animal
        else if (categoryName.equals("animal")and not animalSetupDone) {
            setTargetList(animalList, "Animal Photos");
            animalSetupDone = true;
        }
        // flowers
        else if (categoryName.equals("flower")and not flowerSetupDone) {
            setTargetList(flowerList, "Flower Photos");
            flowerSetupDone = true;
        }
        insert Photo {
            imageName: data.filename
            title: data.title
            xOffset: xOffset
        } into targetList.content;
        xOffset += 222;
    }
}

Stage {
    title: "Wall of Photos"
    scene: Scene {
        fill: Color.BLACK
        height: 700
        width: 750
        content: Group {
            layoutY: 20
            content: photoList
        }
    }
}

loadImages();
```

Listing 8.11 shows CustomNode Photo. Class Photo builds each ImageView component, framing Rectangle, and Text node that holds the image's title. The images are in the local environment ({__DIR__}images/) and all are JPG files with a consistent width and varying heights. Class initialization variables imageName and title are set in the main program from the PhotoData object. Property xOffset reflects the horizontal position of the Photo node, indicating whether it's in the first, second, or third slot in the row of photos. (Variable xOffset is only used when we implement photo dragging, an enhancement shown in the next section.) No scaling is performed with the Image or ImageView components.

Listing 8.11 CustomNode Photo (Photo.fx)

```
public class Photo extends CustomNode {
    public-init var imageName: String;
    public-init var title: String;
    public-init var xOffset: Number;

    def MaxPhotoHeight = 150;
    var group: Group;

    protected override function create(): Node {
        var text: Text;
        var pic: ImageView;

        group = Group {
            content: [
                Rectangle {
                    width: 210
                    height: MaxPhotoHeight
                    stroke: Color.DARKGRAY
                }
                pic = ImageView {
                    layoutX: 5
                    layoutY: 5
                    image: Image {
                        url: "{__DIR__}images/{imageName}.jpg"
                    }
                }
                text = Text {
                    fill: Color.WHITE
                    content: title
                }
            ]
        }
        text.layoutX = (pic.layoutBounds.maxX - pic.layoutBounds.minX) /
                2 - (text.boundsInLocal.maxX - text.boundsInLocal.minX) / 2;
        text.layoutY = MaxPhotoHeight + 20;
        return group;
    }
}
```

8.4 Mouse Dragging

Mouse dragging is a common action with graphical applications. In JavaFX, you can drag any type of node in a scene graph, including groups, layout nodes, text components, shapes, and of course, images (ImageView components).

In this section, you'll see how to add mouse dragging capabilities to the Wall of Photos application. Users can select a photo to drag (with a mouse press event), move the photo (with a mouse move event), and end drag operations (with a mouse release event). The application restricts how you can move the photo, as follows. Although you can drag the photo anywhere on the scene, when you release the mouse (and dragging stops) the photo returns to the nearest slot (first, middle, or last) within its own category row. That is, you can change photo locations only within the same row. Figure 8.7 shows the application during a photo drag operation.

Adding mouse dragging to the Wall of Photos application requires changes to the Photo custom node only. Listing 8.12 shows the updated code with changes in bold. Mouse dragging requires three different mouse event handlers in a press-drag-release gesture. Property onMousePressed specifies the press handler which starts the process. The handler records the current placement of the node as reflected in node properties translateX and translateY.

```
onMousePressed: function(e: MouseEvent): Void {
    startDragX = translateX;
    startDragY = translateY;
}
```

The onMouseDragged handler is continuously invoked as the user drags the mouse. The event includes the x and y offsets (dragX and dragY) relative to the most recent press event if the MouseEvent is part of a press-drag-release gesture (otherwise the value is 0). Updating translateX and translateY with these offsets moves the node in the scene graph.

```
onMouseDragged: function(e: MouseEvent): Void {
    translateX = startDragX + e.dragX;
    translateY = startDragY + e.dragY;
}
```

The onMouseReleased handler is called at the end of the mouse dragging gesture. Here, the node returns to its original vertical position (keeping the node in its own row) by resetting translateY to zero. Function findXPos finds the nearest slot in the row. In this case, the node will be at location 0 (xPos1), 222 (xPos2), or 444 (xPos3) by setting translateX to the new location after adjusting for its original location (in xOffset).

```
onMouseReleased: function(e: MouseEvent): Void {
    translateY = 0;
    findXPos();
}
```

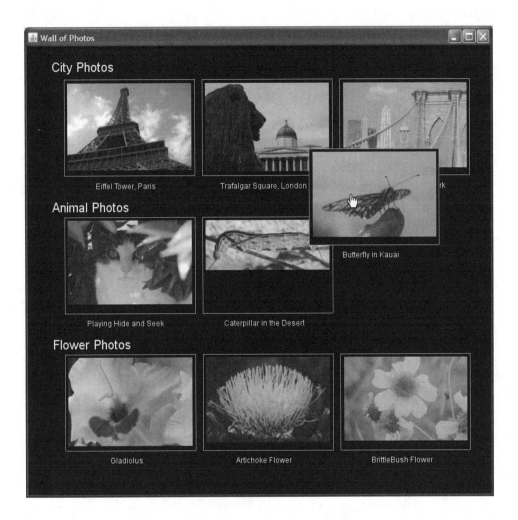

Figure 8.7 Implementing dragging actions

When the user releases the mouse, the node "jumps back" back to its own row and slides into either the first, second, or third slot in the row.

Listing 8.12 Updated CustomNode Photo (Photo.fx)

```
public class Photo extends CustomNode {

    public-init var imageName: String;
    public-init var title: String;
```

```
public-init var xOffset: Number;

def MaxPhotoHeight = 150;
def xPos1 = 0;
def xPos2 = 222;
def xPos3 = 444;

var group: Group;
var startDragX: Number;
var startDragY: Number;

function findXPos(): Void {
    var newX = xOffset + translateX;
    if (Math.abs(newX - xPos1) < Math.abs(newX - xPos2) and
    Math.abs(newX - xPos3) < Math.abs(newX - xPos1)) {
        translateX = xPos3 - xOffset;
    }
    else if (Math.abs(newX - xPos2) < Math.abs(newX - xPos1) and
    Math.abs(newX - xPos3) < Math.abs(newX - xPos2)){
        translateX = xPos3 - xOffset;
    }
    else if (Math.abs(newX - xPos2) < Math.abs(newX - xPos1)) {
        translateX = xPos2 - xOffset;
    }
    else {
        translateX = xPos1 - xOffset;
    }
}

protected override function create(): Node {
    var text: Text;
    var pic: ImageView;

        content: [
            Rectangle {
                width: 210
                height: MaxPhotoHeight
                stroke: Color.DARKGRAY
                cursor: Cursor.HAND
                blocksMouse: true

                onMousePressed: function(e: MouseEvent): Void {
                    startDragX = translateX;
                    startDragY = translateY;
                }
                onMouseDragged: function(e: MouseEvent): Void {
                    translateX = startDragX + e.dragX;
                    translateY = startDragY + e.dragY;
                }
                onMouseReleased: function(e: MouseEvent): Void {
                    translateY = 0;
                    findXPos();
```

```
                    }
                }
                pic = ImageView {
                    layoutX: 5
                    layoutY: 5
                    image: Image {
                        url: "{__DIR__}images/{imageName}.jpg"
                    }
                }
                text = Text {
                    fill: Color.WHITE
                    content: title
                }
            ]
        }
        text.layoutX = (pic.layoutBounds.maxX - pic.layoutBounds.minX) /
                2 - (text.boundsInLocal.maxX - text.boundsInLocal.minX) / 2;
        text.layoutY = MaxPhotoHeight + 20;
        return group;
    }

}
```

8.5 Animated Photo Carousel

Our final example in this chapter is a rotating photo carousel, as shown in Figure 8.8. As each photo fades in, it pauses and then begins a slow trek along a path, shrinking to (approximately) a third of its size half-way through the rotation. As the photo moves towards its starting spot, it returns to its original size. (This simultaneous scaling and movement provide a "3D effect." The image appears to move away as it shrinks and move forward as it grows.) After the photo completes the path animation, it disappears. A new photo fades in every three and a half seconds, so you see a continuous stream of photos appearing, moving and scaling, and finally disappearing. The newest photo always appears on top of the photo right ahead of it.

Although this example uses only nine images stored in the local environment, we'll design the photo carousel so that you can make web service calls to fetch the photos instead (see Chapter 9, "Flickr: Interesting Photos" on page 301). Working with more than just nine photos (the web service example has 100) means we'll have to pay attention to image loading and the scene graph structure. To that end, you'll see that a carousel is initialized with a small number of carousel photo slots (CarouselPhoto objects). The image information is stored separately. As each CarouselPhoto object gets its turn to travel along the carousel, it accepts an image object to display. Of course, Image background loading is also crucial for a smooth-running carousel.

Figure 8.8 Animated Slide Show

Photo Carousel Scene Graph

Figure 8.9 shows a scene graph diagram of the Photo Carousel application. The Scene contains a Carousel object, which includes a sequence of CarouselPhoto objects. The CarouselPhoto is a custom node with ImageView, Text, and Rectangle components. The Carousel also keeps its images in a sequence of CarouselImage objects. A CarouselImage is a convenience class (not a custom node) that includes the Image component and its title. The CarouselPhoto's ImageView component does not initialize its Image component until it is activated in the carousel.

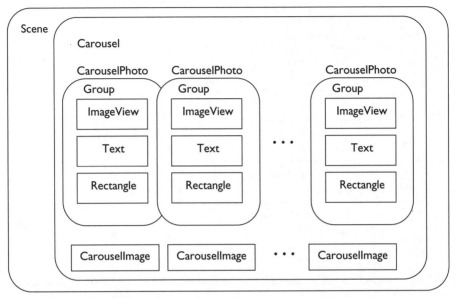

Figure 8.9 Scene graph diagram for the Photo Carousel application

CarouselPhoto Animation

Each CarouselPhoto includes a SequentialTransition object, which defines its animation behavior in the carousel. Figure 8.10 shows a diagram of the CarouselPhoto animation. In the sequential transition, each CarouselPhoto first fades in (from opacity 0 to opacity 1), then pauses. After the pause transition completes, a parallel transition begins. In parallel, the CarouselPhoto scales down as it begins its path transition. Half-way through the path transition, the scale transition completes and auto reverses so that it returns to full size at the same time that the path transition completes.

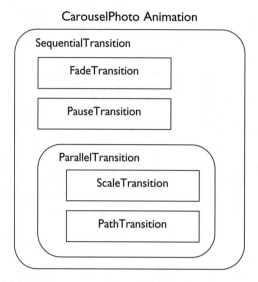

Figure 8.10 Nested transition diagram for the CarouselPhoto animation sequence

CarouselPhoto Custom Node

Listing 8.13 through Listing 8.15 show the code for the CarouselPhoto custom node. Listing 8.13 includes the class variables and the timeline that jump starts a Carousel-Photo animation sequence. Public function play starts the timeline, which makes the node visible and positions it so that the photo is centered when it fades in. Function carouselAnimation.playFromStart starts the CarouselPhoto's animation sequence (shown in Listing 8.14). The timeline has a second key frame object invoked when the animation completes. This key frame makes the node invisible once again.

Listing 8.13 CarouselPhoto Class Variables and Timeline

```
public class CarouselPhoto extends CustomNode {
    // Initialized class variables
    public-init var x: Number;
    public-init var y: Number;
    public-init var carouselElements: PathElement[];

    // Public variables in binding expressions
    public var image: Image;
    public var photoTitle: String;

    // Class variables
    var pic: ImageView;
```

```
var group: Group;
var title: Text;
var rec: Rectangle;
def animationDuration = 26s;

def timeline = Timeline {
    keyFrames: [
        KeyFrame {
            time: 0s
            action: function(): Void {
                opacity = 0.0;
                visible = true;
                translateX = -( layoutBounds.width / 2 ) ;
                translateY = -( layoutBounds.height / 2 ) ;
                carouselAnimation.playFromStart();
                toFront();
            }
        }
        KeyFrame {
            time: animationDuration + 4.0s
            action: function(): Void {
                visible = false;
            }
        }
    ]
}

public function play() {
    timeline.playFromStart();
}
```

SequentialTransition carouselAnimation is responsible for animating the Carousel-Photo. First, a fade transition fades in the node. Next, a pause transition starts. Lastly, the parallel transition begins. The parallel transition starts a scale transition and a path transition. The scale transition completes in half the time, auto reverses, and repeats. The path transition follows a path from the path elements supplied with the object literal initialization variable carouselElements (defined in the Carousel object).

Listing 8.14 CarouselPhoto Animation Sequence

```
def carouselAnimation = SequentialTransition {
  node: this
  content: [
      FadeTransition {
          duration: 1.5s
          fromValue: 0.0
          toValue: 1.0
      }
      PauseTransition {
          duration: 2.5s
```

```
            }
        ParallelTransition {
            node: this
            content: [
                ScaleTransition {
                    duration: animationDuration / 2
                    toX: .4
                    toY: .4
                    autoReverse: true
                    repeatCount: 2
                }
                PathTransition {
                    duration: animationDuration
                    interpolator: Interpolator.EASEOUT
                    path: AnimationPath.createFromPath(Path {
                        elements: carouselElements
                    })
                }
            ]
        }  // ParallelTransition
    ]
};
```

Listing 8.15 includes the CarouselPhoto scene graph (its diagram is shown in
Figure 8.9 on page 275). Note that the ImageView component binds property image to
a public class variable, allowing the underlying image to change under program control. Similarly, the Text component binds its content property to a public class variable. The size of the Rectangle depends on the size of the ImageView component with
bind expressions for height and width. Similarly, the placement of the title (the Text
component) depends on the size of the ImageView component. The title appears
below the image and is centered. Its width depends on the width of the ImageView
component.

Listing 8.15 CarouselPhoto Scene Graph

```
protected override function create(): Node {
    group = Group {
        content: [
            pic = ImageView {
                x: x + 5
                y: y + 5
                image: bind image
            }
            title = Text {
                x: x
                y: y
                fill: Color.LIGHTGRAY
                wrappingWidth: bind rec.width - 10
                textAlignment: TextAlignment.CENTER
```

```
                    layoutX: bind pic.layoutBounds.width /
                        2 - title.boundsInLocal.width / 2
                    layoutY: bind pic.layoutBounds.height + 15
                    content: bind photoTitle
                }
                rec = Rectangle {
                    fill: Color.web("#666666")
                    x: x
                    y: y
                    height: bind pic.layoutBounds.height +
                                title.layoutBounds.height + 10;
                    width: bind pic.layoutBounds.width + 10
                }
            ]
        }
        rec.toBack();
        return group;
    }
}
```

Carousel Custom Node

Listing 8.16 through Listing 8.18 show the Carousel custom node. The Carousel builds the sequence of CarouselPhoto objects and controls the animation by selecting the next slot (CarouselPhoto). This initiates the animation sequence and the next image slides into the selected CarouselPhoto object.

Listing 8.16 includes the Carousel class initialization variables that control the size and placement of the PathTransition path elements. These variables are dependent on screen size and are initialized by the main script.

Programming Tip

The main script supplies the screen size and images to the carousel, which are all the carousel needs to configure itself.

Sequence carouselPhotos is initialized to hold MaxPhotoSlots elements (in Listing 8.18). Sequence images holds the CarouselImage elements. The images sequence is built by successive calls to public function addImage. Thus, the number of images is not dependent on the number of slots in the carousel. There is *not* a one-to-one correspondence between carousel slots and images. This permits a large number of images if needed, or even just one image displayed multiple times.

Listing 8.16 Carousel class variables and function addImage

```
public class Carousel extends CustomNode {
```

```
// Initialized class variables that are dependent on screen size
public-init var centerX: Number;
public-init var centerY: Number;
public-init var radiusX: Number;
public-init var radiusY: Number;

var group: Group;
// How many slots the carousel will have
def MaxPhotoSlots = 12;
// Sequence images includes each Image object
var images: CarouselImage[];

// variables used to grab the next image for
// the carousel photo slot
var imageNumber = 0;
var currentSlot = 0;

public function addImage(filename: String, title: String): Void {
    insert
    CarouselImage {
        filename: filename
        title: title
    } into images;
}
```

Listing 8.17 includes the path elements that initialize each CarouselPhoto's PathTransition (see Listing 8.14 on page 277 for the PathTransition code). The path element
starts with object MoveTo and then defines two ArcTo objects, creating an elliptical
animation path based on the coordinate values supplied by the main script.

Listing 8.17 PathElements that define the PathTransition

```
// PathElements used to control each CarouselPhoto animation
// PathElements are dependent on screen size
def carouselElements = [
    MoveTo {
        x: centerX
        y: centerY + radiusY
    },
    ArcTo {
        x: centerX
        y: centerY - radiusY
        radiusX: radiusX
        radiusY: radiusY
        sweepFlag: false
    },
    ArcTo {
        x: centerX
        y: centerY + radiusY
        radiusX: radiusX
```

```
            radiusY: radiusY
            sweepFlag: false
        }
    ];
```

Listing 8.18 includes the public play function, which starts the carousel by invoking its timeline. The timeline object runs indefinitely. Every three and a half seconds the timeline selects the next image to slide into the next carousel slot and start its animation.

The public create function builds the Carousel node, which includes a sequence of CarouselPhoto objects initialized with the necessary path elements and coordinates.

Listing 8.18 Carousel Animation and Scene Graph

```
// Start the Carousel
public function play(): Void {
    timeline.play();
}

// Control the Carousel's animation
def timeline = Timeline {
    repeatCount: Timeline.INDEFINITE
    keyFrames: [
        KeyFrame {
            time: 3.5s
            action: function(): Void {
                if (imageNumber >= sizeof images) {
                    imageNumber = 0;
                }
                if (currentSlot >= MaxPhotoSlots) {
                    currentSlot = 0;
                }
                var slot = carouselPhotos[currentSlot];
                slot.image = images[imageNumber].image;
                slot.photoTitle = images[imageNumber].title;
                slot.play();
                currentSlot++;
                imageNumber++;
            }
        }
    ]
}

// carouselPhotos is the sequence of CarouselPhoto slots
def carouselPhotos = for (i in [0 .. MaxPhotoSlots - 1]) {
    CarouselPhoto {
        carouselElements: carouselElements
        x: centerX
        y: centerY + radiusY
```

```
            visible: false
        }
    }

    protected override function create(): Node {
        return group = Group {
            content: carouselPhotos
        }
    }
}
```

Class CarouselImage

Class CarouselImage (see Listing 8.19) is a convenience class that includes an Image object plus the title of the image. You initialize it with a title and the image filename (which the class assumes is stored in the local environment).

The Image object sets backgroundLoading to true and provides load-time scaling with properties width and height. Property preserveRatio is set to true, which means the height and width act as maximum limits, not absolute sizes.

Listing 8.19 CarouselImage Class

```
public class CarouselImage {
    public-init var title: String;
    public-init var filename: String;
    public var image: Image = Image {
        url: "{__DIR__}images/{filename}.jpg"
        width: 220
        height: 200
        preserveRatio: true
        backgroundLoading: true
    }
}
```

Main Script

Listing 8.20 shows the main script that initiates the Photo Carousel application. It instantiates the Carousel with dimensions that depend on the size of the application Scene object. The PhotoData sequence contains the same data shown earlier (see Listing 8.9 on page 266). Class PhotoData was also shown earlier (see Listing 8.8 on page 266). Function loadImages accesses each PhotoData object and invokes Carousel function addImage, building the Carousel's image sequence. After all the images are initialized (but not necessarily loaded), the carousel action begins with Carousel function play.

The main script scene graph includes the Carousel in the scene with a linear gradient fill (black to dark gray). Function loadImages is called after the scene graph is defined.

Listing 8.20 Photo Carousel Main Script (Main.fx)

```
def sceneHeight = 500;
def sceneWidth = 400;
var carousel = Carousel {
    centerX: sceneWidth / 2.2
    centerY: sceneHeight / 2.4
    radiusX: sceneWidth * .26
    radiusY: sceneHeight * .24
};

def photoData: PhotoData[] = [ . . . see Listing 8.9 . . . ];


function loadImages(): Void {
    for (data in photoData) {
        carousel.addImage(data.filename, data.title);
    }
    carousel.play();
}

Stage {
    title: "Photo Carousel"
    width: sceneWidth
    height: sceneHeight
    scene: Scene {
        fill: LinearGradient {
            startX: 1
            startY: .2
            endX: 1,
            endY: 1
            stops: [
                Stop {
                    offset: 0
                    color: Color.BLACK
                },
                Stop {
                    offset: 1
                    color: Color.web("#666666")
                }
            ]
        }
        content: carousel
    }
}

loadImages();
```

9 Web Services

Web services open up a whole world of data. Whether you're interested in the weather, real estate values, stock quotes (probably not), videos, buying things, finding restaurants, or finding airline flights and hotels, there's a web service API out there that probably provides the data you're looking for. In this chapter you'll learn how to call web services with JavaFX using HttpRequest to invoke the web service and Pull-Parser to process the response document. You'll see how to do this first without actually invoking a web service. Then, you'll use the Flickr web service API to build examples with "real data." This chapter uses the JavaFX Image and ImageView classes along with concepts presented in the previous chapter for working with images.

What You Will Learn

- XML and JSON document structure

- Using PullParser to process XML and JSON documents

- Using HttpRequest to make asynchronous HTTP requests

- Monitoring HttpRequest execution cycle with callbacks

- Accessing the response InputStream with HttpRequest and PullParser

- Handling errors with HttpRequest

- Using the JavaFX TextBox component

- Build custom PullParser objects to process Flickr web service response data

- Invoking Flickr web service methods

- Integrating Flickr data with the animated photo carousel application

9.1 JavaFX Pull Parsers

The JavaFX PullParser is a class that parses XML or JSON data under program control. As the pull parser parses data, it generates events. When you setup a pull parser class, you specify which events you're interested in. XML and JSON documents are similar in that they both self-describe hierarchical structures. However, PullParser objects differ for each format and each target data source. Both XML and JSON are commonly used to describe data returned from web service calls, but you can use either XML or JSON to describe any sort of configurable data.

To explore the JavaFX PullParser class, we'll present the Wall of Photos application that renders a grid of photos with categories and titles from the previous chapter (see "Building a Wall of Photos" on page 264). To describe the photos, the updated application includes an XML document that specifies the categories, filenames, and titles of each image. Then, we'll modify the PullParser object to parse a JSON document with the same data.

The Advantage of Using Configurable Data

The Wall of Photos application in the previous chapter statically defines the photo data in object literals for each image (see Listing 8.9 on page 266). A PullParser is a better approach, because you can change images and photo information without editing your JavaFX source code.

XML Parsing

XML is a markup language that structures data. XML markup is both easy to parse and human readable. Since XML is a common data format, JavaFX includes a Pull-Parser class that parses XML data under program control. In this section, you'll see how to use the XML parser in an example that describes photos.

XML is a simple, hierarchical structure that is self-descriptive. Here is an XML example that describes a person.

```
<person>
    <name>John Doe</name>
    <address>
        <street>123 Main Street</street>
        <city>OurTown</city>
        <state name="California" abbr="CA"/>
    </address>
    <phone>555-333-1234</phone>
</person>
```

From this XML, it's clear that the above structure describes a person object consisting of name, address, and phone number. Object address, in turn, includes street, city, and state. Objects (or tags) include an open tag (such as <name>) and a pairing close tag (</name>). Nesting within tag objects provides the hierarchical structure (or levels).

The JavaFX PullParser identifies tag `<person>` here as a level 0 `START_ELEMENT`, `<name>` is a level 1 `START_ELEMENT`, and `</name>` is a level 1 `END_ELEMENT`.

Tags can also specify named attributes. In the above example, tag `<state>` specifies attribute `name` and attribute `abbr`. In addition, tag `<state>` uses an alternate form of closure where the closing mark is included with the open tag.

```
<state name="California" abbr="CA"/>
```

The JavaFX PullParser includes function `getAttributeValue` to retrieve these attribute values.

Table 9.1 shows the common properties of class PullParser.

TABLE 9.1 Class PullParser Common Properties

Variable	Type	Description
documentType	String	Type of content handled by parser. Either `PullParser.XML` or `PullParser.JSON`.
encoding	String	Content character encoding.
event	Event	Current parser event, which changes as the parser moves through the XML or JSON document.
ignoreWhiteSpace	Boolean	If true, ignores whitespaces and new lines for a TEXT event.
input	InputStream	Source content to parse. Applications must close the stream when the parser is done.
onEvent	function(e: Event): Void	Callback, reports the current parse event (Event) to the function.
START_DOCUMENT END_DOCUMENT	Integer	Value of `Event.type` indicating the start (or end) of JSON or XML document.
START_ELEMENT END_ELEMENT	Integer	Value of `Event.type` indicating the start (or end) of an XML element or JSON object.
TEXT	Integer	Value of `Event.type` indicating text in an XML or JSON element.
START_ARRAY END_ARRAY	Integer	Value of `Event.type` indicating the start (or end) of a JSON array.
START_ARRAY_ELEMENT END_ARRAY_ELEMENT	Integer	Value of `Event.type` indicating the start (or end) of a JSON array element.

TABLE 9.1 Class PullParser Common Properties *(Continued)*

Variable	Type	Description
START_VALUE END_VALUE	Integer	Value of Event.type indicating the start (or end) of a JSON object value.
TRUE, FALSE	Boolean	Value of Event.type indicating a JSON true (or false) value.

To see how to use the PullParser class to parse XML documents, let's return to the Wall of Photos example from the previous chapter (see Figure 8.5 on page 264). Then, you'll see the PullParser object that parses it.

Listing 9.1 shows the XML document that describes the photos. Tag <?xml> generates a PullParser START_DOCUMENT event type and tag <photo> generates a PullParser START_ELEMENT event type with level 0. Tag <category> generates a PullParser START_ELEMENT event type with level 1. Its attribute (name) specifies the category name, reported with the PullParser event function getAttributeValue, which returns String "city" for the first <category> tag.

Likewise, multiple <image> tags (event type START_ELEMENT with level 2) have attributes filename and title.

Listing 9.1 photo.xml

```
<?xml version="1.0" encoding="UTF-8"?>
<photo>
   <category name="city">
      <image filename="paris" title="Eiffel Tower, Paris"/>
      <image filename="london" title="Trafalgar Square, London" />
      <image filename="newyork" title="Brooklyn Bridge, New York"/>
   </category>

   <category name="animal">
      <image filename="kitty" title="Playing Hide and Seek"/>
      <image filename="catepillar" title="Catepillar in the Desert"/>
      <image filename="butterfly" title="Butterfly in Kauai"/>
   </category>

   <category name="flower">
      <image filename="gladiolus" title="Gladiolus"/>
      <image filename="artichoke" title="Artichoke Flower"/>
      <image filename="brittlebush" title="BrittleBush Flower"/>
   </category>
</photo>
```

The Wall of Photos application displays nine images sorted into three categories (city, animal, and flower). Each image includes its filename (paris, london, etc.) and title.

The application parses this XML document and builds a wall of photos consisting of one row for each category.

Listing 9.2 through Listing 9.4 show the JavaFX code for the XML version of the Wall of Photos application. Only Listing 9.2 is different from the original version (shown in Listing 8.10 on page 267), but the entire **Main.fx** script is included here as well.

Listing 9.2 shows the PullParser class that parses the XML document and builds the image-filled scene graph. The PullParser object (myparser) specifies the document type (PullParser.XML), an input source (photo.xml for property input), and a parsing event handler (property onEvent). The bulk of the code consists of the event handler, a function that includes argument Event e, the parsing event.

The PullParser generates events that include type names, nesting levels, and attributes. In the XML document in Listing 9.1, for example, tag <photo> is event level 0, tag <category> is level 1, and tag <image> is level 2. The event handler uses the event types and levels which determine its corresponding actions. An open tag generates a START_ELEMENT event type and a close tag generates an END_ELEMENT event type.

The event handler looks for level 1 START_ELEMENT events, which include the open <category> tags. Attribute name indicates the category text. The event handler calls function setTargetList with an HBox (horizontal box) layout component (cityList, animalList, or flowerList) and a string for the title of the group. Function setTargetList builds a Text component to display the category name and inserts the component into the appropriate scene graph content node.

The event handler also looks for level 2 START_ELEMENT events. These will be the <image> tags, which include attributes filename and title. The handler initializes the Photo custom node with these attribute values.

You can also look for END_ELEMENT events, although the PullParser object in Listing 9.2 does not need to do this. These END_ELEMENT event types correspond to the closing tags such as </photo> (at nesting level 0), </category> (level 1), and </image> (level 2).

Listing 9.2 PullParser Object for XML (Main.fx)

```
var categoryName: String;
var myparser = PullParser {
    documentType: PullParser.XML
    input: new FileInputStream("photo.xml")
    onEvent: function(e: Event): Void {
        if (e.type == PullParser.START_ELEMENT and e.level == 1) {
            categoryName = e.getAttributeValue(QName{name: "name"});
            // city
            if (categoryName.equals("city")) {
                setTargetList(cityList, "City Photos");
            }
```

```
            // animal
            else if (categoryName.equals("animal")) {
                setTargetList(animalList, "Animal Photos");
            }
            // flowers
            else if (categoryName.equals("flower")) {
                setTargetList(flowerList, "Flower Photos");
            }
        }
        if (e.type == PullParser.START_ELEMENT and e.level == 2) {
            // Build a Photo node using filename and title
            insert
            Photo {
                imageName: e.getAttributeValue(QName{name: "filename"})
                title: e.getAttributeValue(QName{name: "title"})
                xOffset: xOffset
            } into targetList.content;
            xOffset += 222;
        }
    }
}
myparser.parse();
myparser.input.close();
```

Once you define a PullParser object in your program, you invoke it with the parse
member function. To invoke PullParser myparser, for example, use

```
    myparser.parse();
```

PullParser Tip

*It is the responsibility of the caller to close the InputStream specified for PullParser property
input, as shown above with* `myparser.input.close()`.

Listing 9.3 shows the other support components and functions for the Wall of Photos
application.

Listing 9.3 Support Components and Functions (Main.fx)

```
def boxIndent = 20;
def boxSpace = 10;
def categoryFont = Font {
    size: 20
}
var xOffset = 0.0;
// Each category has its own HBox component that
// includes the category title Text node
// and the custom node Photo that displays
// the image
```

```
var cityList = HBox {
    layoutX: boxIndent
    spacing: boxSpace
}
var animalList = HBox {
    layoutX: boxIndent
    spacing: boxSpace
}
var flowerList = HBox {
    layoutX: boxIndent
    spacing: boxSpace
}
// photoList holds all three HBox components
var photoList = VBox {
    spacing: 10
    layoutX: 40
}
var targetList: HBox;

// Create the category title's Text node and set the
// correct category HBox component
function setTargetList(target: HBox, categoryTitle: String): Void {
    insert Text {
        layoutY: 20
        font: categoryFont
        fill: Color.WHITE
        content: categoryTitle
    } into photoList.content;
    targetList = target;
    insert target into photoList.content;
    xOffset = 0;
}
```

Listing 9.4 shows the scene graph for the Wall of Photos application.

Listing 9.4 Scene Graph for Wall of Photos Application (Main.fx)

```
Stage {
    title: "XML Photos"
    scene: Scene {
        fill: Color.BLACK
        height: 700
        width: 750
        content: Group {
            layoutY: 20
            content: photoList
        }
    }
}
```

Listing 9.5 shows the CustomNode Photo that builds each ImageView component, framing Rectangle, and Text node (the image's title). The images are in the local environment ({__DIR__}images/) and all are JPG files with a consistent width and various heights. Note that CustomNode Photo is unchanged from the original Wall of Photos application (as shown in Listing 8.11 on page 269).

Listing 9.5 CustomNode Photo (Photo.fx)

```
public class Photo extends CustomNode {
    public-init var imageName: String;
    public-init var title: String;
    public-init var xOffset: Number;

    def MaxPhotoHeight = 150;
    var group: Group;

    protected override function create(): Node {
        var text: Text;
        var pic: ImageView;

        group = Group {
            content: [
                Rectangle {
                    width: 210
                    height: MaxPhotoHeight
                    stroke: Color.DARKGRAY
                }
                pic = ImageView {
                    layoutX: 5
                    layoutY: 5
                    image: Image {
                        url: "{__DIR__}images/{imageName}.jpg"
                    }
                }
                text = Text {
                    fill: Color.WHITE
                    content: title
                }
            ]
        }
        text.layoutX = (pic.layoutBounds.maxX - pic.layoutBounds.minX) /
                2 - (text.boundsInLocal.maxX - text.boundsInLocal.minX) / 2;
        text.layoutY = MaxPhotoHeight + 20;
        return group;
    }
}
```

JSON Parsing

JavaFX's PullParser can parse JSON (JavaScript Object Notation) data as well as XML data. JSON, like XML, is also used for data exchange applications and is common with web services response data. Like XML, JSON is self documenting. In addition, JSON tends to be more compact than XML.

JSON objects (nodes) consist of name-value pairs with a colon : separator. Braces { } delimit objects and commas separate name-value pairs. Brackets [ ] specify array elements.

Listing 9.6 describes the same set of images as Listing 9.1 (see page 288), using JSON instead of XML. Nodes "city", "animal", and "flower" all contain three array elements each that describe the "filename" and "title" of each image.

Listing 9.6 photo.json

```
{"photo": {"city": [
    {"filename": "paris","title": "Eiffel Tower, Paris"},
    {"filename": "london", "title": "Trafalgar Square, London"},
    {"filename": "newyork", "title": "Brooklyn Bridge, New York"}],

    "animal": [
    {"filename": "kitty", "title": "Playing Hide and Seek"},
    {"filename": "catepillar", "title": "Catepillar in the Desert"},
    {"filename": "butterfly", "title": "Butterfly in Kauai"}],

    "flower": [
    {"filename": "gladiolus", "title": "Gladiolus"},
    {"filename": "artichoke", "title": "Artichoke Flower"},
    {"filename": "brittlebush", "title": "BrittleBush Flower"}]
}}
```

Listing 9.7 is a PullParser defined for this JSON document. It sets property document-Type to PullParser.JSON, property input to file "photo.json", and property onEvent to the event handler that responds to parsing events.

The event handler listens for JSON parsing event level 1 START_VALUE (to get the category names and add HBox components to the scene graph), level 2 TEXT (to parse the title and filename values), and level 2 END_VALUE (to build the Photo object from the saved title and filename values).

No other changes are required in the application to parse the JSON document instead of the XML document.

Listing 9.7 PullParser Object for JSON

```
var imageTitle: String;
var imageFilename: String;

var myparser = PullParser {
    documentType: PullParser.JSON
    input: new FileInputStream("photo.json")
    onEvent: function(e: Event): Void {
        if (e.type == PullParser.START_VALUE and e.level == 1) {
          // city
            if (e.name.equals("city")) {
                setTargetList(cityList, "City Photos");
            }

          // animal
            else if (e.name.equals("animal")) {
                setTargetList(animalList, "Animal Photos");
            }

          // flowers
            else if (e.name.equals("flower")) {
                setTargetList(flowerList, "Flower Photos");
            }
        }
        if (e.type == PullParser.TEXT and e.level == 2) {
          // save the text so we can build a Photo object
            if (e.name.equals("filename")) {
                imageFilename = e.text;
            }
            else if (e.name.equals("title")) {
                imageTitle = e.text;
            }
        }
        if (e.type == PullParser.END_ELEMENT and e.level == 2) {
            var pic: Photo;
            insert
            pic = Photo {
                imageName: imageFilename
                title: imageTitle
                xOffset: xOffset
            }
            into targetList.content;
            xOffset += 222;
        }
    }
}
myparser.parse();
myparser.input.close();
```

Animated Photo Carousel

The previous chapter includes an animated Photo Carousel using the same nine images (see "Animated Photo Carousel" on page 273) with object literals that build the Image objects, as seen here in Figure 9.1.

Figure 9.1 Animated Slide Show implemented with XML PullParser

In the same way we upgraded the Wall of Photos application with PullParser, you can enhance the Photo Carousel application to parse either an XML or JSON document for the image information.

Listing 9.8 shows the upgraded loadImages function that now uses a PullParser object to read the images for the carousel from an XML document. (Listing 8.20 on page 283 shows the original loadImages function.)

Note that the PullParser in Listing 9.8 is much simpler than the XML PullParser used for the Wall of Photos application (shown in Listing 9.2 on page 289) even though the source XML document is the same. The Wall of Photos application must determine the category name for each photo. Here, the Photo Carousel application doesn't use categories.

Listing 9.8 Function loadImages implemented with XML PullParser

```
function loadImages(): Void {
    var myparser = PullParser {
        documentType: PullParser.XML
        input: new FileInputStream("photo.xml")
        onEvent: function(e: Event): Void {
            if (e.type == PullParser.START_ELEMENT and e.level == 2) {
                // Add the image to the carousel
                carousel.addImage(e.getAttributeValue(QName{name: "filename"}),
                        e.getAttributeValue(QName{name: "title"}));
            }
        }
    }
    myparser.parse();
    myparser.input.close();
    carousel.play();
}
```

9.2 JavaFX HttpRequest

Besides PullParser, a second JavaFX class helps you with web service requests: HttpRequest. Class HttpRequest provides an API that makes asynchronous HTTP requests. (The key word here is *asynchronous*. The web service call goes out and your callbacks are invoked during the request and response process.) There are several types of HTTP requests: GET, PUT, POST, and DELETE. Request type GET lets you request data from a URL (a location). For example, browsers use HTTP requests to display markup (returning, for example, XHTML or HTML). You can also use GET requests to invoke RESTful Web Services, which return either XML or JSON data (this is how we'll invoke web services). We'll discuss HttpRequest with method GET.

Using HttpRequest

HttpRequest lets you specify a location (URL) and method (such as GET or PUT) and start an HTTP operation with function start. HttpRequest properties (such as started, connecting, reading and done) change their state as the operation proceeds. You can specify callback functions (for example, onStarted, onConnecting, onRead, onInput, and onException) in your program that respond to specific execution steps in the request and access the appropriate HttpRequest properties. For requests that read or write large amounts of data, you can monitor the percentage progress using properties read and toread.

Table 9.2 shows the callback functions for an HTTP GET request with HttpRequest. Unless indicated otherwise, all callback functions are invoked at most once in a GET HttpRequest operation.

TABLE 9.2 HttpRequest Common Callbacks for Read Operations

Callback	Type	When Callback Is Invoked
onStarted	function():Void	HTTP request has started execution.
onConnecting	function():Void	Request is attempting to connect to location.
onDoneConnect	function():Void	Request is now connected to location.
onReadingHeaders	function():Void	Request is starting to read HTTP response headers, responseCode, responseMessage and error, if any.
onResponseCode	function(:Integer):Void	HTTP response code from the server is available.
onResponseMessage	function(:String):Void	HTTP response message from the server is available.
onError	function(:InputStream):Void	InputStream containing an error response from the server is available. The provided InputStream must be closed when done reading in a finally block.
onDoneHeaders	function():Void	Request is done reading response headers.
onReading	function():Void	Request is starting to read the response body.
onToRead	function(:Long):Void	Indicates total number of bytes to read, if available. (If negative, then not available.)
onRead	function(:Long):Void	Indicates number of bytes read so far. (Invoked possibly multiple times.)
onInput	function(:InputStream):Void	Request body is available. The provided InputStream must be closed when done reading in a finally block.
onDoneRead	function():Void	Request is done reading the response body.
onDone	function():Void	Request has finished execution.

Programming Tip

Note that InputStream must be closed in a finally block with the onError and onInput callback functions when you are done reading. Here is a code snippet that shows you how to do this with the onInput callback function.

```
onInput: function(inputStream: java.io.InputStream) {
    try {
        // process InputStream inputStream
```

```
    } finally {
        // close InputStream inputStream
        inputStream.close();
    }
}
```

Let's perform a simple Get request with URL `http://javafx.com/`. We won't process any input; however, we'll define callback functions that monitor each step in the request. As the HttpRequest object executes the request, various callback functions display output. Figure 9.2 shows the results of running this test application.

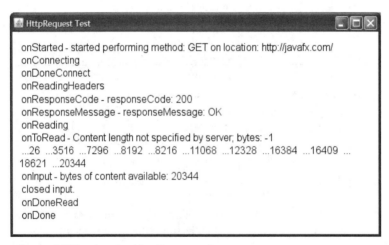

Figure 9.2 Testing the HttpRequest class

Listing 9.9 shows the code for the HttpRequest object literal and the defined callback functions for this test application. Script variable `message` is updated with new content as the request proceeds. The call to initiate the HttpRequest is `getRequest.start();`

Listing 9.9 HttpRequest Test Run

```
var message: String;
def getRequest: HttpRequest = HttpRequest {

    location: "http://javafx.com/"
    method: HttpRequest.GET

    onStarted: function() {
        message = "{message} onStarted - started performing method:
```

```
            {getRequest.method} on location: {getRequest.location}\n";
}

onConnecting: function() {
    message = "{message} onConnecting\n";
}
onDoneConnect: function() {
    message = "{message} onDoneConnect\n";
}
onReadingHeaders: function() {
    message = "{message} onReadingHeaders\n";
}
onResponseCode: function(code:Integer) {
    message = "{message} onResponseCode - responseCode: {code}\n";
}
onResponseMessage: function(msg: String) {
    message = "{message} onResponseMessage - responseMessage: {msg}\n";
}

onResponseHeaders: function(headerNames: String[]) {
    for (name in headerNames) {
        println("    {name}: {getRequest.getResponseHeaderValue(name)}");
    }
}

onReading: function() {
    message = "{message} onReading\n";
}

onToRead: function(bytes: Long) {
    if (bytes < 0) {
        message = "{message} onToRead -
            Content length not specified by server; bytes: {bytes}\n";
    } else {
        message = "{message} onToRead -
            total number of content bytes to read: {bytes}\n";
    }
}

// onRead can be used to show the
// progress of reading the content from the location.
onRead: function(bytes: Long) {
    message = "{message} ...{bytes} ";
}

// The response content is available in argument inputStream
onInput: function(inputStream: java.io.InputStream) {
    // use input stream to access content here.
    // can use input.available() to see how many bytes are available.
    try {
        message = "{message}\n onInput - bytes of content available: "
                  "{inputStream.available()}\n";
```

```
        } finally {
            // close InputStream to free up resources
            inputStream.close();
            message = "{message} closed input.\n";
        }
    }

    onException: function(ex: java.lang.Exception) {
        message = "{message} onException - exception:
            {ex.getClass()} {ex.getMessage()}\n";
    }
    onDoneRead: function() {
        message = "{message} onDoneRead\n";
    }
    onDone: function() {
        message = "{message} onDone\n";
    }
}

getRequest.start();
```

Listing 9.10 includes the scene graph for the HttpRequest test program. Note that the Text object literal content property binds to the script variable message.

Listing 9.10 HttpRequest Test Scene Graph

```
Stage {
    title: "HttpRequest Test"
    width: 600
    height: 350
    scene: Scene {
        content: Text {
            font: Font {
                size: 16
            }
            x: 10,
            y: 30
            content: bind message
            wrappingWidth: 550
        }
    }
}
```

9.3 Flickr: Interesting Photos

With our tools finally assembled (PullParser, HttpRequest, and a modular Photo Carousel application), it's time to integrate HttpRequest with the Photo Carousel to display photos from Flickr's web site.

Flickr

Flickr (`www.flickr.com`) is an online social, photo management, and photo sharing site where people post their favorite photos, tag them, and make them available for friends, groups, or the world to see. Flickr users can tag images, provide titles, and organize images in creative ways. Flickr has a web services API that lets you write programs to manipulate public Flickr data.

You can access the Flickr API using RESTful web service calls. You issue an HTTP GET request using a specific endpoint (location) and include a valid API key.

Flickr Tip

To apply for a Flickr API Key, go to `http://www.flickr.com/services/api/keys/apply/`. *The process is quick and painless. Once Flickr provides you with a key, you can access the Flickr API through a web service call.*

Here's the general format to invoke a RESTful web service call with Flickr.

```
http://api.flickr.com/services/rest/?method=flickr.GROUP.METHOD_NAME
        &api_key=YOUR_API_KEY&argument=ARG
```

where `GROUP` refers to the general Flickr API method group, `METHOD_NAME` is the specific API method, `YOUR_API_KEY` is your API key assigned by Flickr, and `argument` is an argument to the API method with value `ARG`. (Arguments depend on the API method invoked.) You invoke the web service call using JavaFX class HttpRequest.

Interesting Photos

Let's begin our exploration of Flickr by invoking method `flickr.interestingness.getList`, which returns a list of interesting photos from Flickr for the most recent day. The only required argument for this method is `api_key`. Optional arguments include the number of photos per page (default is 100), the number of pages returned (default is 1), a date (default is today), and extras (a comma-delimited list of extra information to include for each returned record).

To use HttpRequest, you specify the endpoint for HttpRequest property `location` as a string.

```
location: "http://api.flickr.com/services/rest/?method=flickr.interestingness"
          ".getList&api_key=YOUR_API_KEY&per_page=3";
```

Listing 9.11 is a sample XML response for method flickr.interestingness.getList
with argument per_page set to 3.

Listing 9.11 Sample Flickr XML Response

```
<rsp stat="ok">
   <photos page="1" pages="167" perpage="3" total="500">
      <photo id="3375155189" owner="35237096496@N01" secret="fcbe3c544f"
         server="3568" farm="4" title="Ray of Light" ispublic="1" isfriend="0"
         isfamily="0"/>
      <photo id="3376883783" owner="22598208@N02" secret="54cc825a1f"
         server="3432" farm="4" title="A Windy Day for Strobists" ispublic="1"
         isfriend="0" isfamily="0"/>
      <photo id="3375633598" owner="66076061@N00" secret="7720f002d4"
         server="3439" farm="4" title="Burleigh Heads Sunset" ispublic="1"
         isfriend="0" isfamily="0"/>
   </photos>
</rsp>
```

Note that Flickr returns an XML response document and expects you to construct the
URL that will fetch each image. You do this by combining <photo> tag attributes id,
secret, server, and farm, and providing an optional photo size specification with a
JPG file extension. Here is an example URL string, assuming that properties farm,
server, id, and secret are stored in JavaFX object meta. (The _m suffix indicates a small
sized photo, 240 pixels on its longest side.)

```
url: "http://farm{meta.farm}.static.flickr.com/{meta.server}/"
        "{meta.id}_{meta.secret}_m.jpg"
```

Listing 9.12 shows a sample XML response if there's an error with Flickr (such as an
invalid API key or an unrecognized method). Note that this is a valid HttpRequest
response (no problem with internet connections or valid web addresses), but Flickr is
unable to generate the requested data.

Listing 9.12 Sample Flickr Error Response

```
<?xml version="1.0" encoding="utf-8" ?>
<rsp stat="fail">
   <err code="[error-code]" msg="[error-message]" />
</rsp>
```

Now let's look at the PullParser object that extracts photo information from the XML
response (and makes sure the response is valid). From the example XML response
document in Listing 9.11 and the error response in Listing 9.12, you see that tag <rsp>

is level 0, <photos> is level 1 and <photo> is level 2. Each <photo> element includes attributes id, owner, secret, server, farm, and title, which are needed to build a JavaFX Image and also store a photo's title. The PullParser Event function getAt-tributeValue returns a value for each of these attributes.

Furthermore, an error response includes tag <err> at level 1 and attribute msg holds the error message.

Assuming the response is error-free, the PullParser builds object literal FlickrMeta to store meta data for each photo. It then passes this information to the carousel with

```
carousel.addImage(meta);
```

When the PullParser sees event type END_DOCUMENT, it indicates completion by setting boolean loadComplete to true.

If an error occurs, the parser calls function alert (shown in Listing 9.15) with the error message and sets script variable error to true. (The PullParser checks for two error situations. First, if the Flickr response returns an error status, and second, if Flickr returns a normal status but no photos are returned.)

Listing 9.13 PullParser to parse Flickr response data

```
def parser = PullParser {
    onEvent: function(event: Event) {
        if (event.type == PullParser.START_ELEMENT) {
            if (event.qname.name == "err" and event.level == 1) {
                error = true;
                alert("Flickr Failed Status",
                        event.getAttributeValue(QName {name: "msg"
                }));
            }
            else if (event.qname.name == "photos" and event.level == 1) {
                if (event.getAttributeValue(QName {name: "total"}) == "0") {
                    error = true;
                    alert("Oops", "No Photos Found");
                }
            }
            else if (event.qname.name == "photo" and event.level == 2) {
                def meta = FlickrMeta {
                    id: event.getAttributeValue(QName{name: "id"})
                    owner: event.getAttributeValue(QName{name: "owner"})
                    secret: event.getAttributeValue(QName{name: "secret"})
                    server: event.getAttributeValue(QName{name: "server"})
                    farm: event.getAttributeValue(QName{name: "farm"})
                    title: event.getAttributeValue(QName{name: "title"})
                }
                carousel.addImage(meta);
            }
        } else if (event.type == PullParser.END_DOCUMENT) {
```

```
                    if (not error) {
                        loadComplete = true;
                        println("photo data loaded");
                    }
                    else error = false;
                }
            }
        }
```

Listing 9.14 shows class FlickrMeta, which is a convenience class to encapsulate the information for each photo.

Listing 9.14 FlickrMeta Class

```
public class FlickrMeta {
    public-init var id: String;
    public-init var owner: String;
    public-init var secret: String;
    public-init var server: String;
    public-init var farm: String;
    public-init var title: String;
}
```

Let's now look at the HttpRequest object that invokes the web service API call. Listing 9.15 includes function makeServiceCall, which builds the HttpRequest object. It accepts arguments parser, the PullParser shown in Listing 9.13, and location, the HttpRequest URL for the RESTful web service. Function alert helps with error handling.

The onRead callback function displays successive "..." strings to provide feedback to the user that response data is arriving. The onInput callback function parses the response using the PullParser object. The finally block closes the input stream when parsing is complete.

Listing 9.15 Function makeServiceCall

```
function alert(alertTitle: String, msg: String): Void {
    loadComplete = false;
    println("{alertTitle}: {msg}");
    description = "{alertTitle}:\n{msg}";
}

function makeServiceCall(location: String, parser: PullParser): Void {
    description = "Loading Photos From Flickr ...";
    var errorMessage: String;
    var httpRequestError: Boolean = false;

    // Submit HttpRequest
```

```
    var request: HttpRequest = HttpRequest {

        location: location
        method: HttpRequest.GET

        onRead: function(bytes: Long) {
            description = "{description} ... ";
        }

        onException: function(exception: Exception) {
            exception.printStackTrace();
            alert("Error", "{exception}");
            httpRequestError = true;
        }

        onResponseCode: function(responseCode: Integer) {
            if (responseCode != HttpStatus.OK) {
                description = request.responseMessage;
            }
        }

        onInput: function(input: java.io.InputStream) {
            try {
                parser.input = input;
                parser.parse();
            } finally {
                input.close();
            }
        }
    }
    request.start();
}
```

Listing 9.16 shows function loadImageMetadata, which constructs the web service end-point (in variable location) and the PullParser for the expected response. It then calls makeServiceCall, shown above in Listing 9.15.

Listing 9.16 Function loadImageMetadata

```
function loadImageMetadata(): Void {
    var errorMessage: String;
    println("Loading image metadata...");
    description = "Loading Photos From Flickr ...";
    var location = "http://api.flickr.com/services/rest/?method="
      "flickr.interestingness.getList&api_key={apiKey}&per_page={perPage}";

    def parser = PullParser {
        . . . see Listing 9.13 on page 303 . . .
    }
    makeServiceCall(location, parser);
}
```

With the details of constructing the PullParser and HttpRequest objects behind us, Listing 9.17 shows the main script and how these pieces all work together. If you compare Listing 9.17 with Listing 8.20 on page 283, you'll see that the structure is similar. While the original Photo Carousel example uses static object literal notation to initialize the photo data, both scripts still add each image to the carousel with function `carousel.addImage` and begin carousel movement with function `carousel.play`.

Listing 9.17 also includes the following trigger block.

```
var loadCarousel: Boolean = bind loadComplete on replace  {
    if (loadComplete) {
        println("starting carousel");
        carousel.play();
    }
}
```

This binds variable `loadCarousel` to Boolean `loadComplete`. Key words `on replace` mean the enclosed block is executed when `loadComplete` changes value. Since the block executes both when `loadComplete` is first initialized (to `false`) as well as when it becomes `true`, we check to make sure the change is to `true` before calling Carousel function `play`.

Listing 9.17 FlickrInteresting Photo Carousel Main Script (Main.fx)

```
def apiKey = "Your Flickr API Key";
var description: String;
def perPage = 100;

def sceneHeight = 500;
def sceneWidth = 400;
var carousel = Carousel {
    centerX: sceneWidth / 2
    centerY: sceneHeight / 2.4
    radiusX: sceneWidth * .26
    radiusY: sceneHeight * .24
};

function makeServiceCall(location: String, parser: PullParser): Void {
    . . . see Listing 9.15 . . .
}

function loadImageMetadata(): Void {
    . . . see Listing 9.16 . . .
}

var loadCarousel: Boolean = bind loadComplete on replace  {
    if (loadComplete) {
        println("starting carousel");
        carousel.play();
    }
```

```
    }

var loadComplete = false;
var error = false;
Stage {
    title: "Carousel Slide Show"
    width: sceneWidth
    height: sceneHeight
    scene: Scene {
        fill: LinearGradient {
            . . . unchanged . . .
        }
        content: [
            VBox {
                visible: bind  not loadComplete
                layoutY: sceneHeight / 4
                layoutX: sceneWidth / 5
                spacing: 20
                content: [
                    Text {
                        fill: Color.WHITE
                        wrappingWidth: sceneWidth - 100
                        content: bind description
                    }
                ]
            }
        carousel ]
    }
}
loadImageMetadata();
```

The Carousel object has not changed with the update that uses Flickr data and it still builds images based on the PullParser. Now, however, the images include the Flickr meta data. Listing 9.18 shows the FlickrImage convenience class, which includes the Image object and the Flickr data. Note that Image property backgroundLoading is true. This lets the (100) images from Flickr load in the background while the carousel starts moving. Since each photo starts its animation in three and a half second intervals, there's plenty of time to load a photo before it is displayed. The Image url property is built from the Flickr data saved in object FlickrMeta (Listing 9.14 on page 304).

Listing 9.18 FlickrImage Class

```
public class FlickrImage {
    public-init var meta: FlickrMeta;
    public def image: Image = Image {
        url: "http://farm{meta.farm}.static.flickr.com/{meta.server}/"
                "{meta.id}_{meta.secret}_m.jpg";
        width: 240
        height: 200
```

```
        preserveRatio: true
        backgroundLoading: true
    }
}
```

Listing 9.19 shows Carousel function addImage, called from the PullParser object (see Listing 9.13 on page 303) for each photo returned by Flickr. Repeated addImage function invocations build a sequence of FlickrImage objects (as many as Flickr returns).

Listing 9.19 Carousel Function addImage

```
public class Carousel extends CustomNode {

    . . .

    var images: FlickrImage[];

    public function addImage(metadata: FlickrMeta): Void {
        insert FlickrImage {
            meta: metadata
        } into images;
    }
    . . .

}
```

9.4 Flickr: Searching with Tags

Flickr has an extensive API. Method interestingness.getList is simple in that there are no required arguments (other than the API key). But let's say you'd like to display photos in a carousel based on a set of tags. Depending on the tags you provide (such as "red,green" or "surfer"), you'll get a different set of photos. Figure 9.3 shows the FlickrTag application as the user provides search tags and then as the carousel is showing photos based on the tag ("surfer").

Figure 9.3 Providing input with component TextBox

Fortunately, Flickr is very consistent with its response data. You can use the same PullParser object, as well as the same HttpRequest object with any of the methods that return photo data. For searching, you just have to change the endpoint (HttpRequest property `location`) and provide a TextBox object to get input from the user. Let's start with the Flickr API `search` method.

Flickr method `flickr.photos.search` returns a list of photos matching the provided tags. The default search criteria matches "any" of the provided tags. (This example supports the default search criteria.) Only public photos are returned. Here is the endpoint for HttpRequest property `location` to use method `flickr.photos.search`.

```
location: "http://api.flickr.com/services/rest/?method=flickr."
      "photos.search&api_key={apiKey}&tags={photoTags}&per_page={perPage}";
```

where `apiKey`, `photoTags`, and `perPage` are script variables containing the API key, search tags, and photos per page information, respectively. (Argument `per_page` is optional.)

The XML response returned is the same format as the response for `flickr.interestingness.getList` (see "Sample Flickr XML Response" on page 302). However, in order to provide the text for the search tags, you'll have to obtain input from the user. JavaFX provides two choices for reading user input: Component TextBox and Swing component TextField. This example uses TextBox, since TextBox is also applicable in the JavaFX mobile environment.

Listing 9.20 shows the changes in project FlickrTag to implement searching Flickr for photos based on tags. New or modified code is displayed in bold.

Function loadImageMetadata defines the URL (location) for method photos.search and specifies argument tags.

The scene graph now includes an additional Text component to display instructions and a TextBox to read user input. The TextBox action function invokes the web service call with function loadImageMetaData. Both components go into the VBox component which becomes invisible after the Flickr response data has been processed.

Listing 9.20 FlickrTag (Main.fx)

```
def apiKey = "Your Flickr API Key";
var description: String;
var photoTags: String;
def perPage = 100;

def sceneHeight = 500;
def sceneWidth = 400;
var carousel = Carousel {
    . . . unchanged . . .
};

function alert(alertTitle: String, msg: String): Void {
    . . . unchanged . . .
}

function makeServiceCall(location: String, parser: PullParser): Void {
    . . . unchanged . . .
}

function loadImageMetadata(): Void {
    var errorMessage: String;
    println("Loading image metadata...");
    description = "Loading Photos From Flickr ...";
    var location = "http://api.flickr.com/services/rest/?method="
                   "flickr.photos.search&api_key={apiKey}"
                   "&tags={photoTags}&per_page={perPage}";

    def parser = PullParser {
            . . . unchanged . . .
        }
    }
    makeServiceCall(location, parser);
}
```

```
var loadCarousel: Boolean = bind loadComplete on replace  {
    . . . unchanged . . .
}

var loadComplete = false;
var error = false;
var textInput: TextBox;
Stage {
    title: "Carousel Slide Show"
    width: sceneWidth
    height: sceneHeight
    scene: Scene {
        fill: LinearGradient {
            . . . unchanged . . .
        }
        content: [
            VBox {
                visible: bind  not loadComplete
                layoutY: sceneHeight / 4
                layoutX: sceneWidth / 20
                spacing: 20
                content: [
                    Text {
                        fill: Color.WHITE
                        wrappingWidth: sceneWidth - 100
                        content: "Type tags separated by commas"
                    }
                    textInput = TextBox {
                        columns: 20
                        action: function(): Void {
                            if (textInput.text != "") {
                                photoTags = textInput.text;
                                loadImageMetadata();
                            }
                        }
                    }
                    Text {
                        fill: Color.WHITE
                        wrappingWidth: sceneWidth - 100
                        content: bind description
                    }
                ]
            }
        carousel ]
    }
}
```

9.5 Flickr: Getting User Photos

Our final Flickr application (FlickrUser) requests a list of photos with a user-supplied Flickr screen name. Public photos are displayed from that user's account. This example is different than the previous two because it requires two web service calls to get the job done. The application, therefore, needs two PullParser objects—one to process the response from each call. The PullParser object that the previous two examples used to parse photo response data can be reused by this application. The other PullParser is new.

The first web service call obtains a user's account ID. People typically know their contacts on Flickr by screen name; accessing a user's account ID is more challenging. This call then, will lookup a user's account ID from the supplied screen name. Here is the endpoint URL for HttpRequest property `location` to invoke method `flickr.people.findByUsername`. This method takes argument `api_key` (of course) and `username`, a user's Flickr screen name.

```
location: "http://api.flickr.com/services/rest/?method="
      "flickr.people.findByUsername&api_key={apiKey}&username={username}";
```

Listing 9.21 shows a sample XML response for this method.

Listing 9.21 Sample XML Response for method findByUsername

```
<rsp stat="ok">
   <user id="FlickrID_here" nsid="FlickrID_here">
      <username>Flickr_username_here</username>
   </user>
</rsp>
```

Listing 9.22 shows function `getAccountName`, which sets the `location` variable with the correct method endpoint and defines the PullParser object that processes the response. It then invokes the web service by calling `makeServiceCall` (see Listing 9.15 on page 304 for the code for function `makeServiceCall`).

Inside the PullParser object, the `onEvent` callback function invokes `loadImageMetadata`, which requests the public photos belonging to the user ID returned in the response.

Listing 9.22 Function getAccountName (FlickrUser)

```
function getAccountName(): Void {
   error = false;
   description = "Getting Username From Flickr ...";
   var errorMessage: String;
   var location = "http://api.flickr.com/services/rest/?method="
         "flickr.people.findByUsername&api_key={apiKey}&username={username}";
```

```
var parser = PullParser {
    onEvent: function(event: Event): Void {
        if (event.type == PullParser.START_ELEMENT and event.level == 1) {
            if (event.qname.name == "user") {
                user_id = event.getAttributeValue(QName{name: "nsid"}) ;
                loadImageMetadata();
            }
            else if (event.qname.name == "err") {
                alert("Flickr Error",
                event.getAttributeValue(QName{name: "msg"}));
                error = true;;
            }
        }
    }
}
makeServiceCall(location, parser);
}
```

The second web service call gets a user's list of photos. Here is the endpoint URL for HttpRequest property location to invoke method flickr.people.getPublicPhotos. This method requires arguments api_key and user_id, the user's Flickr user ID.

```
location: "http://api.flickr.com/services/rest/?method="
          "flickr.people.getPublicPhotos&api_key={apiKey}&"
          "user_id={user_id}&per_page={perPage}";
```

Listing 9.23 shows function loadImageMetadata, which is unchanged from earlier versions (see the PullParser in Listing 9.13 on page 303), except for variable location.

Listing 9.23 Function loadImageMetadata (FlickrUser)

```
function loadImageMetadata(): Void {
    var errorMessage: String;
    println("Loading image metadata...");
    description = "Loading Photos From Flickr ...";
    var location = "http://api.flickr.com/services/rest/?method="
                   "flickr.people.getPublicPhotos&api_key={apiKey}&"
                   "user_id={user_id}&per_page={perPage}";

    def parser = PullParser {
            . . . unchanged from Listing 9.13 on page 303 . . .
        }
    }
    makeServiceCall(location, parser);
}
```

The application is already set up to use component TextBox to gather input from the user. Listing 9.24 shows the updated scene graph for application FlickrUser. Note that if the user supplies an unrecognized screen name, the error flag is set to true. This prevents the application from calling the second web service or starting up the carousel. Instead, an error message is displayed and the user gets another opportunity to provide a screen name.

Listing 9.24 Scene Graph (FlickrUser)

```
var loadComplete = false;
var error = false;
var textInput: TextBox;
Stage {
    title: "Carousel Slide Show"
    width: sceneWidth
    height: sceneHeight
    scene: Scene {
        fill: LinearGradient {
            . . . unchanged . . .
        }
        content: [
            VBox {
                visible: bind  not loadComplete
                layoutY: sceneHeight / 4
                layoutX: sceneWidth / 20
                spacing: 20
                content: [
                    Text {
                        fill: Color.WHITE
                        wrappingWidth: sceneWidth - 100
                        content: "Provide a Flickr screen name"
                    }
                    textInput = TextBox {
                        columns: 20
                        action: function(): Void {
                            if (textInput.text != "") {
                                username = textInput.text;
                                getAccountName();
                            }
                        }
                    }
                    Text {
                        fill: Color.WHITE
                        wrappingWidth: sceneWidth - 100
                        content: bind description
                    }
                ]
            }
            carousel ]
    }
}
```

10 Mobile Applications

The promise of JavaFX to target different screens (desktop, mobile device, or TV) is possible because JavaFX has separate profiles for each platform. Each profile can, and eventually will, have separate extensions that leverage a target device. JavaFX also offers common elements, guaranteed to work with any profile. With this division of runtime systems, you can prepare an application to work anywhere. Alternatively, you can tailor an application for a specific environment.

Preparing an application to run on a mobile device requires two areas of attention. First, make sure your application fits a mobile device form factor. Second, don't use code outside the common profile.

What You Will Learn

- JavaFX common profile
- Targeting a mobile application
- JavaFX mobile emulators
- Discovering the execution environment dynamically
- Responding to orientation changes
- Mouse and key events for mobile applications
- Mobile handset keypad and key press events
- Making an application mobile ready
- Differences between mobile and desktop profiles

10.1 JavaFX Mobile—What Does It Mean?

If you're targeting applications for mobile devices, JavaFX provides three generic mobile device emulators for testing code. But before we show you how to use these emulators, let's discuss what JavaFX Mobile provides today and what it promises for tomorrow.

Figure 10.1 is the big picture for JavaFX. This block diagram shows the various pieces of JavaFX you can leverage when creating applications. As the diagram shows, there are extensions for three environments: Desktop, Mobile and TV. All three environments support the common API (labeled Common Elements in Figure 10.1). As of this writing, the runtime for the JavaFX TV environment does not yet exist. There is a runtime for the JavaFX mobile environment, which supports the common API only.

Mobility Tip

The JavaFX Swing components and the `javafx.scene.effect` *package are not included in the Common Elements. However, the new JavaFX "native" UI components are in the Common Elements and can be used in mobile applications.*

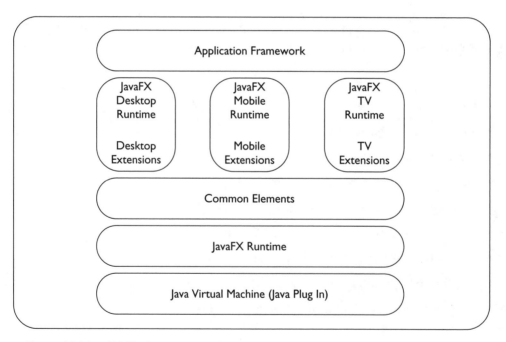

Figure 10.1 JavaFX Platform

Table 10.1 summarizes the current limitations of JavaFX in the mobile environment. Note that some of these limitations are due to the nature of mobile handsets (such as mouse events and applet-specific features).

TABLE 10.1 Limitations in the Mobile Environment

Feature	Not Available with Mobile Runtime
javafx.scene.Cursor	Cursor property (no effect)
javafx.ext.Swing	Swing UI components
javafx.reflect	Provides reflective values
javafx.scene.effect javafx.scene.effect.light	Creates visual effects
ShapeIntersect ShapeSubtract	Composite shapes
AppletStageExtension	Provides browser-specific behavior
FXEvaluator StringLocalizer	From javafx.util package
Mouse Events	onMouseEntered (not relevant), general mouse movements (such as hover, not recorded)

Our first step is to create a simple JavaFX application and deploy it with the JavaFX mobile emulators. We'll start with an application that displays information about its runtime environment.

Mobile Emulator

To deploy this application with the emulator in NetBeans, right click the project name, select the **Properties** menu and choose **Run**. From the radio button choices under Application Execution Model, select **Run in Mobile Emulator**, as shown in Figure 10.2.

Figure 10.2 JavaFX running in the Mobile Emulator

There are currently three JavaFX mobile emulators: Default (DefaultFxPhone1), Touch (DefaultFxTouchPhone1), and Qwerty (QwertyFxPhone1). Figure 10.3 and Figure 10.4 show our simple application running in the standard mobile emulators. In Figure 10.3, View A shows the default emulator and View B shows the touch emulator. Figure 10.4 shows the qwerty emulator.

This application includes a Text component that displays information about the current environment (screen size and profile). Knowing something about the current environment is useful for applications that target both desktop and mobile profiles. A Rectangle shape acts as a background for the Text component.

View A: DefaultFxPhone1

View B: DefaultFxTouchPhone1

Figure 10.3 JavaFX mobile emulator (default emulators)

Figure 10.4 JavaFX mobile emulator (qwerty emulator)

Discovering Your Environment

JavaFX provides several ways for applications to discover their execution environment.

__PROFILE__

The pseudo variable `__PROFILE__` is set to `"browser"` (running as an applet in a browser), `"mobile"` (running in the mobile environment), or `"desktop"` (not an applet and not mobile). Here, Boolean `isMobile` is `true` in a mobile environment.

```
def isMobile = __PROFILE__ == "mobile";
```

FX.getProperty

Object FX is available in all JavaFX applications. FX function `getProperty` returns system-level properties based on a key String argument. In a mobile environment, key argument `"javafx.me.profiles"` returns information on the JavaFX runtime version, as well as the mobile runtime version. In a non-mobile environment, `FX.getProperty` with this key returns null.

```
def isMobile = FX.getProperty("javafx.me.profiles") != null;
```

Stage

The Stage object reflects the mobile device screen height and width.

```
def stage: Stage = Stage {
    title: "Mobility"
    scene: Scene {
        content: [ . . . ]
    }
}
def height = stage.height;          // height of screen
def width = stage.width;            // width of screen
```

Listing 10.1 is the code for the application running in Figure 10.3 and Figure 10.4. After determining whether or not the environment is the mobile runtime, the application builds a profile string. This variable (profileString) includes the screen dimensions and the __PROFILE__ pseudo variable.

Next, the application defines a background Rectangle (r1) and a Text component (t1). The background rectangle binds its dimensions to expressions that depend on the Stage object stage. The Text object sets its location relative to the background rectangle and binds property wrappingWidth to an expression using the rectangle's width. Thus, the dimensions of the background rectangle and the Text wrappingWidth depend on the screen size.

The scene graph includes a Group object that holds the Text and Rectangle. The Groups's horizontal position depends on the Stage width. Grouping Text and Rectangle together makes it easy to maintain the relative position of these two components.

Listing 10.1 MobileTest1

```
def isMobile = __PROFILE__ == "mobile";
def profileString:String = bind "height={stage.height}, width={stage.width}.\n"
 "profile={__PROFILE__}.";

def r1 = Rectangle {
    height: bind stage.height / 2
    width: bind stage.width -  50
    fill: Color.web("#3333ee", .3)
    stroke: Color.CADETBLUE
}

def t1 = Text {
    x: r1.x + 15
    y: r1.y + 15
    wrappingWidth: bind r1.width - 30
    font: Font {
        size: 16
    }
```

```
        textOrigin: TextOrigin.TOP
        content: bind profileString
}

def stage: Stage = Stage {
    title: "Mobility"
    scene: Scene {
        content: [
            Group {
                layoutX: bind stage.width / 2 - r1.layoutBounds.width / 2
                layoutY: 20
                content: [ r1, t1 ]
            }
        ]
    }
}
```

Orientation Changes

When a mobile device changes orientation, you may want your application to respond. This means updating your application's scene graph. Fortunately, JavaFX makes detecting changes in orientation straightforward with binding expressions and/or triggers. Perhaps the more difficult part in responding to orientation changes is deciding what components in your scene graph should change and how.

For example, in the mobility test application from Figure 10.3, the text component should not rotate (you want the text to remain readable), but the Text object literal's dimensions should expand or contract depending on the dimensions of the display.

Figure 10.5 shows an enhanced version of our mobility test application. View A shows the application running in the emulator with normal (0 degree rotation) orientation. The text display includes the word "vertical" at the bottom. View B shows the emulator with a 90-degree rotation, giving a horizontal orientation to the display. You can see that the text component wrapping width and the background rectangle adjust to the change in screen size. The text now includes the word "horizontal" at the bottom.

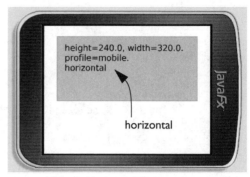

View B: Horizontal Orientation

View A: Vertical Orientation

Figure 10.5 Responding to orientation changes

Listing 10.2 shows the code that responds to these orientation changes. To display the word "vertical" with a vertical display and the word "horizontal" with a horizontal display, we define a new String variable (orientationString) that includes the correct orientation word. The program updates this String using an on replace block that triggers when object stage.height changes. (The dimensions of object stage reflect changes in orientation.) If the height is greater than the width, the phone is oriented vertically and String orientationString is updated with the correct label.

Text component t1 now binds its content property to orientationString so that when the orientation changes, the scene graph reflects the new content. Because property wrappingWidth is already bound to the background rectangle's width (which is bound to stage.width), the text reformats to fit into the new dimensions.

Listing 10.2 MobileTest2

```
def isMobile = __PROFILE__ == "mobile";

def profileString:String = bind "height={stage.height}, width={stage.width}.\n"
 "profile={__PROFILE__}.";

var orientationString: String;
def height = bind stage.height on replace {
    if (stage.height > stage.width) {
```

```
        orientationString = "{profileString}\nvertical";
    }
    else {
        orientationString = "{profileString}\nhorizontal";
    }
}

def r1 = Rectangle {
    height: bind stage.height / 2
    width: bind stage.width -  50
    fill: Color.web("#3333ee", .3)
    stroke: Color.CADETBLUE
}

def t1 = Text {
    x: r1.x + 15
    y: r1.y + 15
    wrappingWidth: bind r1.width - 30
    font: Font {
        size: 16
    }
    textOrigin: TextOrigin.TOP
    content: bind orientationString
}

def stage: Stage = Stage {
    . . . code unchanged . . .
}
```

Mobility Tip

Group components together that respond to orientation changes in the same way. This will simplify your program. For example, Text components are not typically rotated, but you may need to resize them when the display size changes. Similarly, ImageView is also not rotated but may need scaling. Non-text based graphical objects may require a 90-degree rotation.

Mouse and Key Events

The default emulator includes a keypad with a selection button, arrow keys, soft keys, and numeric keys. The default touch phone emulator has no keypad, but includes a virtual keypad with the TextBox component. The mouse mimics touch gestures, which should be viewed as an approximation of real-phone behavior. For example, touch gestures require nice, fat targets, whereas mouse devices can point with precision on the screen.

Let's update the mobile test program to change the rectangle's background color with either a mouse click (emulating the touch phone's touch gesture) or a keypad select key (on the default emulator).

Figure 10.6 shows the default emulator with most of the keys labeled.

Figure 10.6 Mobile emulator key press events

Figure 10.7 shows the qwerty emulator with several keys labeled.

The onKeyPressed property lets you specify a key press event handler, as shown here.

```
onKeyPressed: function(ke: KeyEvent): Void {
    println("keycode={ke.text}, code={ke.code}");
    if (ke.code == KeyCode.VK_ENTER)
        bgColor = if (bgColor == Color.BISQUE) Color.THISTLE else Color.BISQUE
}
```

The println statement displays the key text and key code for each key press. (Figure 10.6 and Figure 10.7 label key press codes.) If the key code is VK_ENTER, the

Figure 10.7 Mobile emulator (qwerty) key press events

background color bgColor alternates between two colors (Color.THISTLE and Color.BISQUE).

Before key events can be detected, the node that has the key press event handler must have focus. Rectangle r1 gains focus with the following statement.

```
r1.requestFocus();
```

Property onMouseClicked lets you change background colors with the touch phone emulator. Here's the mouse event handler.

```
onMouseClicked: function(e: MouseEvent): Void {
    bgColor = if (bgColor == Color.BISQUE) Color.THISTLE else Color.BISQUE
}
```

Listing 10.3 shows the object literal for Rectangle r1 with both the key press and mouse click event handler.

Listing 10.3 Key Press Events

```
var bgColor = Color.BISQUE;
def r1 = Rectangle {
    height: bind stage.height / 2
    width: bind stage.width -  50
    fill: bind bgColor
    stroke: Color.CADETBLUE
```

```
    onKeyPressed: function(ke: KeyEvent): Void {
        println("keycode={ke.text}, code={ke.code}");
        if (ke.code == KeyCode.VK_ENTER)
        bgColor = if (bgColor == Color.BISQUE) Color.THISTLE else Color.BISQUE
    }
    onMouseClicked: function(e: MouseEvent): Void {
        println("mouse clicked");
        bgColor = if (bgColor == Color.BISQUE) Color.THISTLE else Color.BISQUE
    }
}
def t1 = Text { . . . }

def stage: Stage = Stage {
    title: "Mobility"
    scene: Scene {
        content: [
            Group {
                layoutX: bind stage.width / 2 - r1.layoutBounds.width / 2
                layoutY: 20
                content: [ r1, t1 ]
            }
        ]
    }
}
r1.requestFocus();
```

User Input

The JavaFX UI component TextBox gathers text-based user input. When the component has focus, the emulator accepts keyboard input, as shown in Figure 10.8. Select the Enter key to confirm input. With the QwertyFxPhone1 emulator, use the emulator's keypad for input.

Figure 10.8 Text input with the qwerty mobile emulator

10.2 Making a JavaFX Application Mobile Ready

In the previous chapter, we presented three Flickr-based applications that display photos in an animated photo carousel. FlickrInteresting displays photos from today's set of "interesting" photos. FlickrTag displays photos based on a user-supplied search tag. Finally, FlickrUser displays public photos from a Flickr account based on a screenname supplied by the user. Figure 10.9 shows the FlickrInteresting application running in the desktop environment (View A) and in the mobile environment (View B).

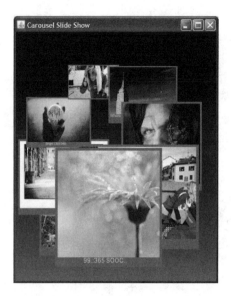

View A: Desktop Environment

View B: Mobile Environment

Figure 10.9 Standard (View A) and mobile (View B) versions of FlickrInteresting

In this section, we'll show you how to make these applications run in both the mobile and non-mobile environments. (Note that the updated applications replace the previous ones; they are not mobile-only, but run in both environments.) Here is a checklist of modifications that make the applications both mobile and desktop friendly.

- Construct the animation path elements based on the screen dimensions determined at run time (**Main.fx**).

- Detect orientation changes and reposition the carousel (**Main.fx**).

- Request 50 images per page instead of 100 in the mobile environment (**Main.fx**).

- Scale the images during load to a smaller size in the mobile environment (**FlickrImage.fx**).

- Scale down the images for the ScaleTransition by factor .3 instead of .4 in the mobile environment (**CarouselPhoto.fx**).

- Shorten the duration of the photo carousel animation in the mobile environment (**CarouselPhoto.fx**).

All three Flickr applications require the same modifications.

Detecting the Mobile Environment

First, add script public variable isMobile, which is true when the application detects the mobile environment. Variable isMobile is used to set the sceneHeight and scene-Width variables, which in turn determine the size of the carousel. The isMobile variable is public so that other classes in the application can access it. Listing 10.4 shows the added code (in bold) that sets isMobile to true if the application is running in the mobile environment.

Listing 10.4 Determine if in Mobile Environment (Main.fx)

```
public def isMobile = __PROFILE__ == "mobile";
def perPage = if (isMobile) 50 else 100;

def sceneHeight = if (isMobile) 320 else 500;
def sceneWidth = if (isMobile) 240 else 400;
def carousel: Carousel = Carousel {
    centerX: sceneWidth / 2.2
    centerY: sceneHeight / 2.4
    radiusX: sceneWidth * .26
    radiusY: sceneHeight * .24
};
```

Because variable isMobile is public, **Main.fx** requires a run function for script-level statements (those not in a function or class). Listing 10.5 shows the added run function.

Listing 10.5 Adding a run Function (Main.fx)

```
def stage: Stage = Stage {
    title: "Carousel Slide Show"
    scene: Scene {
        . . .
    }
}

function run() {
    stage.height = sceneHeight;
    stage.width = sceneWidth;
}
```

Detecting Orientation Changes

The application detects orientation changes with on replace and the stage height (stage.height), shown in Listing 10.6. If the application is vertical, the carousel is positioned at its original location (translateX and translateY are 0). If the application is horizontal, the carousel moves to the right and up in the display (translateX is 45 and translateY is -55). The size of the carousel does not change with a different orientation.

Listing 10.6 Detect orientation changes (Main.fx)

```
def height = bind stage.height on replace {
    if (stage.height > stage.width) {          // vertical
        carousel.translateX = 0;
        carousel.translateY = 0;
    }
    else {    // horizontal
        carousel.translateX = 45;
        carousel.translateY = -55;
    }
}
```

Reducing the Number and Size of Images

The Flickr web services have an optional per_page argument that specifies how many photos to return per page (we get one page back). Set this to 50 in the mobile environment (the default is 100). Listing 10.7 shows the new endpoint with the per_page argument included. (Read-only variable perPage is initialized in Listing 10.4.)

Listing 10.7 Save mobile environment info

```
function loadImageMetadata(): Void {
    var errorMessage: String;
    description = "Loading Photos From Flickr ...";
    def location = "http://api.flickr.com/services/rest/?method="
        "flickr.people.getPublicPhotos&api_key={apiKey}"
        "&user_id={user_id}&per_page={perPage}";
    . . .

}
```

Listing 10.8 shows the updated FlickrImage class that scales its Image component based on whether it's running in the mobile environment or not. Note that the syntax for accessing public variable isMobile must include the package name (flickr) and the class (Main).

Listing 10.8 Scale images (FlickrImage.fx)

```
public class FlickrImage {
    public-init var meta: FlickrMeta;
    public var image: Image = Image {
        url: "http://farm{meta.farm}.static.flickr.com/{meta.server}/"
```

```
            "{meta.id}_{meta.secret}_m.jpg";
        width: if (flickr.Main.isMobile) 180 else 240
        height: if (flickr.Main.isMobile) 160 else 200
        preserveRatio: true
        backgroundLoading: true
    }
}
```

Adjusting the Animation

Class CarouselPhoto builds the transitions that apply to the images as they travel around the carousel. In the mobile environment, the path elements define a smaller path. (The path is built from path elements based on the screen size.) In the mobile environment, the path animation duration is also reduced, since the path size is smaller. Listing 10.9 shows these changes made to **CarouselPhoto.fx**.

Listing 10.9 Modify ScaleTransition and Animation Time (CarouselPhoto.fx)

```
. . .
    def animationDuration = if (flickr.Main.isMobile) 20s else 26s;
. . .

    public def carouselAnimation = SequentialTransition {
        node: this
        content: [
            FadeTransition {
                duration: 1.5s
                fromValue: 0.0
                toValue: 1.0
            }
            PauseTransition {
                duration: 2.5s
            }

            ParallelTransition {
                node: this
                content: [
                    ScaleTransition {
                        duration: animationDuration / 2
                        toX: if (flickr.Main.isMobile) .3 else .4
                        toY: if (flickr.Main.isMobile) .3 else .4
                        autoReverse: true
                        repeatCount: 2
                    }
                    PathTransition {
                        duration: animationDuration
                        interpolator: Interpolator.EASEOUT
                        path: AnimationPath.createFromPath(Path {
                            elements: carouselElements
```

```
                          })
                  }

              ]
          }  // ParallelTransition
      ]
   };
. . .
```

10.3 Mobile-Only Applications

It's not always possible or desirable to have all applications run in both the desktop and mobile environments. Take, for example, the Chutes and Ladders application in Chapter 7 (see "Chutes and Ladders" on page 237). The original application includes buttons that take up precious real estate and drop shadow effects, which are unavailable in the mobile environment. Besides form factor modifications, you also have to change the look of the application. (You can't conditionally apply a drop shadow effect in a mobile environment. The javafx.scene.effect package is unavailable at the compilation level.)

Figure 10.10 shows the desktop version (View A) and the mobile version (View B) of Chutes and Ladders. Not only is the mobile form smaller, the title is removed from the top of the display, inserted in the center, and rotated. There are no buttons. The path balls have numbers instead of drop shadows.

We also changed the way a user selects a path ball for animation. The user can either "touch" the path ball (mouse clicks) or type the number on the phone key pad corresponding to the path ball.

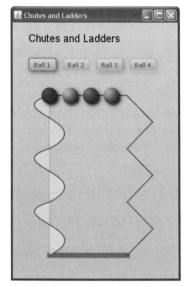

View A: Desktop Environment

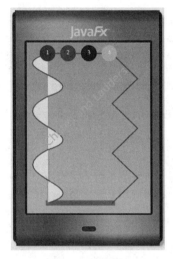

View B: Mobile Environment

Figure 10.10 Standard (View A) and mobile (View B) versions of Chutes and Ladders

As in the previous section, we'll highlight the changes to the original Chutes and Ladders application for the mobile environment. However, this time we create a new program that targets the mobile environment. Therefore, in this case, we don't have to worry about whether or not the application is running in the mobile environment—it always is.

Here's the checklist of modifications.

- Reduce the form factor for the mobile environment.

- Remove the buttons and replace with mouse events and key press events.

- Remove the drop shadows and add numbers to the path balls.

- Move the title from the top of the display to the middle. Add color and a rotation animation.

- Detect orientation changes and rotate all elements of the scene except the title Text component.

For this discussion, we show you only the modifications for key press events, mouse click events, and orientation changes.

Grouping Elements Together

Listing 10.10 shows the Group that includes the path shapes and the sequence of path balls (theBalls) that make up the animated portion of the application. These are all together so that the group can respond to orientation changes. Property transforms defines a Rotate transformation that initializes its angle property to 0. Variable rotateAngle controls the group's rotation.

This group also includes the key press event handler (property onKeyPressed). The handler initiates the animation corresponding to the numbered key (1-4). For example, KeyCode.VK_1 corresponds to "1" on the default mobile phone emulator.

Listing 10.10 Group Scene Graph (Main.fx)

```
var rotateAngle = 0;
def group: Group = Group {
    translateX: 40
    translateY: 20
    transforms: Rotate {
        angle: bind rotateAngle
        pivotX: bind (stage.width / 2) - 20
        pivotY: bind (stage.height / 2) - 10
    }
    onKeyPressed: function(ke: KeyEvent): Void {
        println("keycode={ke.text}, code={ke.code}");
        if (ke.code == KeyCode.VK_1) {
            theBalls[0].play();
        }
         else if (ke.code == KeyCode.VK_2) {
            theBalls[1].play();
        }
        else if (ke.code == KeyCode.VK_3) {
            theBalls[2].play();
        }
        else if (ke.code == KeyCode.VK_4) {
            theBalls[3].play();
        }
    }
    content: [ groundPath, chutePole, chutePath, ladderPath, theBalls ]
} // Group

// listen for keyPress events
group.requestFocus();
```

Listing 10.11 shows the Circle, Text, and Group object literals for the path ball and the mouse click event handler that is added to the path ball object literal.

Listing 10.11 PathBall Group Object Literal (PathBall.fx)

```
def theBall = Circle {
    radius: 15
    fill: ballColor
}
def text = Text {
    x: -3
    y: 2
    content: "{displayNum}"
    fill: Color.WHITE
    font: Font {
        size: 10
    }
}
def theGroup: Group = Group {
    translateX: centerX
    onMouseClicked: function(e: MouseEvent): Void {
        play();
    }
    content: [ theBall, text ]
}
```

Listing 10.12 shows the on replace trigger that responds to orientation changes. If the orientation is vertical, variable rotateAngle is set to 0. If the orientation is horizontal, rotateAngle is set to 90. (Recall that the group's Rotate transformation angle property binds to variable rotateAngle.)

Listing 10.12 On replace trigger for orientation changes (Main.fx)

```
def height = bind stage.height on replace {
    if (stage.height > stage.width) {          // vertical
        rotateAngle = 0;
        group.translateX = 40;
        group.translateY = 20;
    }
    else {  // horizontal
        rotateAngle = 90;
        group.translateX = 45;
        group.translateY = 75;
    }
}
```

Figure 10.11 shows the vertical (View A) and horizontal (View B) rotation. The Chutes and Ladders title is not affected by orientation changes.

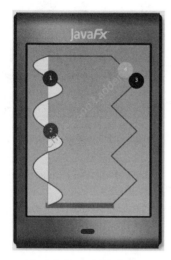

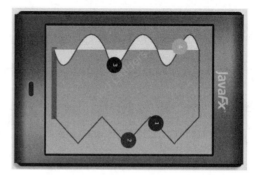

View B: Rotated 90 degrees

View A: Rotated 0 degrees

Figure 10.11 Chutes and Ladders orientation changes

Index